The Baroque Wind Band and Wind Ensemble

Books by David Whitwell

Philosophic Foundations of Education
Foundations of Music Education
Music Education of the Future
The Sousa Oral History Project
The Art of Musical Conducting
The Longy Club: 1900–1917
A Concise History of the Wind Band
Wagner on Bands
Aesthetics of Music in Ancient Civilizations

The History and Literature of the Wind Band and Wind Ensemble Series

Volume 1 The Wind Band and Wind Ensemble Before 1500
Volume 2 The Renaissance Wind Band and Wind Ensemble
Volume 3 The Baroque Wind Band and Wind Ensemble
Volume 4 The Classic Period Wind Band and Wind Ensemble
Volume 5 The Nineteenth-Century Wind Band and Wind Ensemble
Volume 6 A Catalog of Multi-Part Repertoire for Wind Instruments or for Undesignated Instrumentation before 1600
Volume 7 Baroque Wind Band and Wind Ensemble Repertoire
Volume 8 Classic Period Wind Band and Wind Ensemble Repertoire
Volume 9 Nineteenth-Century Wind Band and Wind Ensemble Repertoire
Volume 10 A Supplementary Catalog of Wind Band and Wind Ensemble Repertoire
Volume 11 A Catalog of Wind Repertoire before the Twentieth Century for One to Five Players
Volume 12 A Second Supplementary Catalog of Early Wind Band and Wind Ensemble Repertoire
Volume 13 Name Index, Volumes 1–12, The History and Literature of the Wind Band and Wind Ensemble

www.whitwellbooks.com

David Whitwell

The Baroque Wind Band and Wind Ensemble

THE HISTORY AND LITERATURE OF THE WIND BAND AND WIND ENSEMBLE, VOLUME 3

EDITED BY CRAIG DABELSTEIN

WHITWELL PUBLISHING • AUSTIN, TEXAS, USA

Whitwell Publishing, Austin 78701
www.whitwellbooks.com

© 1983, 2011 by David Whitwell
All rights reserved. First edition 1983.
Second edition 2011

Printed in the United States of America

PAPERBACK
ISBN-13: 978-1-936512-24-9
ISBN-10: 1936512246

All images used in this book are in the public domain except where otherwise noted.

Composed in Bembo Book

Contents

Foreword — vii
Acknowledgements — ix

PART 1 THE HAUTBOISTEN TRADITION AND THE BIRTH OF HARMONIE MUSIK — 1

PART 2 COURT WIND BANDS

1. Court Wind Bands in France — 25
2. Court Wind Bands in the German-Speaking Countries — 57
3. Court Wind Bands in Italy — 71
4. Court Wind Bands in Spain — 75
5. Court Wind Bands in England — 77

PART 3 THE ORIGINS OF WESTERN 'TURKISH MUSIC' — 101

PART 4 MILITARY WIND BANDS

6. Military Wind Bands in the German-Speaking Countries — 117
7. Military Wind Bands in France — 133
8. Military Wind Bands in England — 145
9. Military Wind Bands in Italy — 151
10. Military Wind Bands in the Low Countries — 153
11. Military Wind Bands in Russia — 155

PART 5 CIVIC WIND BANDS

12. Civic Wind Bands in the German-Speaking Countries — 159
13. Civic Wind Bands in England — 175
14. Civic Wind Bands in the Low Countries — 187
15. Civic Wind Bands in France — 191
16. Civic Wind Bands in Italy — 193
17. Civic Wind Bands in Russia — 195

PART 6 CHURCH WIND BANDS

18. Church Wind Bands in the Low Countries — 199
19. Church Wind Bands in England — 201
20. Church Wind Bands in the German-Speaking Countries — 207
21. Church Wind Bands in France — 217
22. Church Wind Bands in Italy — 219
23. Church Wind Bands in the Spanish-Speaking Countries — 221

Notes On The Instruments	223
Bibliography	229
Index	239
About The Author	247

Foreword

THIS VOLUME IS THE THIRD of several which together attempt a general History and Literature of the Wind Band and Wind Ensemble. At the time these volumes were first written there was no comprehensive history of the wind band. In addition these volumes together provide library identification and shelf-marks for more than 30,000 wind band manuscripts and early prints before 1900 found in more than 450 libraries. Over several decades it was my practice when conducting in Europe to add some weeks to my trip to visit libraries and examine early works for wind band and many of these scores I worked into the repertoire of my own concerts.

The story of the wind band during the 150 years [1600–1750] known as the Baroque Period is very interesting in several respects. First, in terms of instrumentation the first half of this period consists of a continuation of the Renaissance consorts, while the second half consists of the spread of the new modern instruments. This change is particularly personified in the *Hautboisten* band, which consisted of oboes, bassoons and horns. In terms of instrumentation it is Classic Period *Harmoniemusik*, differing only in the style of the music. Historically, the importance of the *Hautboisten* band lies in its function as a bridge between the repertoire of Renaissance consorts and the repertoire of *Harmoniemusik*. In addition, the *concerto da camera* of the *Hautboisten* repertoire was the form which gave birth to the Classic Period symphony and partita. And the *Hautboisten* Ouverture had the same relationship with the Classic Period Divertimento.

The second interesting hallmark of Baroque band music is the first modern appearance of military bands. It was the creation of standing armies, as opposed to the use of mercenary troops, which made possible for the first time since ancient Rome coordinated marching. This, in turn, required the employment of military bands.

David Whitwell
Austin, Texas

Acknowledgments

This new edition would not have been possible without the encouragement and help of Craig Dabelstein of Brisbane, Australia. His experience as a musician and educator himself has contributed greatly to his expertise as editor of this volume.

> David Whitwell
> Austin, 2011

PART I

The Hautboisten Tradition and the Birth of Harmoniemusik

The Hautboisten Tradition and the Birth of Harmoniemusik

For the wind band the Baroque Period was one of dramatic events! The kinds of wind bands and wind ensembles, and the very instruments themselves, which had been at the very forefront of European instrumental music throughout the late Middle Ages, Renaissance, and early Baroque now came to their final chapters.

Out of the death of these noble institutions came, at the same time, a metamorphosis: the emergence of the Baroque Hautboisten ensemble which would develop into the Harmoniemusik of the Classic Period, an enormously important medium not only for its own extensive repertoire but for its role as the wind choir in the first generation of the modern orchestra. It is the knowledge of the history of this development which allows the reader to see that the canzoni of Gabrieli and the octets of Mozart are not isolated phenomena, but are linked in a natural development like all other important musical institutions of this period.

The important late Baroque Hautboisten ensemble began in the last decades of the seventeenth century as a reflection of the German courts' desire to follow the taste of the great French court of Louis XIV. The German Hautboisten ensemble was directly modeled on the Parisian court's *Les Grands Hautbois* and this included the forms of its repertoire, the size of the ensemble and even the importation of the new French oboe. The French *Les Grands Hautbois* itself was a direct metamorphosis of the sixteenth-century Italian church wind ensemble repertoire by way of the *concerto da camera*, as the reader will see below.

The Story of the Hautboisten Ensemble

While the focus of the following volume is on the new wind bands and their literature, the reader should perhaps be reminded that during the first third of the seventeenth century the earlier wind band traditions continued in full strength in nearly all countries in Europe. Johann Schein, writing in 1609, said,

> Summon with the noise of cornetts, the sound of sackbuts, curtals and sorduns, with pommers too, the gentle sound of recorders, with crumhorns.[1]

Similarity, in Italy, Cerone writes in 1613 that ensembles (*Conciertos*) are found made of sackbuts, curtals or bassoons, doppioni, recorders, dulcaynas, cornetts, cornamuse, and crumhorns.[2] Iconography confirms such texts and one need only point to the beautiful ivory coin cabinet made by Christoph Angermaier for Elizabeth, wife of Maximilian I of Bavaria in ca. 1618–1624. Here Pan and a group of shepherds are playing the crumhorn, sackbut, treble and bass recorders, and panpipes.[3] (see image below)

[1] Johann Schein, 'Frisch auf, du edle Musikkunst,' from *Venus Kräntzlein* (1609).

> Mit Zinkenschall,
> Posaunenhall,
> Dulzan und den Sordanen,
> Mit Pommern auch,
> Flötengerauch
> Krummhörnern thu anmahnen.

[2] Domenico Pietro Cerone, *El Melopeo y Maestro* (Naples, 1613 and Bologna, 1969), 1038.

> Sacabuches, Fagotes ò Baxones, Doblados, Flautas, Dulçaynas, Cornetas, Cornamusas, y Cornamudas.

[3] Munich, Bayerisches National Museum.

Carving on an ivory cabinet by Christoph Angermaier.

One must acknowledge, of course, the arrival of the new string instruments and their ensembles which most musicians today associate with Baroque instrumental music. English scholars insist this new medium was firmly established in their country by the beginning of the seventeenth century. While this may have been true, one can say there is no evidence in the surviving instrumental manuscripts of anything approaching exclusive domain; while many English manuscripts are designated for the string, or mixed, consort, most of the manuscripts I have examined are still for ensembles of undesignated instruments. Be that as it may, in some parts of Europe this new force arrives later in the seventeenth century. Praetorius, in 1619, in presenting his discussion of the kinds of instrumental choirs available for use in large church concerti, adds the string choir almost as an after-thought and only, he says, for the purpose of making his account complete.

> But it is up to anyone's pleasure to use this *capella*, or leave it out. For, as mentioned above, I have only added it (to this discussion) because of the approbation of certain listeners and would not otherwise have deemed it very important. If one would thus want to compose and arrange such a *capella fidicinia* ... one would attract those listeners in Germany who still do not know what to make of (this) new style.[4]

[4] Michael Praetorius, *Syntagma Musicum*, trans. Hans Lampl, vol. 3 (California State University, Long Beach, 1957), 154.

I believe this entire question of the emergence of the modern string ensemble and especially the development of the Classical string orchestra as a *medium*, apart from the development of the symphonic literature, deserves more detailed study than it has thus far received. The important point to keep in mind for now, however, is that the entire string question is *irrelevant* with regard to the development of the wind band medium. During the Baroque they coexisted as instrumental mediums, even though, of course, it can be said the quality of the string literature did have an increasing impact on the role of the wind band in society.

The *real* crisis in the wind band medium came from within. The success of the twelve-member oboe–bassoon band, *Les Grands Hautbois*, under Louis XIV in France, together with the development of the new French oboe, was imitated by courts throughout Europe, exactly as the same courts imitated so many other facets of the 'Sun King's' court (one need mention only architecture). Indeed it seems to have been a necessary part of every German aristocrat's cultural education to spend some time in the court of France. 'Everyone in Germany goes there,' wrote Frederick the Great in 1750, 'The French taste rules our food, our furniture, and our clothes.'[5]

When this new French style oboe–bassoon band appeared in Germany, late in the seventeenth century, it was known as the *Hautboisten*, and one notices even the name is French! Traditional studies treat this new ensemble only as a military unit (and indeed the name continues to mean military musicians for a long time in Germany), but as the following volume will document there was a concurrent court *concert* band existing at the same time, under the same name, and with the same instrumentation. It was this concert wind band which would develop into Harmoniemusik and not its military counterpart.

In Germany the appearance of the new Hautboisten band can be documented widely by the last two decades of the seventeenth century, as for example in Stuttgart (680),[6] Weissenfels (695),[7] Dresden and Gotha (1697),[8] and Gottorf (1699).[9] According to Braun, by 1700 almost every great German residence had such a band.[10]

In many cases the arrival of the new French oboe in Germany came in the hands of French players. We know of their names in the court records in Celle (1681), Bonn (1697), Dresden (1699, 'Françoise le Riche'),[11] and Berlin (22 December 1681, 'Pierre Potot and François Beauregard').[12]

The impact of the new French oboe was such that even in those cases where some players continued to play the older shawm (even as late as 1749), they were now invariably called 'Hoboisten.'[13]

The actual creation of this new oboe in France, the development of a more cylindrical instrument as opposed to the more conical shawm, remains an important question which has never received definitive study. I should like to venture the hypothesis that the factor which may have served as the catalyst was the musette, which became very popular in the French court at about the same time. It shares a bore more similar to the modern oboe and was played by the oboists of the French oboe-band. It was an entirely new sound, as one can see in the testimony by Martin Mersenne in 1635.

[5] Frederick II von Brandenburg, *Memoires pour servir a l'histoire de Brandenbourg* (1750), 2:771.

> Toute l'Allemagne y voyageoit
> ......
> Le goût des François regla nos Cuisines, nos Meubles, nos Habillements...

[6] Josef Sittard, *Zur Geschichte der Musik und des Theaters am Württembergischen Hofe* (Stuttgart, 1891), 2:13.

[7] Arno Werner, *Städtische und fürstliche Musikpflege in Weissenfels* (Leipzig: Breitkopf & Hartel, 1911), 95.

[8] Arno Werner, *Vier Jahrhunderte im Dienste der Kirchenmusik* (Leipzig: Carl Merseberger, 1933), 246–248.

[9] Bernhard Engelke, *Musik und Musiker am Gottorfer Hofe*, II (HSS, Universitätsbibliothek Kiel).

[10] Werner Braun, 'Entwurf für ein Typologie der "Hautboisten",' in *Der Sozialstatus des Berufsmusikers vom 17. bis 19. Jahrhundert* (Kassel: Barenreiter Verlag, 1971), 47.

[11] Braun, ibid., 46.

[12] Curt Sachs, *Musik und Oper am kurbrandenburgischen Hof* (Berlin: J. Bard, 1910), 61.

[13] Peter Panoff, *Militärmusik* (Berlin: K. Siegismund, 1944), 87.

When one has heard the musette in the hands of those who play it perfectly, as does M. Des Touches, one of the Royal Oboists, it must be admitted that it yields to none of the other instruments, and that there is a singular pleasure in hearing it.[14]

Additional examples of French influence on these later German wind bands can be seen in the fact that some were formed with exactly the same number of players (twelve) as Louis XIV's *Les Grands Hautbois*, as in Halle (1676),[15] Jena,[16] and Eisenberg, a band known as the 'Apostles.'[17] In Weissenfels (1695) the Hautboisten were organized as was that of Louis XIV, with each wind player doubling on a string instrument.[18]

Another imitation of the French model can be seen in the division of parts (regardless of the number of players), into two soprano oboes, a tenor oboe (taille) and bassoon.[19]

The appearance of the other member of the Hautboisten bands, the modern bassoon, is more difficult to date, due to the fact that the name (from *bassus* in Latin) was used long before to include other kinds of bass wind instruments. One can see, however, that by the seventeenth century it was clearly associated with the oboe family. Mersenne wrote, in 1635,

> I treat of these species of basses because they can be joined in the concert of oboes, and are different from the preceding bass (oboe) only in that they break into two parts to be able to be managed and carried more easily; that is why they are called Fagots, because they resemble pieces of wood.[20]

Similarly, Mattheson wrote in 1713,

> The stately bassoon, Basse de Chormorne, Ital. Fagotto, common name Dulcian, is the normal bass, the foundation or accompaniment of the oboe.[21]

It is, by the way, this association with the Hautboisten band which explains a reference in the Weissenfels court records[22] to a musician in 1698, 'An oboist who plays (blies) the bassoon.' It means, of course, 'a member of the oboe-band' who plays bassoon.

Regular bassoon players appear in court records in Germany simultaneously with the Hautboisten itself, the final third of the seventeenth century. One sees them in court records in

[14] Martin Mersenne, *Harmonie Universelle* [1635], trans. Roger Chapman (The Hague: M. Nijhoff, 1957), 359.

[15] W. Serauky, *Musikgeschichte der Stadt Halle* (Halle-Berlin: Buchhandlung des Waisenhauses, 1939), 2:423.

[16] Braun, 'Entwurf für ein Typologie der "Hautboisten",' 47.

[17] Werner, *Städtische und fürstliche Musikpflege in Weissenfels*, 96.

[18] Ibid., 95.

[19] Ibid., 59, 94.

[20] Mersenne, *Harmonie Universelle*, 372.

[21] Johann Mattheson, *Das Neu-Eröffnete Orchestre* (Hamburg, 1713), 269.

> Der stoltzte Basson, Basse de Chormore, Ital. Fagotto, vulgò Dulcian, is der ordinaire Bass, das Fundament oder Accompagnement der Hautbois...

[22] Quoted in Werner, *Städtische und fürstliche Musikpflege in Weissenfels*, 74.

Saxony in 1666 and 1680[23] and in Wissenfels by 1667.[24] The Berlin court had four bassoons by 1708, which together with four oboes constituted the Hautboisten.[25]

It might seem at first quite astonishing to modern readers to find music for large ensembles of bassoons during the Baroque, but this can be understood in view of the long tradition of consorts, which was not entirely dead. Gottfried Pepusch composed (ca. 1700–1713) a work for six bassoons, labeled 'porco primo, porco secondo,' etc., to be performed before Friedrich Wilhelm I in a Tabacco collegium. Friedrich, we are told, was quite taken by this 'Schweinsextet.'[26]

The Kapellemeister of the Württemberg court in Stuttgart, Reinhard Keiser, wrote a work in 1720 for eight bassoons, which he describes in a letter to the prince.

> There are two suites which I have composed in all respect for your majesty a few days ago. When the players had practiced them on their instruments they produced harmony of a special effect. The two bassoonist of your band have expressed the greatest satisfaction with them ... The 'La Chasse' and the 'Granadier-Marsch' produced good humor ... The King of Denmark had eight such bassoons and 'bassonetten' in his Granadier-Guarde which were ceremonious and pleasant to hear.[27]

As the reader will find below, there was even a work performed in London, in 1744, for twenty-four bassoons and four contra-bassoons! An example of music for these bassoon ensembles which seems to have survived is the manuscript by Johann Trost (in Mügeln, Pfarrarchiv) for six bassoons (two octavo, two quarto, and two regular bassoons) and two horns.

The Hautboisten band, then, existed from ca. 1680 to ca. 1730 in an instrumentation of oboes and bassoons. It is important to remember that whereas the *Les Grands Hautbois* in Paris consisted of twelve members, so the new German Hautboisten (indoor) bands also consisted of twelve players. Perhaps a clue to the choice of twelve as the number of members can be seen in the fact that one German ensemble used the nickname 'The Apostles.' This becomes a long tradition which includes the original twelve wind parts of the Handel *Fireworks music*, the Gossec *Te Deum* and the Mozart *Gran Partita*.

---

[23] Panoff, *Militärmusik*, 84.

[24] Werner, *Städtische und fürstliche Musikpflege in Weissenfels*, 57ff.

[25] Sachs, *Musik und Oper am kurbrandenburgischen Hof*, 66. One of these oboists, Peter Glösch, was called 'celebrated' by Walther and had a composition dedicated to him in 1716 by Telemann. (Ibid., 69)

[26] Quoted in Georg Thouret, *Friedrich der Grosse als Musikfreund und Musiker* (Leipzig, 1898).

[27] Quoted in Sittard, *Zur Geschichte der Musik und des Theaters am Württembergischen Hofe*, 1:107ff.

> Euer hochgräfl. Excellenz übersende hierbey, mit allem Respect 2 Suiten von 8 Bassons, so ich vor wenigen Tagen erst componiret. Wenn die Leute alle auf diesem Instrument so exerciret wären, thut solche harmonie einen besonderen Effect. Die beiden Bassonisten unter Ihrer Bande, gbftr. Herr, Schäffer und noch einer, haven mir die beste Satisfaction von allen geben. Und wenn selbe es à propos finden möchten, dergleichen Schnarr Werck Serenissimo hören zu lassen, musten gedachte bende Bassonisten von dero Regiment darben sein. La chasse und ein Granadier-Marsch durfften I.D. bei gutem humeur vielleicht contentiren. Freundenberger könnten F. hochgefl. Excellenz die Ordre dazu ertheilen, welcher auch mit blasen muss, und auch die übringen Weiss, so mit dazu gehoren. Der Konig in Dänemarck hat 8 solche Bassons und Bassonetten bey Seiner Granadier-Guarde, welche uberaus gravitätisch und angenehm zu hören.

The real proof of the indoor concert form of the Hautboisten is found in the very large number of surviving repertoire of lengthy, major works which have no military application whatsoever.[28] Perhaps the most extraordinary example of this literature is a complete library for such a band now in Herdringen, Schloss Herdringen, Bibliotheca Fürstenbergiana. Here six original leather bound volumes are labeled in gold printing: Hautbois I, II, III, Taille, Basson I, and Basson II. This collection, dated ca. 1720, contains twenty-one multi-movement works, including Concerti (a form which will be discussed below), Symphonias, and an Intrada. Another important collection is the set of twelve *Sonatas* for oboes in three parts, taille, and bassoon by Johann Müller, printed in Amsterdam, ca. 1709. An example of real musical value is the set of three (French) *Overture-suites* by Venturini, composed in 1723 and scored for two oboe parts, hautcontre, taille, and two bassoons.[29] There is even an extant work for two Hautboisten bands in Germany, Rostock, Universitätsbibliothek. Finally, there is an excellent example of Dutch iconography which shows an Hautboisten ensemble of two oboes, taille, and bassoon performing from music, indoors.[30] (see image following page)

The next crucial development occurs shortly after the dawn of the eighteenth century when horns began to be added to the Hautboisten, for then one has an ensemble with the precise instrumentation of the early Harmoniemusik—pairs of oboes, bassoons, and horns.

Horns of one sort or another had been used much earlier in Germany, as elsewhere, for the hunt.[31] Indeed Mersenne, in 1636, even includes a surprising passage regarding consorts of these more primitive prototypes.

> If the hunters wish to have the pleasure of performing some concerts in four or more parts with their horns, it is rather easy, provided they know how to make their tones exact, and they so proportioned the length and thickness of their *trompes* that they maintain the same rations as the organ pipes.[32]

The important fact is that until the eighteenth century these early horns were not accepted in the indoor, 'concert' ensembles. Even in France, where their history is perhaps the most

[28] Sources for these works and others are given in full in volumes seven and twelve of this series.

[29] 'Hautcontre' and 'Taille' were used for both wind and string parts during this period, in this context winds are clearly intended. A similar example is the Cantata by Lehmann (in Mügeln, Pfarrarchiv) scored for SATB and two violins, viola, together with a wind choir of 'Hautbois, Hautbois contre, Taille, and Bassoun.'

[30] Reproduced in Eric Halfpenny, 'A Seventeenth Century Oboe Consort,' *The Galpin Society Journal* 10 (May 1, 1957): 62.

[31] The history of these earlier, pre-indoor, horns has been traced by Reginald Morley-Pegge, *The French Horn* (London: Ernest Benn, 1973), 12ff., and by Horace Fitzpatrick, *The Horn and Horn-Playing* (London: Oxford University Press, 1970), 1ff.

[32] Mersenne, *Harmonie Universelle*, 318.

10 The Hautboisten Tradition and the Birth of Harmonie Music

The engraved bell of a Dutch oboe showing an Hautboisten ensemble of two oboes, taille, and bassoon performing from music, indoors.

ancient for field music, it is significant that they are not found anywhere in the Chapelle Musique or Grande Écurie of Louis XIV. Even as late as 1717, in Vienna, an aristocratic lady writes, in describing a court ball,

> the music good, if they had not that detestable custom of mixing hunting horns with it, that almost deafen the company.[33]

33 Lady Mary Wortley Montagu, quoted in Morley-Pegge, *The French Horn*, 16.

Traditionally, the introduction of the more modern (single-coil) horn into indoor use is credited to a very cultured Bohemian aristocrat and supporter of the arts, Franz Anton, Count von Sporck, Lord of Lissa, Gradlitz, Konoged, etc. The best account of this event was written in 1792:

In the year 1680 he set out upon a tour of foreign countries, according to the custom of the Bohemian nobility. He visited the foremost royal and princely courts, where he noted everything which struck him as beautiful, artistic, or useful; and brought them back with him for the ornament and benefit of his native land. In this connection we must not omit mention of an incident which forms a proper part of the history of music in Bohemia. In Paris he heard the hunting-horn for the first time, an instrument which had been invented there a short time before. He found this instrument so agreeable that he caused two men from his retinue to be instructed in the art of playing it, which they brought shortly to the highest degree of perfection, and upon their return to Bohemia taught it to others.[34]

Whatever is the case, the idea of using the horns in the indoor ensembles does seem to come to Germany from the East as one can see in one of the earliest references to this expanded Hautboisten wind band as the 'Sächsische Variante.'[35] This new wind band, which was Harmoniemusik in all but name, seems to have rapidly replaced the short-lived Hautboisten. One finds mention of the new band (oboes and Waldhörnern) in Zeitz by 1715;[36] in the Bavarian military (six oboes and two horns) in 1722;[37] the 'Sächsische Variante,' mentioned above, of ca. 1730 (two oboes, two horns, and two bassoons);[38] and in a performance for the Nürnberg Carpenter's Guild in 1731 by three bands, each consisting of three oboes, two horns, and a bassoon.[39]

The extant literature for this new wind band of oboes, horns and bassoons includes both military music, as for example in the oldest extant Saxony military music (for two oboes, two horns, and two bassoons), dated 1729,[40] and non-military music as well. Outstanding examples of the latter include the eight important compositions by Telemann, probably written for the court in Hamburg, and the several works by Handel.

Once horns were added to the oboes and bassoons of the Hautboisten ensembles the instrumentation was now the same as that of the first generation of Harmoniemusik of the Classic Period. But the instrumentation is only half the story, for the names and style of the repertoire had its own separate metamorphosis in becoming the forms and style of the Classic Period, as the reader will find in the following section.

[34] Quoted in Friedrich Hirsching, *Historisch-Litterärisches Handbuch Beruhmter und Denkwürdiger Personen* (Leipzig, 1792), xiii, 146.

[35] Braun, 'Entwurf für ein Typologie der "Hautboisten",' 59.

[36] Werner, *Städtische und fürstliche Musikpflege in Weissenfels*, 96.

[37] Johannes Reschke, 'Zur Geschichte der Deutschen Militärmusik des 17. und 18. Jahrhunderts,' in *Deutsche Musik-Kultur* (1937), Nr. 2, 15.

[38] Braun, 'Entwurf für ein Typologie der "Hautboisten",' 59.

[39] Ibid., 54.

[40] *Die Infanterie Märsche der vormaligen Chürfurstl. Sachsischen Armee 1729.*

Before continuing we might mention that by 1780 the new Harmoniemusik name had become reserved for the ensemble of pairs of oboes, clarinets, horns and bassoons, with an optional contrabassoon. Any other collection of wind instruments at this time went under the name, *blasmusik*. The center for the new Harmoniemusik repertoire was Vienna and one finds that the further away one gets geographically from Vienna the fewer manuscripts one finds under that name. In England, for example, in the final decade of the eighteenth century there appears to have been no Harmoniemusik movement at all.

The Origin of Hautboisten Repertoire

The key to understanding the origin of Harmoniemusik literature, and a very large part to understanding the function of the pre-Harmoniemusik wind band in the courts of the German Baroque, is found in a considerable body of extant German literature for wind band under the name of 'Concerto.' These works are neither solo concerti nor concerto grossi, but are examples of an almost never discussed form, the *concerto da camera*. It is this form which provides proof of a continuous and direct development in wind literature from sixteenth-century Italy to the Harmoniemusik of the Classic Period.

In order to chart the course of this development, I should like to review briefly the use of the word 'concerto' itself, beginning, of course, in Italy. The word 'concerto' was first used only to mean a group of musicians, as we might today use the word 'ensemble.' Thus Doni wrote of singing 'sopra un concerto di Viole.'[41] 'Concerto' was frequently used as part of the title of an Italian wind band in the late sixteenth and seventeenth centuries, as for example in the famous 'Concerti delli stromenti di fiato della Illustriss. Signoria di Venetia,' conducted by Girolamo Dalla Casa (ca. 1584); the wind band called 'Concerto di Palazzo' in Siena (1559); again in Siena, the civic wind band, the 'Concerto della Signoria' (1621); the 'musici del concerto di Campidoglio,' an ensemble of shawms, trombones, and cornetts under the Pope's jurisdiction in Rome (1702); the important Roman civic wind band of the Baroque,

[41] Quoted in Franz Giegling, *Giuseppe Torelli* (Kassel: Barenreiter, 1949), 12.

the 'Concerto Capitolino', etc. The word seems to have had only this meaning in the oldest extant appearance in a musical composition, the *Concerti di Andrea, et Gio. Gabrieli* of 1587.[42]

By the time of Gabrieli, and certainly evident in the music of Gabrieli, the term seems to designate music in which there is some nature of contrast, either of instrumental textures or of dynamics. This is confirmed both by Bottrigari in 1594, who wrote that 'If you inquire into the word Concerto you will find that it signifies "contention" or "contrast",'[43] and by Praetorius, who pointed out in 1619 that 'concerto' derived from *concertare*, to compete, and not from *conserere*, to consort.[44]

The word 'concerto' at this time did not seem to refer at all to form, as we understand it, which has contributed to some misleading scholarly commentary on the music of this period.[45] In particular, sonata, sinfonia, and concerto are all synonyms between ca. 1580 and the early part of the seventeenth century and all tend to have fugal first movements. Indeed, as Bukofzer points out[46], even the vocal and instrumental styles are identical which is of no particular surprise as the first multi-part instrumental music was taken from prior vocal works. Bukofzer also reminds us[47] that canzonas appeared frequently under the title Sinfonia or Sonata and that 'Sonata,' is in fact nothing but an abbreviation of 'canzon da sonar.'

According to Hutchings[48] the word 'concerto' did imply what we might call today 'concert' music.

> In 1730 a symphony might still be an Italian overture, a passage for organ in an English anthem, a march, battle, storm or pastoral piece in an opera or oratorio, or a ripieno concerto served under another name; but if a work were called concerto it was intended for 'absolute' listening, for use at a concert.

It is also important to point out that these various 'form' names did not imply any particular size of performing medium. As Hutchings observes,

> Until well after 1700 purely instrumental pieces might be called sonatas, concertos, or sinfonias, without apparent distinction of structure. What Torelli would have called *sinfonie con trombe* at Bologna, and Bach

[42] Manfred Bukofzer, *Music in the Baroque Era* (New York: Norton, 1947), 20.

[43] Ercole Bottrigari, *Il desiderio ovvero De' concerti de varii stromenti musicali* (1594).

[44] Praetorius, *Syntagma Musicum*, vol. 3.

[45] See Henry Mishkin, 'The Italian Concerto before 1700,' *Bulletin of the American Musicological Society*, no. 7 (October 1, 1943): 20ff., for a review of the mistaken paths some writers have taken.

[46] Bukofzer, *Music in the Baroque Era*, 21.

[47] Ibid., 51.

[48] Arthur Hutchings, *The Baroque Concerto* (New York: Scribner, 1979), 29.

Konzerte at Cöthen were called *Sonatae Grossae* by Molter, director of the orchestra at Gotha. The choice of designation was not affected by the number of performers.[49]

[49] Ibid., 27–28.

Indeed, with regard to the concerto, one can identify four basic types: the large and small church concerti and the large and small chamber concerti.

The large Italian church concerti, often called *Missa concertata*, *Motetti concertati*, or most often, *Concerti ecclesiastici* are very familiar to musicians in the compositions by Gabrieli and in the extensive discussion by Praetorius in *Syntagma Musicum*, volume 3.[50]

[50] Praetorius' discussion is presented in detail in volume two of this series.

During the early years of the seventeenth century there also appeared church concerti for smaller ensembles, of both voices and instruments. Examples of church concerti for small vocal ensembles are Fattorini's *Sacri concerti a due voci* (1600) and Viadana's *Cento concerti ecclesiastici* (1602). Small church concerti for instruments appear for both strings, as Felice dall'Abaco's *Concerti da chiesa*, op. 2 (in which both violin parts are written on the same stave, indicating only two players) and Alberti's *Concerti da chiesa e da camera* (1713), and for winds, as in the example 'Concerto a cinque,' for four trombones and tenor in Franzoni's *Appartato Musicale de Messa …* (1613). One should add, of course, that the entire body of Italian instrumental canzonas are actually small church concerti.

The chamber concerti, *concerto da camera*, also existed in considerable numbers during the Italian Baroque, even though the reader will scarcely find a single reference to them in musicological publications. The vocal *concerti da camera* were called *Concerti da Pastori* or *Concerti d'Amore*.[51]

[51] Giegling, *Giuseppe Torelli*, 12.

It is of course the instrumental form of the seventeenth-century Italian *concerto da camera* which is the subject of our interest here for it is this form which, with the intrada, aria, sonata, symphonia, canzona, et.al., travels to the North and will be found in the form of German *concerti da camera* for wind bands. Perhaps the earliest extant Italian example of this title is the *Concerto da camera* by Torelli (1686), which is followed by such examples as Tagietti's *Concerti a quattro* (1699), Albergati's *Concerti varii da camera* (1702), Manfredini's *Concerti per Camera* (1704), Alberti's *Concerti da chiesa e da camera* (1713), and Abaco's

Concerti a piu Istrumenti (1730), to name a few examples. An example of such a work designated for wind band is the Albinoni *Concerto* for three oboes, bassoon, trumpet, and bass.

That fact that nearly all the surviving examples of music using this title are prints from late in the seventeenth or early eighteenth century does not, it seems to me, preclude the existence of this form much earlier during the seventeenth century. First of all, it seems to me that most scholars would conclude that the instrumental concerti had their origin in the church sonatas, as Hutchings points out.

> The Italian concertos had come from church sonatas and were used at High Mass. We speak of concerts and recitals, but in the seventeenth and eighteenth centuries music was named after the places in which it sounded—church, theatre, chamber ... Church sonatas became chamber music at sessions of the Bologna academies, in court music rooms ...[52]

In the case of the Italian wind instrument *concerto da camera* I believe the use of this word as a synonym for the wind band itself during the sixteenth and seventeenth centuries implies a continuity of the literature as well. Evidence of this continuity can be seen in Cerone's *El Melopeo y Maestro* of 1613 (Naples), mentioned above, which gives a list of wind instruments which he says were used in the *concertos* ('que entran en los Conciertos'):

> Sackbuts, curtals or bassoons, doppioni, recorders, dulcaymas, cornetts, cornamuse and crumhorns.[53]

Given what is known today of early seventeenth-century Italian instrumental music, I believe one can assume that many more compositions once existed which were known as 'concerti,' whether *da chiesa* or *da camera*, all quite similar in style.

It also seems quite obvious that both wind ensembles and string ensembles coexisted as completely separate mediums at this time. The coexistence of these different kinds of ensembles was one of the characteristics of the new concerto grosso late in the seventeenth century. This new form differed with the earlier instrumental music first as a distinction in size of ensemble.

[52] Hutchings, *The Baroque Concerto*, 17.

[53] Cerone, *El Melopeo y Maestro*, 1038.

Corelli, Gregori, Valentini and Torelli—all the early concertists except Dall'Abaco—called their works concerti grossi to distinguish them from instrumental *concerti sacri* or *concerti ecclesiastici* and from *concerti da camera*, which might employ five or six instrumental parts but were not orchestral conceptions.[54]

Second, as Schering points out, while the new concerto grosso symbolizes the transformation of the 'up to now predominate wind orchestra to the homogeneously organized and technically dependable string orchestra,'[55] the essential characteristic was the 'contrast of bodies of sounds, as strings against winds, as opposed to early forms, such as the sonata, where they might be mixed.'[56] Bukofzer adds that the original idea was not only a contrast of mediums, but the spatial factor was fundamental to it.[57]

Given this characteristic of the contrast of bodies of sound, one should not be surprised to find many Italian concerti grossi with real wind bands in the concertino. Schering gives the manuscript source[58] for twenty-two such works by Torelli, some for two to four trumpets, with and without oboes; others for two horns or trombones. Vivaldi also wrote a number of concerti grossi with from four to six winds standing alone in the concertino. These works represent only the very logical use of the two most prominent ensembles of the day and should not be looked on as mere experimentation in the use of wind color.[59]

As is commonly known, all of these Italian forms traveled to the North during the seventeenth century. Not only did the various representatives of these forms for wind bands also travel north, but they found a very receptive atmosphere in Germany, for as Schering points out, 'In general, Germany cultivated in the first place Blaserkonzerts.'[60] Bukofzer adds that not only did the Germans prefer winds to strings for the ensemble canzona, but winds were considered more noble than strings.[61]

Thus church works for voices and wind instruments, both the large and small *concerto da chiesa*, appear in Germany as is documented in Praetorius and so gloriously represented in the works of Andreas Hammerschmidt and Heinrich Schütz (who was, let us not forget, Gabrieli's student).

[54] Hutchings, *The Baroque Concerto*, 21.

[55] Arnold Schering, *Geschichte des Instrumentalkonzerts* (Leipzig, 1927), 8.

[56] Ibid., 39.

[57] Bukofzer, *Music in the Baroque Era*, 223.

[58] Schering, *Geschichte des Instrumentalkonzerts*, 61.

[59] As for example in Bukofzer, *Music in the Baroque Era*, 229. One of the origins traditionally given for the concerto grosso itself are the trumpet sonatas of the Bologna school. See Schering, *Geschichte des Instrumentalkonzerts*, 60, and Hutchings, *The Baroque Concerto*, 20:

> When the music of Bologna reached its zenith during the last decade of the century the most magnificent pieces heard in St. Petronio, and probably at sessions of the *Accademia Filarmonica*, were the *sinfonie con due trombe, concerti per trombe* and *sonate con trombe* by Torelli, Perti, Domenico Gabrielli and Jacchini.

Another origin for the concerto grosso, given by Schering, in his introduction to *Denkmaler Deutscher Tonkunst*, vols. 29/30, v, are the trio sonatas for either strings or two oboes/flutes and bassoon. (See also, Schering, *Geschichte des Instrumentalkonzerts*, 60, and Bukofzer, *Music in the Baroque Era*, 223ff.)

[60] Schering, *Denkmaler Deutscher Tonkunst*, viii.

The Italian church sonata now appears in Germany for all kinds of wind bands: the civic wind bands, represented by the brass sonatas of Briegel, Kindermann, Pezel, Reiche, Speer, and Störl; sonatas for Hautboisten bands by Fasch, Finger, Keller, Müller, and Schulz; and sonatas for the new 'Harmoniemusik' ensemble by Molter. Also one finds for winds the Italian intrada, aria, and symphonia (especially Molter and Kindermann).

Instrumental concerti are also found in great number in Germany, but now they are no longer church music, but music of the court—chamber music.[62] This is made very clear in the introduction to Georg Muffat's collection of concerti grossi, *Ausserlesene Instrumental-Music* of 1701. First he informs the reader that the concerti are in a style he learned in Italy, but then adds,

> These concertos, suited neither to the church (because of the ballet airs and the airs of other sorts which they include) nor for dancing (because of other interwoven conceits, now slow and serious, now gay and nimble, and composed only for the express refreshment of the ear) may be performed most appropriately in connection with entertainments given by great princes and lords, for receptions of distinguished guests, and at state banquets.[63]

Although this particular collection is intended for strings, Muffat makes an additional observation of interest:

> Should there be among your musicians some who can play and modulate the French oboe or shawm agreeably, you may with the best effect use two of these instead of the two violins, and a good bassoon player instead of the French bass, to form the concertino.

In the German concerto grosso one can again find many examples of the use of the independent wind bands in the concertino, due, as Krüger points out,[64] to the abundance of these ensembles in the German courts. Krüger gives the locations of a large number of concerti by Fasch with independent wind bands, sometimes Hautboisten, sometimes 'Harmoniemusik,' in the concertino, with strings alone in the ripieno.[65] The *Denkmäler deutscher Tonkunst*, vol. 29–30, includes a concerto by Graupner with an Hautboisten ensemble in the concertino and a striking concerto by Stölzel with three wind concertino

---

[61] Bukofzer, *Music in the Baroque Era*, 115ff., 406. There is some evidence that by the late seventeenth century winds had begun to fall in social status in Italy. This can be seen in the often quoted remark by Scarlatti that he did not like wind instruments as they all played false (See Walther Krüger, *Das Concerto grosso in Deutschland* [Wolfenbüttel-Berlin, 1932], 125). Also Wolfgang Caspar Printz, in his *Historischen Beschreibung der Edelen Sing- und Klingkunst* (1690), quotes an unnamed author of *Gymnasmatis de Exercitiis Academicorum* as commenting on the rejection in Italy of the 'pfieffer' and 'trommeten,' because,

> they contort the mouth, disarrange the face, impede the speech and conversation and, beyond this, the intellect and judgement is impared. The manner of blowing by so many civic wind players often causes them to lose their common sense … Yes the winds expand the lungs apart, fatigue the body, expend the spirit of life. (Quoted in Krüger, *Das Concerto grosso in Deutschland*, 125)

[62] Hutchings, *The Baroque Concerto*, 29, 'From about 1715 very few concertos can have been composed with any thought of church use.'

[63] Quoted in Oliver Strunk, ed., *Source Readings in Music History* (New York: Norton, 1950), 449ff.

[64] Krüger, *Das Concerto grosso in Deutschland*, 125.

[65] Grove (6:414) lists twenty concerti grossi by Fasch with five to eight winds in the concertino.

choirs accompanied by strings. Here one sees an Hautboisten band of three oboe parts, bassoon, and flute in one concertino and two typical royal trumpet choirs, each with timpani, in the other two concertinos. This work perfectly spot-lights the current German court wind ensembles as solo ensembles. Works in this tradition may have also appeared in France, for the *Mercure de France*, of 23 April 1728, speaks of a *concerto* for trumpets and timpani, horns, and oboes, accompanied by orchestra 'which gave great pleasure.'

Of greater interest, with regard to the birth of Harmoniemusik, is the appearance in Germany of the *concerto da camera* for winds, nearly all of which seem to have been composed for the Hautboisten band with no horns. There are fourteen such works in the Herdringen, Schloss Herdringen, Bibliotheca Fürstenbergiana collection, as well as contributions by Fasch (not to mention his work for *three* Hautboisten and *three* trumpet choirs!), Foerster, Hasse, Hertel, and seven by Prowo. German concerti for wind bands with horns are very rare (Molter [1695–1765] is the principal exception), but one must mention the two double wind band concerti, each accompanied by strings, by Händel, for they stand at the very point in time when the new ensemble with horns was beginning to appear in Germany. Händel acknowledges this transformation by composing one concerti for double Hautboisten bands (oboes and bassoons) and the other for double 'Harmoniemusik' bands (oboes, horns and bassoons). In general, however, one can say that the *concerto da camera* for winds in Germany are identified with the Hautboisten period and are completely indebted to the Italian models.

Toward the end of the seventeenth century a new instrumental form appears briefly in Germany called the 'Overture' (usually referred to today as the 'French Overture-suite'). The wind band music which appeared under this title is, I believe, of considerable historical value. First, this literature documents the continued presence of the 'concert' Hautboisten through the end of the Baroque, for even a cursory glance at this music reveals that it had nothing to do with the functions in society of the concurrent military Hautboisten. Second, and more important, the transformations which occur in this body of wind band literature reveal clearly the emergence of the classical Harmoniemusik and the relationship of that literature to earlier forms.

The earliest generation of wind band overtures seem to have been written for the Hautboisten band (without horns), as can be seen today in the extant works by Burckart, Venturini, Wieland, and Witt. In the three (of an original six) extant *Overtures* for Hautboisten by Francesco Venturini (d. 1745), composed in 1723, one sees the typical form for this period: an 'overture' first movement followed by four to six freely composed dance movements. Here one finds the typical Minuets, Gavottes, and Allemandes, but also in each of these works the more ancient 'Aria,' one of the forms which migrated from sixteenth-century Italy. There is another important stylistic relationship with the past here, an idea which Schering found at work in an earlier group of works by Venturini.

> A mixture of the Concerto and French Orchestra-suite had been attempted by Corelli, Muffat, and Venturini, who in one case in his *concerto da camera* of 1713, had substituted a concerto movement for the Overture.[66]

In the present works Venturini apparently attempts the same end by introducing the concertato principle, although retaining the title 'Overture,' for the first movement.

In summary, here is wind band music in a new form, but with strong stylistic hallmarks of the Italian heritage and composed for the older medium (Hautboisten).

In the next generation, one finds Overture-suites for the new medium, the Hautboisten with the addition of two horns. Representative of these are ten anonymous overtures in Schwerin Wissenschaftliche Allgemeinbibliothek, three by Graun, six by Telemann, and examples by Fick and Roellig. In the wind band works by Telemann (1681–1767) one can see the new horns but also, as compared with Venturini, an important new step forward. Here the internal content is entirely German; there are no traces evident of the Italian past. Here is purely German baroque music composed for the instrumentation of 'Harmoniemusik.'

[66] Arnold Schering, 'Einleitung,' *Denkmäler Deutscher Tonkunst*, vol. 29/30 (1906), xiii.

> Eine Verschmelzung des Konzerts mit der französischen Orchestersuite hatte ausser Corelli, Muffat und anderen schon Franc. Venturini in seinen Kammerkonzerten von 1713 versucht, indem er in einigen Fällen die einleitende Overtüre durch einen Konzertsatz ersetzte.

In the following generation, one suddenly finds oneself caught up in that cross currents of style which we call the 'Pre-Classic' Period, as is clearly evident in the wind band works by Wagenseil. Wagenseil (1715–1777) has left wind band works with older sounding titles (Suites) and wind band works with the new titles we associate with the Harmoniemusik of the Classic Period (Divertimenti and Partitas). It is the works with the new titles which interests us more, as they reflect the very moment when the new Harmoniemusik begins to emerge. The three extant works in question (Austria, Wien, Gesellschaft der Musikfreunde in Wien, VIII 8540) are scored for two oboes, two 'Corni Ingl,' two 'Corni di Caccia,' and two fagotti. The appearance of English horns here is no surprise for they had already made themselves regular members of the Baroque Hautboisten band, where in the repertoire they are called *taille* (not to be confused with the later viola). The appearance of the term 'Corni di Caccia,' of course, only reminds us that it was the single-coil French hunting horn which had so recently made its indoor appearance in Germany.

It is however the stylistic features here which are so interesting and so revealing. The form of both a *Divertimento in F* and the *Partita in C* seem at first glance to be nothing more than the old Overture-suite under a new title, for they consist of eight and seven movements, respectively. Closer examination reveals important new formal characteristics: the dance titles have given way completely to Italian tempo markings and the first movements are clearly the early, two-part sonata form. Here are compositions which are truly half-Baroque and half-Classical, with the multi-movement form and the very heavily ornamented slow movements pointing toward the Baroque and with the new titles and sonata first movements pointing toward the Classic Period. Another *Divertimento in F*, in four movements (Allegro/Minuetto/Andantino/Chase), seems much closer to the Classic style, but retains the Baroque slow movement (in spite of the title, it is actually an 'Adagio,' performed in a sub-divided common time).

These 'half-way' Harmoniemusik compositions can be found in great numbers throughout Bohemia, in particular. Often they appear with the new title, 'Partita,' while retaining the old pair of taille instruments. It is interesting to note, parenthetically, that in this first generation of music under the new Classic titles works were composed for both the indoor wind band ('a la Camera') and the military counterpart ('di Campagna'), but examples of the latter soon die out.

If some works during this transition period seem more old fashioned, there were, of course, some which had an entirely new sound and breathed a new spirit. Let me only note that it was still during the lifetime of both Telemann and Wagenseil that Haydn composed his Divertimenti for two oboes, two horns, and two bassoons in 1759–1761. These compositions belong in every respect to the Classic Period and announce that the metamorphosis of the *concerto da camera* has ended and a new kind of music had arrived: Harmoniemusik!

PART 2
Court Wind Bands

1 Court Wind Bands in France

Louis XIII

Neither nature nor history has been kind to Louis XIII. He was very thin, with an oversized head and nose and a great lower lip which caused his mouth to hang open. Most of his life he was physically weak, suffering from tuberculosis, intestinal inflammation, and doctors.[1] History treats him poorly because he was king in name only; the real power was the famous Cardinal Richelieu. Because Louis had a preference for the male sex, he went for periods of up to thirteen years without visiting the bed of his wife and thus there was fear he would fail to produce an heir. But he did, thereby making his greatest single contribution to France: Louis XIV, who would tower over the century.

There seems to be sufficient evidence to suggest that the *Les Grands Hautbois*, a twelve-member royal wind band established at least as early as 1580, under Henry III,[2] continued throughout the reign of Louis XIII, although an engraving of his coronation (17 October 1610) pictures only an eight-member wind band.[3] Shortly after the coronation, in any case, the twelve-member band can again be documented, consisting of two shawms and two cornetts playing treble parts, four alto or tenor shawms playing *haute-contre* and *taille* parts, two trombones playing *basse-taille*, and two bass shawms playing a *basse* part.[4]

For Louis XIII's more private entertainment one may assume that smaller wind ensembles were drawn from the larger one. A contemporary engraving of a ballet given for Louis XIII shows a wind ensemble of two cornetts, shawm, sordun, and trumpet.[5]

Louis XIII also maintained a separate body of trumpet players for ceremonial and state appearances. One finds them, for example, performing in the great Carrousel of 1612, held in honor of Louis' marriage. On this occasion the trumpets provided three day's worth of music in a series of horse ballets depicting a variety of Greek gods, the legends of Amadis of Gaul and Perseus, the Seasons, and the Hours of the Day. The

[1] In a single year they bled him forty-seven times and gave him two hundred fifteen enemas! See Arvède Barine, *La Grand Mademoiselle* (New York, 1902), 15, and Jacques Boulenger, *The Seventeenth Century* (New York: Putnam, 1920), 37.

[2] The development of this wind band in the sixteenth century is discussed in volume two of this series.

[3] Several extant examples of the repertoire of this wind band are in six-parts (see volume seven in this series).

[4] See Jules Écorcheville, 'Quelques Documents sur la Musique de la Grand-Écurie du Roi,' in *Sammelbande des Internationalen Musikgesellschaft* (1903), 3:608ff., and Grove, 17:242.

[5] Grove, 17:535.

Coronation of Louis XIII, 17 October 1610

celebration ended with a final triumphant entry of Roman warriors leading captive kings of Africa and Asia, mounted on elephants, and a model palace exploding in fireworks.[6]

Apparently some of the other lords of France maintained large wind bands in imitation of the king. De la Ruelle's illustrated chronicle of the funeral ceremonies for Charles III, Duke of Lorraine, includes two engravings with wind bands, both of which are quite extraordinary. One pictures the singers in the church on a balcony together with shawm and trombone players. One of the shawms is a huge bass instrument with an up-turned bell, looking like a seven-foot bass clarinet. Another engraving shows the entire interior of the church during the principal funeral ceremony. Here a large balcony supports some thirty musicians, of whom at least twelve are clearly wind players and the rest (largely obscured) are perhaps singers, while a separate balcony contains the string players.[7]

[6] Robert Isherwood, *Music in the Service of the King* (Ithaca, NY: Cornell University Press, 1973), 95.

[7] Claude de La Ruelle, *Obsequies of Charles III* (*Pompe funèbre de Charles III, Duc de Lorraine*) (Nancy, 1608).

Louis XIV

Everyone has read of the almost incredible opulence of the court of Louis XIV. Like its symbol, the buildings at Versailles, everything about this court was bigger and richer than any court in Europe during modern history.

But Louis XIV was also an extraordinary man and king. Although his formal education was incomplete, he had penetrating judgement, worked very hard as an administrator, and, when not at play, was a most effective head of government. He had outstanding personal qualities as well, being well built, robust, and a skillful dancer and horseman. France was delighted to have so great a king at last and, at the same time, a man of such charm. Duke Saint-Simon recalled,

> Never did man give with better grace than Louis XIV ... Never did disobliging words escape him; and if he had to blame, to reprimand, or to correct, which was rare, it was nearly always with goodness, never ... with anger or severity. Never was a man so naturally polite ... Never did he pass the humblest petticoat without raising his hat.[8]

[8] Louis de Rouvroy Saint-Simon, *Memoirs of Louis XIV and the Regency* (London: Dunne, 1901), 2:369.

As his court had exceeded everything in recent history, so was his musical establishment larger and better, including numerous wind players organized into several distinct ensem-

28 Court Wind Bands

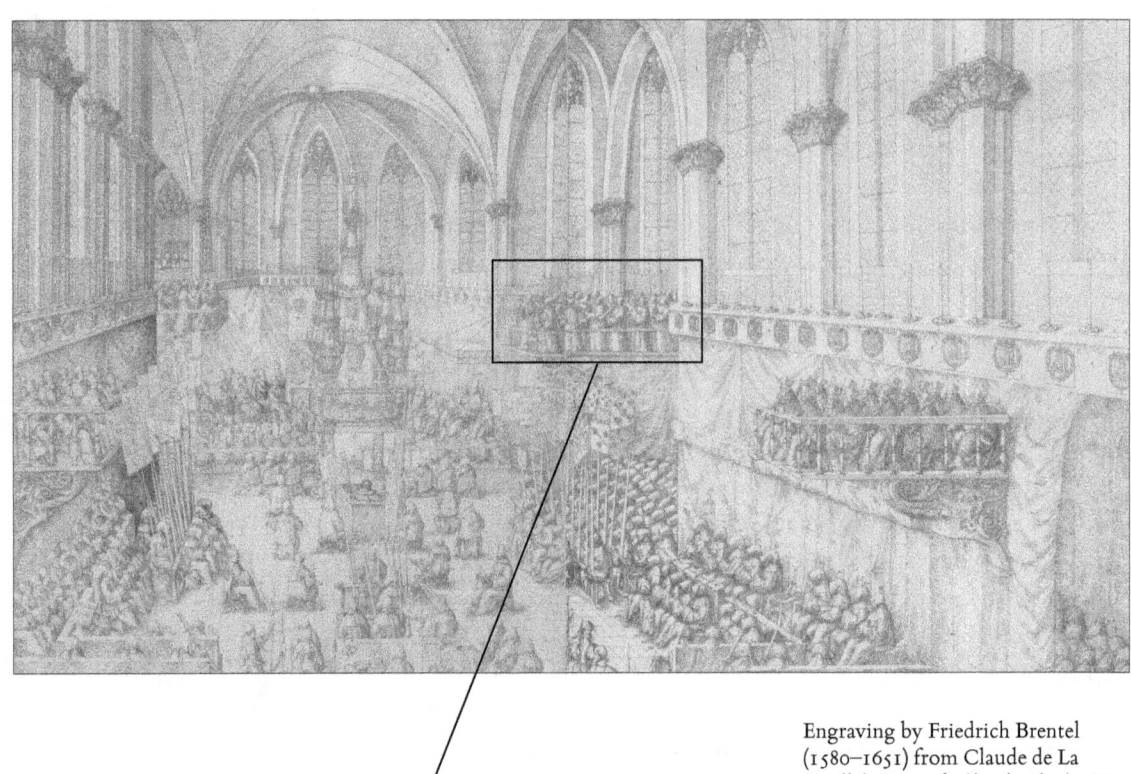

Engraving by Friedrich Brentel (1580–1651) from Claude de La Ruelle's *Pompe funèbre de Charles III, Duc de Lorraine*

Detail of the musicians; see larger image pp. 30–31

COURT WIND BANDS IN FRANCE 29

Engraving by Friedrich Brentel (1580–1651) from Claude de La Ruelle's *Pompe funèbre de Charles III, Duc de Lorraine*

Detail of the musicians; see larger image pp. 32–33

30 Court Wind Bands

COURT WIND BANDS IN FRANCE 31

Detail of the musicians in an engraving by Friedrich Brentel (1580–1651)
from Claude de La Ruelle's *Pompe funèbre de Charles III, Duc de Lorraine*

32 Court Wind Bands

Detail of the musicians in an engraving by Friedrich Brentel (1580–1651)
from Claude de La Ruelle's *Pompe funèbre de Charles III, Duc de Lorraine*

bles. These musicians were organized under four broad administrative divisions: the *Écurie*, the Chapelle, the Chambre, and the Maison Militaire.

I begin this discussion with the *Écurie*, where the most interesting wind bands were found. The *Écurie*, an ancient title meaning 'stable,' included not only musicians, but riding masters, heralds of arms, sword bearers, and officers of the royal household; it might better have been named the 'Department of Ceremony.'

The musicians under the *Écurie* enjoyed high prestige: they possessed the right of *commensaux* (meal companions of the king), they were exempt from many taxes and obligations to church-wardens and civic officials, and they were not required to quarter soldiers in wartime. They received gifts of food and clothing, in addition to regular income and bonuses for special ceremonies. During their time off they could live and work in Paris.[9]

They were free to accept private students and this assumed special significance with regard to employment at the palace. There seems to have been no formal audition process for members of the *Écurie* wind bands, as players were hired only on the basis of recommendation. Thus study with one of the current members of a court band was the only direct route to success for a young musician. The importance of such teacher–pupil relationships can be seen in the formal contracts which were drawn upon the initiation of study, as one can see in the following agreement between Jean Baptiste Desjardins, a member of the *Les Grands Hautbois*, and one, François Gillotot.

> Today it has appeared in front of the notary of Paris that the undersigned Jean B. Desjardins ... is obligated to Francois Gillotot, servant of M. The Abbey Bouchart, ... to show him how to play the oboe, flute and instrumental music which this entails. Gillotot may be free to obtain this goal and do his profession without being obligated. Mr. Desjardins will furnish him with instruments. This contract entails the sum of 185 livres [about $1200 in 1983 dollars] ... (the final payment) is made when Mr. Desjardins succeeds in placing Gillotot in a quality position as an oboist. Desjardins must try to place Gillotot ... Gillotot must go precisely all the days to take his lessons with Desjardins.[10]

[9] Isherwood, *Music in the Service of the King*, 251, 284–285.

[10] Dated 3 October 1702, and quoted in 'Documents du Minutier Central,' in *Recherches sur la Musique francaise classique* (Paris, 1968), 245. In the 1963 edition of the same publication, Norbert Dufourcq and Marcelle Benoit have published extensive additional legal notices which reveal insights into the private lives of these musicians.

Les Grands Hautbois

The band which interests us the most, among those of the *Écurie*, is the *Les Grands Hautbois*, which was one of the most important wind bands in the history of music. Because in previous publications there have been so many misconceptions about the instrumentation and function of this band, we must first review its history.

Long thought to have been created during the reign of Louis XIV, we now know that it dates from the reign of François I, near the beginning of the sixteenth century, and continues to appear as an independent wind band until the French revolution.[11] One source of confusion has been the title of this band as it appears in the court pay documents. Until about 1715, when it was called 'Hautbois et saqueboutes,' it had been recorded as 'Joueurs de violons, haultbois, saqueboutes et cornetz,' a title carried over by scribes from the time of François I (ca. 1530). The title was in fact accurate for the first period (the reign of François I), for it was then an ensemble of six oboes and (Italian) trombones and a separate ensemble of six violins. By the second-half of the sixteenth century the violins disappeared from this ensemble, joining the Chambre administrative section.[12] By 1580, under Henry III, one can document a band of twelve 'hautbois, sacquebutes, et cornets à bouquin.'[13]

This ensemble of twelve winds continues as a pure wind band into the seventeenth century. It is here, however, that the name 'violin' reappears in the records. Furthermore, several records list each member as playing a specific secondary string instrument. As one will see among the civic musicians in seventeenth-century Germany, it was not uncommon for players to play several instruments. Benoit, who has considered this question in depth, concludes that the band was basically a twelve-member wind band. Its members probably did in fact have a doubling ability on strings (before 1715), but Benoit believes the evidence is that if they played strings to augment the already large group of string players, it must have been only very occasionally, for they were clearly primarily wind players.[14]

But if, in spite of the title, it was a true wind band during the seventeenth century, it was not, on the other hand, an *oboe* band! *Les Grands Hautbois* must rather be taken to mean some-

[11] For the first period, see Henri Prunières, 'La Musique de la Chambre et de L'Écurie sous le Regne de François Ier,' in *L'Année Musicale* (Paris, 1911), 240ff. For the periods of Louis XIII–Louis XIV, the definitive work on the musicians of the court has now been published in two volumes by Marcelle Benoit: *Versailles et les Musiciens du Roi* (Paris, 1971) and *Musiques de Cour* (Paris, 1971). While these volumes conclude with 1733, the present writer has seen documents (in particular, MS.Bundle 01/878) in the National Archives, Paris, which carry the history of the band as far as 1791.

[12] Prunières, 'La Musique de la Chambre et de L'Écurie sous le Regne de François Ier,' 248–249; also, Benoit, *Versailles et les Musiciens du Roi*, 220ff.

[13] Prunières, 'La Musique de la Chambre et de L'Écurie sous le Regne de François Ier.'

[14] Benoit, *Versailles et les Musiciens du Roi*, 221. Écorcheville, 'Quelques Documents sur la Musique de la Grand-Écurie du Roi,' and more recent writers such as Susan Sandman, in 'Wind Band Music under Louis XIV' (Unpublished dissertation, Stanford, 1974), 111–112, give a mistaken impression that the band performed equally in time and ability as a string or wind band. The court records simply do not support this hypothesis.

thing more like 'the double-reed family' band. It consisted of three sizes of oboes: *dessus* (the modern size instrument), two larger forms, *haute-contre* and *taille* (two players played each of these instruments), and two more who performed on 'basse de hautbois,' which most scholars take to mean bassoon. To these eight double-reeds were added two cornetts and two trombones.

This was the basic wind band instrumentation, but it should be remembered that these players probably performed on a variety of other wind instruments. The estate of Jacques Danican Philidor, a member of the *Les Grands Hautbois*, upon his death in 1708, indicates he owned fourteen oboes (dessus, quintes, tailles), twenty-one flutes (dessus, quintes, tailles et basses), two bassoons, two flageolets, one violin, one tambour, and one great pair of timpani.[15]

According to an ancient tradition, the *Les Grands Hautbois* performed when the king awoke on the first day of the year, on his name-day, and on May One. This often quoted tradition has led some writers to imply that these were among the rare occasions these players appeared as a wind band.[16] Actually they made numerous appearances, both private and public, in the chamber, the chapel, and outdoors.[17] The rather large gifts of food they received (bread, wine, meat, poultry, and lard) six times a year alone suggests they were a busy ensemble.

One contemporary (ca. 1665) description of the performance of this wind band seems to suggest fine musicians struggling with less than perfect (or perhaps newly developed) instruments.

> The oboes, whom one can now hear at the king's palace and in Paris, have stately repertoire and style. Their cadences are correct, their vibrato is sweet, their ornaments are just as correct as the more educated vocal ones and those of the most perfect instruments. We have seen their success in the theater; especially in certain entrées. They had a marvelous effect in one Pastorale. But one can never be confident of the air; the shortness of breathe, the thickening of the lungs, the fatigue of the stomach and finally, one is conscious of a notable difference in beginnings and endings; here one could discover more exactness.[18]

When these players joined the 'twenty-four Violins' of the king, they played their wind instruments, yet doubled the string parts. Rousseau, who had been a professional music

[15] Benoit, *Versailles et les Musiciens du Roi*, 360. The original document can be seen in Norbert Dufourcq and Marcelle Benoit, *Recherches sur la Musique francaise classique* (Paris, 1963), 195. This original document lists in one place two oboes, followed by an indication that 'one is old and one is of the Écurie.' Perhaps this suggests that by the time of Louis XIV, these players were using the modern oboe.

[16] As for example in Sandman, 'Wind Band Music under Louis XIV,' 112, and Grove, 14:206.

[17] Benoit, *Versailles et les Musiciens du Roi*, 222.

[18] Abbé des Pures, quoted in J. Écorcheville, *Vingt suites d'orchestre* (Psris, 1906), 1:92.

> Les hautbois ont un chant élevé et de la maniere dont on en joue maintenant chez le roi et à Paris il y aurait peu de chose à en désirer. Ils font des cadences aussi justes, les tremblements aussi doux, les diminutions aussi régulières que les voix les mieux instruites et que les instruments les plus parfaits. Nous en avons même vu le succès sur le théâtre et en certaines entrées particulières. Je ne doute point qu'ils ne fissent un merveilleux effet dans une Pastorale. Mais on ne peut jamais s'assurer sur le vent; l'haleine manque, les poumons s'épaississent, l'estomac se fatigue, et enfin on sent une notable différence de la fin et des commencements; on n'y trouve plus de justesse.

copyist during his varied career, later made a commentary on this practice which is revealing, especially with regard to the early modern oboe.

> The parts for the oboe that one extracts from the violin of the grand orchestra can not be exactly copied as they are in the original, since the tessitura is less than the violin and there are soft notes it can not produce; it is also not as agile at slow speeds: the force of the oboe must be handeled gently so as not to obscure the accents of the music. If I had to judge a symphonic copyist without hearing (his work), I would give him the task of extracting an oboe part from the violin. Every copyist should know how to do it.[19]

[19] Jean-Jacques Rousseau, 'Copiste,' in *Dictionnaire de Musique* (Paris, 1767), 130.

Musettes et Hautbois du Poitou

This wind band of six players is one of the strangest and most enigmatic in character. Both the musette and hautbois de Poitou were pastoral, folk instruments and their popularity in the court of Louis XIV reflects the pretense by members of that court that they had a natural sympathy with the peasant. Relics of this curious form of play can be seen still today at Versailles in the miniature farm buildings at the back of the estate, where the queen used to play at being a simple peasant's wife.

The musette was a small, highly decorated, bagpipe, which played the treble in this ensemble, according to Mersenne.[20] The hautbois de Poitou was used in three sizes (alto, tenor, and bass) and differed in construction with the chanter of the bagpipe only in size and with its windcap. Since no examples of this instrument are known to be extant, our only insight into it comes from references in contemporary literature.

> But without getting involved in detailed discussions concerning the names of shawms, suffice it is to say that there are two types used nowadays in France: some are simply called *haubois*, others *haubois de Poitou*; the difference between them is that the former look more like recorders.[21]

> The *hautbois de Poitou* are similar (to the Hautbois) and only differ in length, in the placing of the holes, and in having windcaps.[22]

> There are two types of old-fashioned shawms: one type was called *hautbois de Poitou*, the other simply hautbois … It is unnecessary to comment on the *hautbois de Poitou*: these are the same instruments as we have just described (simple oboes) apart from some minor difference in the way they are made.[23]

[20] Martin Mersenne, *Harmonie Universelle* [1635], trans. Roger Chapman, (The Hague: M. Nijhoff, 1957), 380.

[21] Pierre Trichet, *Traité des Instruments de Musique* (Bordeaux, ca. 1640).

> Mais, sans entrer en plus grande contestation touchant la dénomination des haubois, disons maintenant qu'il y en a de deux sortes usités aujord'hui en France, les uns nommés simplement haubois, et les autres haubois de Poitou entre lesquels il y a cette différence que les premiers resemblent mieux aux flutes d'Angleterre …

[22] Antoine Furetière, *Dictionaire Universel* (The Hague, 1690).

> … Les hautbois de Poitou sont de même figure, & ne different des grands hautbois qu'en longeur, & en la disposition de leurs trous & de leurs boëstes.

[23] Denis Diderot, *Encyclopédie* (Neufchastel, 1765).

> Il y a deux sortes de hautbois anciens: les uns qu'on appelloit hautbois de Poitou; les autres simplement hautbois … Il est inutile de s'étendre sur les hautbois de Poitou: ce sont les mêmes instrumens que nous venons de décrire, si l'on veut négliger quelque legere différence de facture.

An engraving by Thomas Blanchet for the frontispiece of Pierre Borjon de Scellery's *Traité de la musette*, 1672.

Suffice to say, all these instruments were performed by regular oboists in the *Écurie* and in 1661 they were described in court records as two players on 'dessus de haulbois,' one 'dessus de muzette,' one 'basseconte de muzette,' and two players on 'taille de haulbois.'[24]

Did they always play together as an ensemble? *The L'État de la France* for 1697 says they were used for large divertissements given in celebration of virtually every kind of court event.[25] But it remains unclear if they had their own repertoire, as a band, or only joined in as additional players in the large ensembles used for such festive events. The flutist, Michel de La Barre, was asked in 1730, by M. De Villiers, Secretary to Prince Charles of Lorraine, Grand Écuyer, to investigate

[24] Benoit, *Musiques de Cour*, 4.

[25] Écorcheville, 'Quelques Documents sur la Musique de la Grand-Écurie du Roi,' 641.

the history of this band. In his report²⁶ there is unfortunately nothing of historical substance and from it one concludes that if there was a tradition, it was already lost by the beginning of the period of Louis XIV. The report does indicate that during the reign of Louis XIV the 'positions' in this band were being given to flute players, in particular Philbert and Descoteaux.²⁷

This band, at least in name, is found in the records of the National Archive through 1784. Our interest in this band today lies in our curiosity in the role these instruments may have had in influencing the design of the modern oboe.²⁸

Les Cromornes

Another wind band in the *Écurie* is somewhat enigmatic, in this case because there is some question regarding what the *Cromorne* itself was. Until recently scholars have assumed this was an ensemble of crumhorns, even though in the rest of Europe the period of the crumhorn was very near its end. One has to take note that a present day authority on the crumhorn, Barra Boydell, rejects this idea in favor of an unknown instrument of the bassoon family.

> The *cromorne* as used in the French court has little (if any) connection with the Renaissance instrument of the same name but referred to an instrument the bass size of which was close enough to the bassoon to be identified with it in the early eighteenth century. The identity of the *cromorne* is most probably to be found in some member of the bassoon family.²⁹

In a passage discussing Jean Hotteterre, Borjon's *Traité de la Musette* (Lyon, 1672) includes the cromorne as one of the wind instruments in which complete consorts were made. This can be taken as another confirmation of the ensemble itself and, perhaps, that it was a unique instrument made for the court by Hotteterre.

> ... a unique man for making all types of wooden, ivory, and ebony instruments such as bagpipes, recorders, flageolets, oboes, cromornes; and even for making perfect sets of all these same instruments.³⁰

---

²⁶ 'Memoire de M. de La Barre, sur les musettes et hautbois,' National Archives, Paris (Bundle 01/878, Nr. 240).

²⁷ Francois Descoteaux (1640–1723) was also a famous plant breeder, who was painted by Watteau and immortalized as *L'Amateur de Tulipes* by La Bruyère, often dining in his garden with such men as Molière and Racine. See Josef Marx, 'The Tone of the Baroque Oboe,' *The Galpin Society Journal* 4 (June 1, 1951): 11.

²⁸ Several European oboist friends of mine believe that the musette was not always played as a bagpipe, but rather the chanter may have been removed and played as a small oboe; they consider the musette literature as part of the oboe literature.

²⁹ Barra Boydell, *The Crumhorn and other Renaissance Windcap Instruments* (Buren: Knuf, 1982), 195. An example of the eighteenth-century literature referred to by Boydell is Johann Walther's *Musikalisches Lexikon oder musikalische Bibliothek* (Leipzig, 1732), 193:

> Cromorne (gall.) s.m. bedeutet (1) einen Basson. s. Ménage, Dictionaire Etymologique. (2) ein Orgel-Register ...

On page 78 of this work, Walther defines the 'Basse de Cromhorne oder Cromorne' simply as 'ein Fagott.'

³⁰ Quoted in Georg Kinsky, 'Doppelrohrblatt-Instrumente mit Windkapsel,' *Archiv für Musikwissenschaft* 7 (June 1, 1925): 271.

> ... un homme unique pour la construction de toutes sortes d'instrumens de bois, d'yvoire et d'ébeine, comme sont les musettes, flûtes, flageolets, haubois, cromornes; et mesme pour faire des accords parfaits de tous ces mêmes instrumens.

Whatever the instrument was, the band usually appeared in the court records of Louis XIV as an ensemble of five players, consisting of two dessus, one quinte, one taille, and a basse. In a few records it appears with a sixth player, but was permanently set at five in 1689.³¹

Like the other wind bands in the *Écurie*, the *Les Cromornes* seem not to have had specific musical functions, but rather appeared in a great variety of court ceremonies.

> They all have their livery and are sometimes used in balls, ballets, comedies in the King's household and elsewhere where they are required. There are also two of them in the Chapel Music.³²

The ensemble appears again in connection with the preparations for the funeral of Louis XIV.

> Full suits of mourning with crepe bands for the trumpets, drums and fifes of the Chamber, oboes, musettes, and cromornes.³³

Les Fifres et Tambours & Les Trompettes

Two small ensembles of wind players were maintained under the *Écurie* solely for ceremonial needs, which of course were almost without pause. The fifes and drums had consisted of only four members during the sixteenth century, but under Louis XIV they grew to eight players, four of each. Although this organization had little musical significance, it was an indispensable part of court life during the seventeenth century. Virtually every moment of the king's day was defined in elaborate ritual and each ritual was carefully spelled out in court organizational documents. Consider, for example, the planning for a rather routine court function, the announcing of new laws to the public. The fifes and drums are instructed to,

> come to the antichamber of the King to receive the orders from the grand Master of Ceremonies who then designates precisely the King's door, so, at the exit they can lead His Majesty to the place where he must read the law; and to march at the head of the princes of blood, in the center, in front of the trumpets, after whom marches the Grand Squire and finally the King and his retinue.³⁴

---

³¹ National Archives, Paris (Bundle 01/872, Nr. 13, 17–20).

³² *État de la France* (1702).

> (Les Cromornes et Trompettes Marines) ont tous leur habillemens de livrée et sont quelquefois emploïez aux Bals, Balets, Comédies, aux Appartemens chez le Roy et autres endroits ou ils sont nécessaires. Il y en a aussi deux à la Musique de la Chapelle.

Sandman apparently misreads this reference in stating that there was a separate crumhorn ensemble in the chapel (Sandman, 'Wind Band Music Under Louis XIV,' 110).

³³ Benoit, *Musiques de Cour*, 273.

> Des habits complets de deüil avec des crespes, aux Trompettes, Tambours et fifres de la chambre hautbois, musettes et cromornes.

³⁴ Écorcheville 'Quelques Documents sur la Musique de la Grand-Écurie du Roi,' 44.

One is not surprised to find trumpets continuing their long association with kings and here they also participate in virtually every event which included Louis XIV. Under the *Écurie* there were usually twelve, of which four were nearly always near the king and thus more honored than their colleagues. When ceremonial demands required additional trumpets, there were four 'Trompettes des Plaisirs' organized under the *Maison Militaire*.

Additional Court Winds

Aside from all these wind bands under the administrative accounts of the *Écurie*, there were still more wind players employed in the court of Louis XIV. In the *Chambre*, another administrative wing, there were musette and flute players and in the *Chapelle*, serpent and cornett players, all of whom seem to have been independent of those in the *Écurie*.

Finally, under still another administrative section, the *Maison Militaire*, one finds numerous additional wind players who played, from time to time, at court. The various regiments of the king's guards maintained a total of twenty-four trumpets and four timpanists at Versailles.[35] In addition, the *Cent-Suisses*, the honorary Swiss Guards, included a fife and three drums.

Musically, the most interesting units under the *Maison Militaire* are found associated with the troops known as *Les Mousquetaires*. Reorganized in 1657, the music of the two companies of Mousquetaires had at first consisted of only a trumpet, which was replaced in 1663 by a fife and five drums. In 1665 the fife was replaced by three oboes and soon after a fourth.

Toward the end of the seventeenth century the '8 hautbois des Mousquetaires' appear frequently in the court pay records for both Versailles and Fontainebleau. As above, these eight oboes, four from each company, should be thought of as oboes in several sizes, including no doubt bassoons.

Because of the separate departments in which the various band's pay records are found, it is not always possible to say if these eight oboes of the Mousquetaires are being used as additional players together with those of the *Écurie* or if they are being used as a substitute band.[36] Of these various entries relative to the performance of the eight oboes of the Mous-

[35] Benoit, *Versailles et les Musiciens du Roi*, 234.

[36] Some independent music composed for the Mousquetaire bands is extant.

quetaires, one is very striking. We know oboes, in general, doubled the violins when the court ballets and comedies were performed. On one occasion, in 1698, these oboes were with the court at Fontainebleau, performing with the 'twenty-four violins' in the comedy, 'Bourgeois gentilhomme.' For some reason the 'Violins of the King' had to return early to Versailles and the oboes alone apparently played the final production of the comedy.[37]

Music for State Celebrations

It appears that many of the above components were drawn together for the great state celebrations. The newspaper, *Mercure*, in describing the celebration of the peace with the Dutch in 1679 mentions, 'aussi-bien que des Fifres, Hautbois, Tambours, & Trompetes de la grande *Écurie* du Roy.'[38] A similar ceremony in 1713 used an even greater number of players.

> We ... certify ... that the twelve trumpets, twelve players of large oboes, eight players of fifes and drums and the five cromornes and marine trumpets of the King's Chamber and Grande *Écurie* have all served his Majesty and carried out their duties at the ceremony in Paris on Monday the 22nd May publishing the treaty concluded between his Majesty the King, the Queen of Great Britain, the King of Prussia, the Duke of Savoy, and the Assembly of the Provinces of the Netherlands.[39]

Visiting aristocrats from other nations also offered the occasion for appearances by large numbers of the court wind players. Government delegates from Russia brought, in May 1681, their own wind players to Versailles, including eight trumpets, five drummers, and several oboists and bagpipe players. These ambassadors were treated to the usual processions, banquets, and large-scale court entertainments. Of particular interest is the evening of 12 May, when the visitors were taken to a window in the royal apartments to observe a 'concert' performed in the garden below by 'drums, trumpets, and oboes.'[40]

On some occasions musicians from outside the court musical establishment must have been engaged as well, for the reported numbers exceed those of the Versailles ensembles. One example is the ceremonies surrounding the unveiling of a statue of Henry IV, in March 1686. The procession which began the celebration is said to have included one hundred and

---

[37] National Archives, Paris (MS. Bundle 01/2830, Nr. 86, 88).

> Aux 8 Aubois des Mousquetaires, ... pour avoir esté aud. Fontainebleau les 2 derniers jours pour jouer a la derniere comedie, parce que les Violons du Roy estoient partis pour retourner a Versailles.

[38] *Le Nouveau Mercure* (Paris, January, 1679), 5.

[39] Benoit, *Musiques de Cour*, 256.

> Nous ... certifions ... que les douze Trompettes, douze joüeurs de grands hautbois, huit joüeurs de fifres et tambours et les cinq cromornes et trompettes marine de la chambre et grande Écurie du Roy, ont tous servy sa Majesté et fait les fonctions de leurs charges à la cérémonie de la Publication faite en la Ville de Paris le lundi vingt deux du present mois de may, de la Paix faite et conclüe entre sa Majesté, la Reyne de la grande Bretagne, le Roy du Prusse, Monsieur le Duc de Savoye et les Etats géneraux des Provinces unies de païs bas.

[40] Isherwood, *Music in the Service of the King*, 303.

seventy-four players of oboes, trumpets, and drums.[41] When the procession reached the statue, the trumpets played as some of the four hundred participating military troops conducted military drills. Apparently even the violins were stationed at the statue of this popular king, for an account mentions the 'very agreeable symphony of violins, oboes, trumpets, and timpani of the Chambre.'[42] The statue was illuminated by torches and fireworks; the oboes remained throughout the night, playing periodically. An account of a similar unveiling, of a statue of Louis XIV himself in 1699, mentions the performance by 'tambours, trompettes, flûtes et hautbois.'[43]

Any ceremony in which the members of the royal family were the center of attention was also a state ceremony and involved the various wind bands. The coronation of Louis XIV must have included all the court musicians, although an engraving of the actual ceremony in the church pictures only the twelve members of the *Les Grands Hautbois* standing prominently in the foreground.[44]

The tone for many of the later court festivals was set by the lavish celebration of the king's wedding in 1660. The central event was a spectacular parade throughout the city with numerous allegorical arches placed at key intersections. The first of these arches was Roman in style, with figures representing Faithfulness, Obedience, Joy, Gratitude, Concord, and Constancy. Upon this arch an ensemble of eighteen oboes performed a concert for the king. Similar arches later on the route included one with a violin ensemble and another, at Notre Dame, featuring an ensemble of bagpipes.[45]

The births of royal children also received very ostentatious celebrations, beginning with Louis XIV's first son. These festivities included a concert at the city hall by an ensemble of oboes and cromornes.[46] An even greater celebration occurred, with processions, concerts, and fireworks, on the birth of Louis XIV's grandson, the Duke of Bourgogne, in 1682. This seems to have been more national in character, for one reads that in Lyons there was a concert by flutes, oboes, trumpets, and drums at the College de Notre Dame, a procession, and the following day, a carrousel which included a chariot bearing 'crumhorns,' oboes, flutes, and drums.[47] These celebrations continued for a year and had barely run their course when the king's daughter gave birth to yet another son and everything had to begin all over again!

---

[41] Ibid., 301.

[42] Ibid., 302.

[43] Georges Pillement, *Paris en Fête* (Paris: B. Grasset, 1972), 135ff.

[44] Antoine Lepautre, National Bibliothèque, Paris (Foto-Nr. 64 c 23590).

[45] Isherwood, *Music in the Service of the King*, 291–292.

[46] Ibid., 295. Here 'crumhorn' is given for cromorne.

[47] Ibid., 296.

44 COURT WIND BANDS

Detail from the bottom right of *Sacre de Louis XIV* by Antoine Lepautre showing *Les Grands Hautbois*.

During the celebrations for the birth, in 1704, of the final grandchild, known as the Duke of Bretagne, one reads of the oboes, trumpets, and drums of the *Écurie* performing in the procession, two days later from the balcony of the Church of the Monastère-Royal, a concert in the Place du Collège, and finally from the balcony of the College itself. At Versailles, this child's coming was celebrated by an illuminated chariot which appeared 'like a globe of fire,' from which the allegorical figure of Mars appeared to pay his respects. Two trumpeters announced the birth and when Louis xiv himself appeared on the balcony an ensemble of oboes and musettes began to play.[48]

[48] Ibid., 297–298.

All of these musicians appeared as well at royal funerals. One is of particular interest, for an eye-witness recalls,

> the oboes of the army began a lugubrious concert which was marvelously suited to the ceremony.[49]

[49] Quoted in ibid., 299

The Entertainment of Louis xiv

Judging by the frequency and scale of his entertainments, one concludes that a considerable staff must have been necessary just to see that not a single moment of Louis's life went unfilled. Even so simple a thing as a walk, was planned as if it were a state voyage. As Louis would leave the building trumpets would play their fanfares and then as he made his way through those extraordinary gardens at Versailles he heard constant background music, for hidden among the trees, carefully out of sight, would be an oboe ensemble here and a violin ensemble there. The ensembles would play until the king had passed and then run ahead to be in position a bit further in the route to play again![50]

[50] Ibid., 259, 279.

Because of the size of the court, entertainments for the entire court had, of necessity, to be on vast scales. Among these were the carrousels, relics of the age of armed tournaments. By this time these were in part state processions, horse ballets, tilting matches, and allegorical pageants. Trumpets and drums were ever present in order to announce each aristocratic participant and to mark the beginning and end of each race or match. An engraving of a carrousel in 1662 pictures six separate ensembles, each consisting of seven trumpets and three timpani players, all on horse and placed equidistant around a great square. One also sees vast bleachers constructed of wood, forming a great bowl, which are filled with people.[51]

Larger wind bands were also used at some of these carrousels, as we know from the extant four-movement composition by Lully[52] for three oboes, bassoon, four trumpets and timpani, composed for a carrousel in 1686.

The largest of the court entertainments were called *divertissements* and three of these were of such a magnitude that they are known today as the *grands divertissements*. The first of the *grands divertissements* was given in 1664 ostensibly to honor two queens, Anne of Austria and Marie-Thérèse, but actually as a vehicle for Louis to announce to the aristocratic world that he intended to lay claim to the Spanish crown, as the lawful inheritance of his wife (Louis himself was half-Spanish and only a quarter-French).

This *divertissement* was called, 'Les plaisisrs de l'île enchantée,' taken from Ariosto's tale of the imprisonment of the knight, Roger, by the sorceress, Alcine. The *divertissement* began with a carrousel on the first day, with the king, dressed as Roger, participating.[53] Other members of the court appeared as Apollo, the Centuries, the Twelve Hours, and the Signs of the Zodiac. Lully marched into the carrousel stadium dressed as Orpheus, followed by thirty-four musicians. I assume these were all wind instruments for following a dance by the Four Seasons (who entered riding four different animals: a horse, an elephant, a camel, and a bear!), Lully conducted a concert of 'oboes and flutes' (which probably meant a full consort of recorders and several sizes of oboes and bassoons). Next a machine operated forest of artificial trees lifted dancers into the air. Finally a ballet was performed by the twenty-four dancers of The Hours and the Zodiac. The allegorical figures of Abundance, Joy, Propriety, and Good Cheer carried in a table of food for the hungry royal observers.

[51] Reproduced in Pillement, *Paris en Fête*, 124–125.

[52] Among the extant wind band compositions of the court of Louis XIV are a large number composed by Lully; the sources and incipits for these are given in volume seven of this series.

[53] This description is taken from Isherwood, *Music in the Service of the King*, 265ff.

The second day featured a play by Molière, 'La princesse d'Élide,' with musical intermezzi by Lully. A sextet at the end sang the theme, 'A heart begins to live only on the day that it knows love.' During this song, another machine operated tree lifted sixteen 'fauns' into the air, each faun playing a flute.

On the final day the royal audience saw a palace, which had been constructed near the small lake behind Versailles, illuminated, while Lully conducted a concert. Trumpets then announced the entrance of Alcine and her nymphs, who were riding mechanical sea monsters. Next was a ballet battle between dwarfs, giants, and Moors against the monsters and knights. In the end Roger conquers Alcine, breaking her spell of sorcery with his magic ring. In the background, the palace disappears in a blaze of fireworks!

A newspaper, reporting on this *divertissement*, said nothing so magnificent had been seen for several centuries—the same could have been said for Louis XIV.

Louis XV

Louis XV became king at age five, thus one can forgive him in his youth for being selfish, lazy, and spoiled by adoration. He had a fine mind and as he grew he managed to absorb some education in spite of himself. His youthful entertainments, wood carving, needlework, milking cows, etc., soon gave way, as he developed into a handsome young man, to the usual pursuits of his contemporaries. In this regard, he was unusually organized, maintaining a cottage on the edge of Versailles called, 'Parc aux Cerfs,' where a stable of young girls were prepared for royal service.

The coronation of Louis XV occurred in 1722 when he was twelve years old. An administrative order,[54] to 'Les trompettes, tambours, hautbois, musettes' of the *Écurie*, provides an insight into a portion of the role of the wind instruments on this occasion. They were instructed to appear at six o'clock in the morning at the king's lodging and then to march to the church, two by two between files of the Swiss Guards. In the church they were to stand near the doors of the choir, but were cautioned to remain silent. When the king was crowned, they were ordered to shout, 'Vive le Roy,' and then play a fanfare as part of the performance of the 'Miserere.' They were then

[54] National Archives, Paris (MS. Bundle 01/878, Nr. 28).

48 COURT WIND BANDS

Above and details opposite: An engraving by Nicolas Gabriel Dupuis (1698–1771), *The Royal Feast*, Plate 39 in *Coronation of Louis XV, King of France and Navarre in the church of Reims, Sunday October 25, 1722 XXV* by Antoine Danchet.

Court Wind Bands in France

50 Court Wind Bands

Above and detail opposite: An engraving by Nicolas de Larmessin, (1684–1753): *The King going to church*, Plate 10 in *Coronation of Louis XV, King of France and Navarre in the church of Reims, Sunday October 25, 1722* by Antoine Danchet.

Court Wind Bands in France 51

52 COURT WIND BANDS

Above and details opposite: An engraving by Nicolas Henri Tardieu (1674–1749): *The Coronation of the King*, Plate 27 in *Coronation of Louis XV, King of France and Navarre in the church of Reims, Sunday October 25, 1722* by Antoine Danchet.

Court Wind Bands in France 53

instructed to remain silent for the rest of the ceremony and to participate in the procession back to the palace. The same players performed for the coronation banquet as well.

All the separate wind bands discussed above, under Louis xiv, continued throughout the reign of Louis xv, although unfortunately little music has survived. A document of 1724 suggests that the financial support for this music was not as forthcoming as it had been in the past.

> The oboes, musettes, cromornes, drums and fifes request the Prince to pay them their wages in clothing as in the previous year, and should the Prince decide not to grant them this grace, they beseech him to fix their clothing at 120 lt, like those of other officers, instead of only 90 lt or 100 lt, which the tailors allow each one for their clothes.[55]

It was during this period that the musette became especially popular in the court, as well as another folk instrument, the hurdy-gurdy (vielle). The extant music composed for the members of the *Les Grands Hautbois* includes music for these instruments, although usually it is scored for only two, and rarely three, parts.[56]

It had been previously arranged for Louis xv to marry the Infanta of Spain, but court intrigue led to her replacement by Marie Leszczyńska of Poland. Thus, in 1725, Louis, at age twelve, was married at Fontainebleau. Once again, all of the wind bands of the *Écurie* were taken there for this ceremony.[57] Three days later, on 8 September 1725, a much larger celebration was held at Notre Dame in Paris. For the Te Deum sung there, six separate wind ensembles were employed: the cromornes, trumpets, and fifes and drums of the *Écurie*, together with three civic ensembles, the 'Tambours de la Ville,' the 'Trompettes de la Ville,' and the 'Hautbois de la Ville,' the civic wind band of Paris.[58]

The extant pay documents from the reign of Louis xv are concerned mostly with various court ceremonies of an honorary nature, rather than the great entertainment productions of Louis xiv. For the presentation of the Order of Saint-Esprit, in 1722, pay records indicate 'trompettes, tambours, hautbois et musettes,' who once again march to and from the church but do not play inside.[59] Similarly, the ceremony to award the

---

[55] Benoit, *Musiques de Cour*, 345.

> Les hautbois, musettes, cromornes, tambours et fifres demandent au Prince de leur accorder leurs habits en nature, comme l'an passé, et en cas que le Prince ne juge pas a propos de leur faire cette grace, ils le suplient de fixer leurs habits a 120 lt, comme ceux des autres officiers, au lieu de 90 lt seulement ou 100 lt, que les tailleurs leur rendent a chacun pour leur habillement.

[56] As for example, the *Simphonies* for 'musette, vielles, fluttes à bec, flutes traversières, et hautbois,' by Esprit Chédeville (see volume seven in this series).

[57] Benoit, *Versailles et les Musiciens du Roi*, 48–49.

[58] National Archives, Paris (MS. Bundle 01/878, Nr. 401).

[59] Ibid., (MS.Bundle 01/878, Nr. 28).

'cordon bleu,' in 1724, specified performance by the twelve *Les Grands Hautbois*, four 'musettes ou flûtes,' and eight fifes and drums.[60]

An engraving of the proclamation of peace in 1738 pictures both trumpets and oboes playing while riding horses in a procession, with triumphal arches and fireworks in the background.[61]

[60] Ibid., (MS.Bundle 01/953, Nr. 87).

[61] Reproduced in Pillement, *Paris en Fête*, 187.

2 Court Wind Bands in the German-Speaking Countries

IN PART I ABOVE, 'The Hautboisten Tradition and the Birth of Harmoniemusik,' I have discussed the most significant development of the seventeenth-century court wind band in Germany, the appearance of the Hautboisten bands a little after the mid-point of what is known today as the Baroque Period in music.

In terms of wind instruments, the date the Hautboisten bands begin to appear (ca. 1680) marks the point where the old Renaissance instruments are replaced by the new ones we associate with the Classic Period.[1] One can still clearly see the old Renaissance wind band in the examples of early Baroque literature and iconography quoted above,[2] and this characteristic of the early Baroque court wind bands can also be seen in the extant court inventories. The court of Johann Schweickard von Kronberg, in Mainz, maintained a band of cornetts and trombones in 1604, but the winds in the inventory of 1745 were only the modern flutes, oboes, clarinets, horns, and bassoons.[3] Extant inventories which reveal complete Renaissance consorts of winds can be found in Weimar (1623)[4] and Kassel (1613, 1638):[5]

> A case of crumhorns containing eight crumhorns of different sizes ...
> ...
> Four Schreyerpfeifen, a basset, tenor, alto and soprano.

An example of perhaps the final generation of these old consorts can be seen in the court wind band, the 'Hof-Schalmey-Pfeiffer,' at Halle in 1676. Here one finds twelve players of shawms all dressed in their uniform of green coats.[6]

The appearance of the new Hautboisten band dates from the final two decades of the seventeenth century, as can be seen in documents from Stuttgart (1680),[7] Weissenfels (1695),[8] Dresden and Gotha (1697),[9] and Gottorf (1699).[10] In the case of Weissenfels, it is quite interesting to note that the Elector was apparently dissatisfied with the Hautboisten he hired in 1695 and was able to replace them by engaging an entire band (Kam-

---

[1] In isolated cases the old Renaissance instruments and even their guilds proved slow to die. Josef Sittard, *Zur Geschichte der Musik und des Theaters am Württembergischen Hofe* (Stuttgart, 1890), 1:330, quotes in full thirty-five articles of a constitution set down in 1721 for the 'Zinckenisten-Profession.'

[2] Pages 2–3.

[3] Adam Gottron, *Mainzer Musikgeschichte* (Mainz, 1959), 43, 219. An inventory of a fairly small court, that of Sayn-Wittgenstein at Berleburg, in Westphalia, in 1741, reflects the interesting mixture of Renaissance and 'new' instruments during the period of transition. In addition to sixteen string and six keyboard instruments, one finds fifty winds:

> 3 bassoons
> 8 large recorders
> 4 small recorders
> 2 bass recorders without crooks
> 1 ivory flageolet
> 2 transverse flutes
> 1 piccolo
> 1 pair of 'Flaute traversières d'amours
> 1 large 'Flaute traversière d'amour'
> 2 oboes
> 2 pair of 'Hautbois d'amours'
> 1 pair of 'Wald-Hautbois,' without brass crooks
> 1 taille, without the brass crook
> 2 pair of clarinets, in a recorder case
> 2 trumpets with crooks
> 10 horns, with crooks
> 1 small horn

(Anthony Baines, *Woodwind Instruments and their History* (London: Faber, 1957), 302–303)

merpfeifer) in Vienna in 1697.[11] Courts which did not yet have one of the new Hautboisten bands could hire visiting bands for important court events. Thus we see the twelve-member Hautboisten band from Jena performing for the Weissenfels court (1676) and the twelve-member band from Eisenberg ('the Apostles') performing in Zeitz (1686–1689).[12] In any case, according to Braun, by 1700 virtually every major court possessed one of the new bands.[13]

I wish to stress once again that while almost every mention of the Hautboisten bands in current literature has been with respect to military functions, it is clear that there were either separate *chamber* Hautboisten or, in some cases, these bands worked in both spheres. The indoor 'concert' existence is clear first and foremost, it seems to me, from the extant literature which is nearly always 'concert' and not military in nature; and from the use of such terms as, 'Kammerpfeifer' (as in the case in Weissenfels, above) or 'Hofkunstpfeifer' (as in the case of Berlin, below). This concert function can be clearly seen in a complete 'band library' of original concerti da camera, ouvertures and symphonies for Hautboisten band now housed at the State Archiv in Kassel. Each composition consists of five of more movements and are scored for oboes in three parts, English horn and bassoons. A few works have horn parts and one features the post-horn. This collection is notable for the improvisation written in the parts by the original players.

It may be true that the wind players in some courts were considered rather lowly as musicians, as was apparently the case in Zeitz,[14] but on the other hand, there were also Hautboisten bands which were highly esteemed and even made concert tours. One of these Hautboisten bands which gave concert tours was from the Brandenburg court in Berlin, led by an oboist-director called 'Lubuissière,' 'La puisier,' or 'La Bassire.' These tours can be documented between 1693 and 1700, when he left the court, and one appearance, for the birthday in 1698 of Duke Friedrich Heinrich von Sachsen-Zeitz indicates an ensemble of seven oboes and recorders.[15]

His successor was Gottfried Pepusch, who with a wind band of seven players even made a tour to London in 1704. A review of his concert (4 April) in the *Daily Courant* calls him 'the famous Godfrede Pepusch' and mentions they played 'new music by his Brother, that Eminent Master, Mr. John Christo-

[4] Adolf Aber, *Die Pflege der Musik unter en Wettinern und wettinischen Ernestinern Von den Anfängen bis zur Auflösung der Weimarer Hofkapelle 1662* (Bückeburg: C. F. W. Siegal, 1921), 139.

[5] Ernst Zulauf, *Beiträge zur Geschichte der Landgräflich-Hessischen Hofkapelle zu Cassel bis auf die Zeit Moritz des Gelehrten* (Cassel: Druck von L. Doll, 1902), 115, 133–135.

> Ein Krumbhörner futter darinnen acht Krumbhörner vnderschiedener Grosse...
> ...
> Vier Schriari, ein basset, Tenor, Alt und Soprano.

[6] Walter Serauky, *Musikgeschichte der Stadt Halle* (Halle-Berlin: Buchhandlung des Waisenhauses, 1939), 2:423ff.

[7] Sittard, *Zur Geschichte der Musik und des Theaters am Württembergischen Hofe*, 2:13.

[8] Arno Werner, *Städtische und fürstliche Musikpflege in Weissenfels* (Leipzig: Breitkopf & Härtel, 1911), 95.

[9] Arno Werner, *Vier Jahrhunderte im Dienste der Kirchenmusik* (Leipzig: Carl Merseberger, 1933), 246–248.

[10] Bernhard Engelke, *Musik und Musiker am Gottorfer Hofe* (Mss, Universitätsbibliothek Kiel), II.

[11] Fürstenau II, 12, quoted in Werner, *Städtische und fürstliche Musikpflege in Weissenfels*, 95.

[12] Braun, 'Entwurf für ein Typologie der "Hautboisten",' 47.

[13] Braun, ibid., 47.

[14] Arno Werner, *Städtische und fürstliche Musikpflege in Zeitz* (Bückeburg & Leipzig: Siegal, 1922), 90.

pher Pepusch (Johann Christoph Pepusch).'[16] Pepusch seems to have also been a famous teacher of the Hautboisten medium, for an entire band from Ansbach came to Berlin to study with him in 1703.[17] In another case six of his students were hired as a Hautboisten band in Hannover in 1705.[18] When Johann Mattheson visited Hannover in 1706 he was astonished by the 'Virtuosen,' especially the 'exquisite Bande Hoboisten.'[19]

Another oboe-band which seems to have trained other wind players was the 'Passauer Hubuisten,' of Bavaria. An account from 1697 mentions their instruction in oboe and bassoon given two young musicians from Stift Kremsmünster.[20]

The better of these court wind players were no doubt paid as well as any musician during the Baroque. Even Bach, in 1730, admired the well-being of the court musicians in Dresden.

> Let anyone visit Dresden and observe how the royal musicians there are paid. They have no anxiety regarding their livelihood, and consequently are relieved of chagrin; each man is able to make himself a competent and agreeable performer on it.[21]

Sachs gives a pay document for the Berlin 'Hofkunstpfeifer' as including a basic salary, clothing, and extra pay for service in the church.[22] An interesting document relative to a bassoonist in the Weissenfels court gives his food allowance for one year as '20 pounds of beef, 9 portions of bread, 9 portions of wine and 18 portions of beer.'[23]

While I have attempted to establish above that there was a concert facet to the existence of these Hautboisten bands in Germany, one does have to acknowledge that the broader range of their duties must have been quite wide, as it had been for court wind bands since the fifteenth century. Even the fine 'Hofkunstpfeifers' of Berlin were required to perform from the palace tower at ten o'clock in the morning and five o'clock in the evening during the Summer (four o'clock in the evening during the Winter). But even in this case, we note the seven-member band was instructed to perform 'not only artistic and good works, but Psalms.'[24]

Not only did the Hautboisten perform in a wide variety of situations, but also on whatever instrument was required at the moment[25] and, furthermore, had to always be ready to travel with their prince.[26]

---

[15] Braun, 'Entwurf für ein Typologie der "Hautboisten",' 46.

[16] Friedrich Blume, ed., *Die Musik in Geschichte und Gegenwart* (Kassel, 1949–1968), 10:1030.

[17] Gunther Schmidt, *Die Musik am Hofe der Markgrafen von Brandenburg-Ansbach* (Kassel: Barenreiter-Verlag, 1956), 72.

[18] H. Sievers, *Die Musik in Hannover* (Hannover: Sponholtz, 1969), 58.

[19] Mattheson, *Ehren-Pforte* (Hamburg, 1740), 195.

[20] Altmann Kellner, *Musikgeschichte des Stiftes Kremsmünster* (Kassel: Barenreiter-Verlag, 1956), 285.

[21] Charles Sanford Terry, *Bach: A Biography* (London: Oxford University Press, 1933), 203.

[22] Curt Sachs, *Musik und Oper am kurbrandenburgischen Hof* (Berlin: J. Bard, 1910), 73.

> 130 rtl. Gehalt,
> 70 rtl. Kirchendienstentschädigung
> ———
> 200 rtl.
> Hofkleidung und Neujahrsakzidenz bei der Domgemeide

[23] Werner, *Städtische und fürstliche Musikpflege in Weissenfels*, 74.

[24] Sachs, *Musik und Oper am kurbrandenburgischen Hof*, 73.

> nicht allein zu jederzeit künstliche und zierliche gute Stücke, sondern auch insonders allemal einen Psalm aus dem Lobwasser.

[25] Extant records in Zeitz show the oboists at one time or another had to play violin, flute and horn. (See Werner, *Städtische und fürstliche Musikpflege in Zeitz*, 90)

No wonder the Konzertmeister of the Weissenfels court, Johann Beer,[27] wearily expressed,

> With the court you've got to be in one place today, tomorrow in another. Day and night, unfortunately, makes no difference. Tempest, rain, sunshine—it's all the same. Today you've got to go into church, tomorrow to the dining hall, the day after tomorrow to the theatre. Compared to all this disturbance, life is somewhat more peaceful in the towns.[28]

Among the required performances for these Hautboisten players were the court festivities surrounding the aristocratic family ceremonies. For the baptism, in 1616, of Friedrich, son of the Duke of Württemberg, one finds a rather rare performance of a composition already a hundred years old, the 'Ecce nunc benedicite Domino,' for eight voices, four bassoons, and four bass shawms, by Ludwig Daser. After an organ fugue, another motet, 'Laudate Dominum,' by Grégor Aichinger, was performed with two cornetts, four trumpets, and two bassoons.[29]

The celebration of the birthday of Duke Christian of Weissenfels (1712–1736) was probably a typical example of the coordination of a noble's entire music establishment. The celebration began with the duke's eight trumpets playing 'Feldstücke' from a castle tower while both his and the civic militia fired canon salvos. When the shooting ended the trumpets played 'morning songs.' During the day church bells rang and services were held in the court chapel. During the procession to the church, the trumpets and timpani played intradas until all the nobility and visiting guests were in their places.[30] The civic trombones played from the city hall tower followed by a performance by the duke's wind band ('Hautboisten und Waldhornisten').

Another duty of the court wind bands was to help out with church music on the great festival days. The Berlin Hautboisten ('Hofkunstpfeifers') on such occasions would play on cornetts and trombones.[31]

Hunting remained a popular court entertainment and one can conclude that the court wind band also participated, indeed can the Konzertmeister mentioned above, Johann Beer, was accidently shot and killed during a hunt in the year 1700!

[26] Sittard, *Zur Geschichte der Musik und des Theaters am Württembergischen Hofe*, II, 173.

nicht nur bey Hof, sondern nach Hochfstl. gnädigstem Belieben mehrmals auf dem Land.

[27] His biography and picture are given in Werner, *Städtische und fürstliche Musikpflege in Weissenfels*, 69ff.

[28] *Musicalische Diskurse* (Nürnberg, 1719), 18; and the British Museum/Library (MS. 785.b.40,18).

Heute muss man mit dem Hof da-, morgen dorthin. Tag und Nacht leiden da keinen Unterschied. Sturmwind, Regen und Sonnenschein gilt da eines wie das andere. Heute muss man in die Kirche, morgen zu der Tafel, übermorgen aufs *Theatrum*. Gegen dieser Unruhe gehet es in Städten etwas ruhiger zu.

[29] Jean Jacquot, ed., *Les Fêtes de la Renaissance* (Paris, 1973), 3:400.

[30] This account taken from Werner, *Städtische und fürstliche Musikpflege in Weissenfels*, 55.

… wird in der Kirche präambuliert und mit Trompeten und Pauken eine Intrade gemacht und damit so lange *continuiret*, bis die Herrschaft ins Kirchstübchen und die fremden Herren Cavaliere in ihre Stände gekommen sind.

[31] Sachs, *Musik und Oper am kurbrandenburgischen Hof*, 73.

Some courts maintained separate hunting bands, as one can see in Weissenfels ('Jägerband')[32] and Berlin ('Jägdmusik').[33] One rare hunting song for wind band is extant (in Schwerin, Landesbibliothek Mecklenburg-Vorpommern Musikaliensammlung), composed in 1606 by Vöckel for the Duke, and later Elector, Johann Georg I of Saxony, and scored for two cornetts, two tenor and a bass shawms. This music may have been appreciated by a prince who maintained five hundred huntsmen and a thousand hunting dogs in his court. This is not to say he encouraged hunting by his peasants, however, for any of those who shot game on his estate faced the death penalty.[34] He must have done something besides hunting, because the French Ambassador, Grammont, wrote,

> His sole occupation was drinking immoderately every day; only on the days when he went to the Holy Communion did he keep sober in the morning at any rate; to make up for this, however, he drank all through the night till he fell under the table.[35]

Finally, during the Baroque there was an active competition between these court wind bands and the civic wind bands for the right to perform local weddings, casual jobs, etc.[36]

Musical Emperors

A long period of the cultivation of music by the emperors in Vienna begins with Ferdinand III (1637–1657). He was a composer and his works include the *Hymnus de Nativitate* (ca. 1649) for SATB and ten wind instruments.

It was Ferdinand III who imported from Italy the horse ballets, which became an important fixture in Viennese life.[37] The first of these was given as part of the wedding festivities for the marriage of Ferdinand and Maria Anna, daughter to Philip III of Spain. One aspect of this horse ballet would be familiar to American readers: vast numbers of cavalry spelled out the names of Ferdinand and his bride on the floor of the stadium.

In Leopold I (1658–1705) one finds another composer and he composed a *Beatus vir* for voices and wind instruments. Court records are more complete by the end of the century and one can see that in 1700 Leopold I had a Hautboisten band of five oboes and four bassoons, together with six trombones and two

[32] Werner, *Städtische und fürstliche Musikpflege in Weissenfels*, 99.

[33] Sachs, *Musik und Oper am kurbrandenburgischen Hof*, 67.

[34] Johannes Janssen, *History of the German People* (New York: AMS Press, 1966), 15:213, 218.

[35] Ibid., 236–237.

[36] This is outlined by Werner, in *Vier Jahrhunderte im Dienste der Kirchenmusik*, 247–248.

[37] The tradition continues today under the name of the 'Spanish Riding School.'

cornetts for use in church music. According to Köchel, strings begin to appear in larger numbers in the extant records only in ca. 1707–1708.[38]

In January 1667, Leopold sponsored a great horse ballet to celebrate his wedding to Margareta Theresa of Spain, for which published descriptions and engravings were sent all over Europe. Here is also a rare case where some of the actual music is extant, consisting of a few movements for trumpets and timpani by Johann Heinrich Schmelzer.[39] An idea of the seriousness of purpose which these horse ballets entailed can be seen in the fact that the first rehearsal for the one given in January 1667, occurred in August 1666! This production, called 'The Contest between Air and Water,' was given in a vast stadium constructed in the Burghof. First various gods debated on behalf of Water, others on behalf of Air, and finally, after the contention became increasingly violent, the equestrian ballet.

Another great horse ballet held during the reign of Leopold I survives in a published description, but without the original music by Cesti. This event began with the emperor leading the first dance, mounted on a richly decorated horse. The contemporary description relates that next the Duke of Lorraine entered with his party and after the two groups had ridden around the arena, one heard 'a strepitosa armonia da un pianissimo *concerto* di Timpani e Trombe guerriere.'[40] Following this was an elaborate procession, centering on the allegorical figure, 'Germania,' then a tilting contest, with the target being sea-monsters and savages. The music for this, again for trumpets, was described as 'warlike fanfares.'

Finally comes the final horse ballet proper, to dance music by the trumpets. Here the emperor, Counts Dietrichstein and Preiner, and the Duke of Lorraine, to a *corrente*,

> execute the first figure of the ballet in the greatest variety of curvets and volts; after which the ballet is ridden—first by four, then by six, and finally by eight knights, the figures changing as the music changes. Thereupon the riders are seen to press forward to the strains of the fiery *giga* taking the barrier by twos—a magnificent feat never before seen at festivals of this sort. Then some gallop to the center of the field, while the rest are performing their volts and curvets. Their ballet is now carried on by threes in the four corners of the arena, while two others execute new figures in the center. Around these two the twelve entwine the round dance 'treccia' (or, as it is known in Vienna, 'Trezza'), which

[38] Ludwig Köchel, *Die Kaiserliche Hof-Musikkapelle in Wien* (Hildesheim: G. Olms, 1976), 65ff. One should add Köchel's records are not complete.

[39] Schmelzer is given in most books as a violinist, but he was also a cornettist and appears as such in the records of St. Stefan (Vienna) from 1643.

[40] *La Germania esultante, Festa a Cavallo …* (Vienna, 1677).

has its counterpart in another winding dance by eight riders. The two convolutions uncoil themselves, the knights reappear in the center and thence betake themselves toward the spectator's seats, making way for nine knights who execute the figures of the *sarabanda*. They form a crescent, in the center of which the Emperor and the Duke of Lorraine take their stand. Again we behold the knights confronting each other in pairs, executing elaborate steps, at first on the spot and then in motion. The two groups part and stride across the arena, greeted by the tumultuous applause.

Under Karl VI (1711–1740) the large Hautboisten band appears to remain and in 1725 consisted of eight oboes and seven bassoons. Horns now appear in the Viennese court, but are still called hunting horns ('Jägerhornisten'). The consort of trombones and cornetts are also present as well as a large corps of trumpets, now called, 'Musicalische Trompeter,' meaning, I believe, that they could now *read* music.

Beginning with Maria Theresia, there is apparently somewhat of a retrenchment of the wind bands in favor of the instruments of the new classical orchestra. In 1741 one finds only three oboes, four bassoons, five trombones, one cornett, together with a corps of six trumpets. She was a singer and nurtured the environment in Vienna, preparing it for the end of the century and one of the great moments of civilization.

During the reign of Maria Theresia, the composer Dittersdorf visited the court and recorded an eyewitness account of a great entertainment, perhaps one of the last in the old Renaissance and Baroque tradition of vast allegorical festivals. This was a water festival, held on an artificial lake designed by Prince Eugene and built under his personal supervision.

> (The artificial lake) was eighty feet broad and a hundred long. From bank to bank, in the center of the lake, two galleries were thrown across; on each of these were seated a number of trumpeters and drummers, with other players on wind instruments; they were heard playing alternate strains.
>
> In the lake itself, at a little distance from the shore; there stood, at regular intervals on each side, eight pedestals, painted so as to look like stone, and adorned with bronzed grotesques. On the first two pedestals, two live bears stood opposite each other, dressed as clowns; on the second two, two wild-boars, dressed as columbines; on the third, two big goats, dressed as harlequins; and on the fourth were two huge bulldogs.
>
> You may fancy the noise made by growling bears, grunting pigs, bleating goats, howling dogs, and the music going on at the same time!

After allowing his guests an interval in which to enjoy the scene, the Prince waved his handkerchief as a signal, and the show began.

Two gondolas emerged at either end of the gallery, and made towards the cottage; each was manned by four gondoliers, dressed in Venetian fashion. One of them sat on the beak of the vessel, with a bundle of spears, lances, and similar weapons, laid crosswise before him; two others rowed, and the steerer, turning the gondola wherever he chose, sat behind them. These two gondolas advanced, circling in different ways round the pedestals; there were afterwards joined by two others, then by two more, and then the last two. The eight went through their manoeuvres with such accuracy, that no ballet-master, marshalling his *danseuses*, could have improved upon them. When they had gone their rounds, they were ranged face to face, and a tournament began, in which each water-knight, seated on the beak, broke from four to five lances; then they went once more round the pedestals on which the comic actors stood. At one and the same moment, each knight, armed with a staff, struck at one of the grotesque masks, a spring gave way under the blow, and a trap-door fell. Numbers of white ducks and geese, and one swan as well, were concealed in each of the hollow pedestals, and you may fancy the alacrity with which these winged creatures took to their native element, though a marionette rode upon each of them. These marionettes were various figures, proportioned to 'the size of the birds which they bestrode—clowns, harlequins, Anselmos, Doctors, Leanders, Pasquins, Scaramouches, and other Carnival mummers.

A fray ensued, and the knights seized their clubs and threatened one another. The gondolas darted about in studied disorder. When one collided with another, the knights dipped their clubs, which were hand-syringes, into the lake, and squirted the enemies. Whenever they neared a pedestal, the creature on it got the whole benefit of a shower bath, and the animals loudly resented the rudeness of the whole proceedings. The effect on the audience may be imagined, for orders had been given to the musicians in either band to blow in any key they chose. Directly after the skirmish had begun one trumpeter blew a shrill blast in D, whilst another, with the aid of a crook, did the same in C, and another in E *la fa*. Some of the drummers had tuned up, others had tuned down; oboists, clarinettists, bassoonists followed suit. What an infernal discord it was! The beasts growled, the ducks and geese quacked and spluttered, coming into collision with the moving gondolas every moment, and the three thousand spectators roared with laughter. Show me the hypochondriac who could remain unmoved by such a spectacle![41]

[41] Karl von Dittersdorf, *The Autobiography of Karl von Dittersdorf*, trans. A. D. Coleride, (London, 1896), 64ff.

The Golden Age of the Trumpet

As the previous volumes in this series have documented, the trumpet had long been the instrument which was associated with the person of the noble. In Germany even the smallest courts maintained trumpets for this symbolic purpose. Beginning with the seventeenth century there was a dramatic increase in the numbers of these instruments maintained, as one can see in almost every court in the German-speaking nations.[42]

[42] Detlef Altenburg, *Untersuchungen zur Geschichte der Trompete im Zeitalter der Clarinblaskunst* (Regensburg: G. Bosse, 1973), 1:24. This three-volume study is the most distinguished on the subject.

Wolfenbüttel	1553: 2 trumpets	1622: 14 trumpets
Darmstadt	1569: 1 trumpet	1629: 6 trumpets
Dresden	1548: 10 trumpets	1629: 14 trumpets
Graz	1567: 8 trumpets	1611: 13 trumpets
Innsbruck	1554: 12 trumpets	1593: 14 trumpets
Kassel	1538: 8 trumpets	1613: 12 trumpets
Schwerin	1550: 1 trumpet	1609: 7 trumpets
Stuttgart	1550: 6 trumpets	1610: 16 trumpets

In the larger courts the trumpets were often arranged in two choirs, as for example in Berlin, under Friedrich III (1688–1713) where there were two choirs of twelve trumpets and a timpani in each choir.[43]

This great preference for the trumpet during the Baroque is of course also reflected in literature. Looking back on this proud chapter in the long history of the trumpet, Altenburg observed in 1795,

[43] Sachs, *Musik und Oper am kurbrandenburgischen Hof*, 67.

> A sovereign may have ever so good an orchestra, venery, royal stables, and other such ministrations, but if he does not retain at least one choir of trumpeters and timpani, there is, in my opinion, something lacking in the perfection of his household.[44]

[44] *Versuch einer Anleitung zur heroischmusikalischen Trompeter- und Pauker-Kunst* ... (Halle, 1795).

The players themselves were no doubt greatly envied by other musicians and admired by even the nobles, as can be seen in a madrigal in praise of Fantini (found in the preface of his famous trumpet treatise of 1638) by Signor Alessandro Adinari.

> And now Girolamo is here, playing every hour
> With such amazing art,
> That he can by his fiery song arouse Mars;
> And (to make such sweet and pleasant sounds) he takes
> Fame's trumpet and the winds from the air.

Finally, Andreas Werckmeister, to whom Bach was indebted for equal-tuning, saw, in 1691, the instrument in harmony with nature itself.

> God should be praised with them. Yes, the trumpet contains the correct order of all the consonances in itself and is the foremost instrument.[45]

[45] Quoted in Wilhelm Ehmann, *Tibilustrium* (Kassel: Barenreiter-Verlag, 1950), 56.

> Gott will damit gelobet sein. Ja, die Trompete hält eine recht Ordnung aller Konsonanzen in sich und ist ein Hauptinstrument.

What brought on so rich a climax to this art during the seventeenth century? First, the full acceptance of the trumpet in the church, epitomized by the glorious music of Gabrieli and a hundred others, not only gave a higher approval but lifted the instrument above even its high secular associations. Second, advances in metallurgy in the sixteenth century brought a generation of instruments, often made of pure silver and kept in the king's treasure house, which were treasures of art in their own right. This must have contributed to the glamor of the art and the ego of the artist.

These factors and others contributed to a stronger sense of identity in the trumpeter and his guild, called *Kameradschaft*, and these guilds became much more vocal during the seventeenth century in attempting to guarantee their 'rights' and to protect their domain from infringement by other musicians. During this century they frequently called upon the aristocracy itself to help set down these rights in legal definitions. Indeed, in the first important example of such a document, by Ferdinand II, in 1623, it seems as if the aristocracy genuinely shared in these concerns.

> No honourable trumpeter or timpanist shall allow himself to be employed with his instrument in any way other than for religious services, Emperors, Kings, Electors and Princes, Counts, Lords and Knights and nobility, or other persons of high quality: It shall also be forbidden altogether to use a trumpet or a timpani at despicable occasions; likewise the excessive nocturnal improper carousing in the streets and alleys, in wine- and beer-houses. He who transgresses in this way shall be punished.[46]

[46] Quoted in Don Smithers, *The Music and History of the Baroque Trumpet* (London: Dent, 1973), 115.

In 1653, Ferdinand III issued another imperial edict of the same kind.[47] In the introduction, the emperor refers to the edict of his father in 1623, but points out that in the interval 'various difficulties, errors and abuses' had been experienced relative to it. The new rules were arrived at after a discussion, 'as usual in an atmosphere of friendliness,' and everyone was now expected to abide by them.

[47] Antonium Fabrum, *Europäischer Staats-Kantzley* (Leipzig, 1700), part IV, 848–865.

The new edict first deals with the apprentice system in considerable detail. One may not take a student without first obtaining adequate information about the student's 'honorable ancestry and birth.' The apprentice pays a fee at the beginning of a two-year period of study, at the end of which an examination was given.

> Each master shall instruct his apprentice very diligently in his art, and shall not send him into the field (a reference to a period of service in the army) until he knows his field pieces (Feldstücke) perfectly. In order to test this, the apprentice must present himself beforehand to the highest and oldest trumpeter and play his test piece for him. If this is not done, then as a bungler he will not be allowed to go into the field.

Very specific obligations are defined in the case that either student or teacher should quit during the two-year period of instruction. It is also very interesting that strict limitations were placed on how many students one could teach and how often—an obvious attempt at guarding against over-crowding the profession. If a trumpeter gives up his art for a higher position; he also gives up the right to teach. If, however, he retires to become a farmer, he may continue to teach so long as he is not caught 'making the boy work in the fields or the wine cellar and not at his music.'

Several articles deal with the standards of behavior for the trumpeters.

> No honorable trumpeter shall let himself be heard or play the trumpet at night after the curfew hour in the alleys or cross roads, nor in public houses or wine bars, nor anywhere else, except in the houses of princely lords and noble families.

Since only a student who could demonstrate an honorable birth, as mentioned above, could be an apprentice, the trumpeter is warned that if he 'behaves dishonorably toward a widow or an honest man's daughter and makes her pregnant,' even though it is his own acknowledged child, he may not instruct him in trumpet playing. A strong hint is given that if one marries 'a person of public ill repute' he will no longer be permitted to be a trumpeter. He would be immediately thrown out of the profession, should he, lose his skill at the trumpet, play in the company of jugglers, court mutes, town watches or at lotteries and the like … (or) give up his art to become a watchman on a tower, or join the jugglers or comedians.

Finally, a framework for discussion is established, 'if the lord's affairs permit,' to handle problems that may arise, disputes, etc., as well as discussion of fines and fees.

A particular fear of the trumpet guilds was that their positions might be taken over by the civic musicians, who read music and, judging by the extant music, were better musicians.[48] The trumpet guilds tried to protect their domain first by attempting to define the kinds of playing which belonged to them, as opposed to that which belonged to the civic musician. There were so many restatements of this one must conclude that the idea was never accepted outside the trumpet guild.

Next, the trumpet guilds tried, and largely succeeded for a time, to restrict to themselves the trumpet, leaving to the civic musicians the old S-trumpet and the cornett. As a reflection of the importance this issue held for the trumpet guilds, one finds several documents during the seventeenth century[49] which suggest that they were even concerned that another instrument, especially the trombone, might try to *sound* like a trumpet! In 1671, the court trumpeters from Altenburg, having heard something of this nature at the local carnival, lodged a complaint with their prince. In this case, the city fathers made a strong defense of the civic players. One notes here also the stress on the fact that the civic players were *reading* music, as opposed to the memorized repertoire of simple, triadic, and short pieces of the trumpeters, and that this need to adhere to the page seems to be taken as an argument in their favor.

> (The civic players) used their instruments, such as trombones, cornetts, also strings, according to the music, as well as they could in all places for celebrations, weddings, and other honourable gatherings. It is also customary everywhere that they perform, from the music set down, on the instruments discussed here, and if town's people and other music lovers requested a tune in the manner of trumpets on trombones, cornetts, or strings, they could not help but oblige them in this way the best they could. All of which has been customary here and in other places according to their art for countless years.[50]

[48] I disagree with Smithers, *The Music and History of the Baroque Trumpet*, 114, and others who characterize the civic wind players as if they were still in the state of development they were during the twelfth century.

[49] For example one from the Reichstage in Regensburg (October 24, 1630), quoted by Werner, *Städtische und fürstliche Musikpflege in Zeitz*, 42.

[50] Quoted in Smithers, *The Music and History of the Baroque Trumpet*, 115. How strong is the rule of the printed page among musicians today!

The members of the trumpet guilds also were concerned with maintaining the standards of their art among their own members. One Caspar Hentzschel, in 1620 comments on the misuse of their art, especially in the performance of the military signals, 'Toccetten, Sonaden' and 'Serosoneten.' These, he reminds the trumpeter, should be performed in an 'artful' manner and never in beer houses. One must recognize the correct musical art, in view of this 'ancient art which was used by the Jews and was communicated to me by an old Jew from Padua.'[51]

Some accounts of the ceremonies surrounding the life of the Baroque noble indicate large numbers of trumpets could be assembled, as in the example of the visit to Leipzig by Duke Johann von Sachsen-Halle, in 1671, when one heard forty-seven trumpets.[52] These court trumpeters must have been a colorful addition to court life during the Baroque, with their uniforms and banners. An eyewitness describes the trumpeters of the Duke of Württemberg, who brought them with him to England in 1603 when he was made a member of the Order of the Garter.

> As to the order of the proceeding, it was in this manner: first went two trumpeters belonging to the troops of horse, whose trumpets were adorned with silk banners, painted with the arms of Wirtemberg in their proper colours, and after them ten other trumpeters in the same equipage. Next a flute player and a drummer, the military musik belonging to the foot. These fourteen musitians were clad in silk intermixt white and red at equal intervals, and caps of black velvet on their heads.[53]

Another English chronicle gives an indication of how the aristocratic listeners could respond to these trumpet corps. Describing the wedding of the Count Palatine of Germany and Elizabeth, daughter to James I, in the Winter of 1612–1613, in London, he reports:

> Before the Palsegrave, at his return from the Chappell, went six of his owne country gallants, clad in crimson velvet, laide exceedingly thicke with gold lace, bearing in their hands six silver trumpets, who no sooner comming into the Banquetting-house, but they presented him with a melodious sound of the same, flourishing so delightfully, that it greatly rejoyced the whole Court, and caused thousands to say at that instant time, 'God give them joy!'[54]

[51] Quoted in Johannes Reschke, *Studie zur Geschichte der brandenburgisch-preussischen Heeresmusik* (Berlin: VDI-Verl, 1936), 5.

> Nun aber/ ob gleich unsere Kunst von vielen wird missbraucht/ die daher leuren und döhnen/ das sie den Hirten und Heherr blasen, der Sawen/ als einem Trommeter/ ehnlicher scheinen: Jedoch wenn wir unsere Putreselle, Allstandare, Acawale, Cawalche und Auget, neben den Toccetten; Sonaden, Serosoneten und Clarien ansehen/ und artlch gebrauchen, wollen/ so wird fuerwar solche kunst und Musicalische zier/ darinnen gespueret/ das, auch darueber ihr viel in die verdacht der Nigromantia kommen und gelangen. Denn das wir solches nicht beweisen auhs unsern Stücken,/ die wir billich in geheim behalten/ und nicht in alle Bierschenken ausbreiten lassen/ so muessen wir der Trommeter gethoen vor eine rechte Musicalische Kunst erkennen/ wann wir nur der uhralten art ansehen/ welche bey den Jueden in gebrauch gewesen/ und mir von einem alten Jueden zu Padua in Italia communicieret und mitgetheilt worden/ den ich billich gegleubet/ und auch daher setzen/ und jedermaenniglich zuerkennen geben wollen.

[52] Arnold Schering, *Musikgeschichte Leipzigs von 1650–1723* (Leipzig, 1926), 298.

[53] Quoted in John Nichols, *The Progresses of King James the First* (London, 1828), 286. An anonymous engraving of the same ceremony, also showing twelve trumpets, is in Nürnberg, Germanisches Nationalmuseum (Sign. HB 116).

[54] Ibid., 548.

In larger courts the trumpet corps were often used for performing during the princely meals. In Berlin, Friedrich Wilhelm I had twenty-four trumpets and two timpani divided into two choirs in order that they could alternate performing the announcement of the meal and for the entertainment of the guests.[55] Sittard says that these 'Kammer-' or 'Concert-trompeter' played on these occasions 'Bicinium, Tricinium or Quadricinium.'[56]

As the reader will find below, the trumpeters also played vital roles in military and diplomatic service. Having an official court trumpeter along gave a traveler safe passage in foreign nations and even a high ranking official traveling without a trumpet or passport risked imprisonment.

[55] Peter Panoff, *Militärmusik in Geschichte und Gegenwart* (Berlin: K. Siegismund, 1944), 86.

[56] Sittard, *Zur Geschichte der Musik und des Theaters am Württembergischen Hofe*, 7.

> The Earl of Feversham the general of the forces: who going without Trumpet or passeport is detained prisoner by the Prince.[57]

[57] *The Diary of John Evelyn* [1673–1689] (Oxford: Clarendon Press, 1955), 4:610.

For the trumpet, it was indeed a golden age, but it would all come to an abrupt end with the Enlightenment movement of the Classic Period.

3 Court Wind Bands in Italy

THE ITALIAN NOBLES also had their private trumpet players and a few of their names are known today, in particular Girolamo Fantini who served under the Grand Duke Ferdinando II of Florence. Fantini's famous trumpet treatise was no doubt taken from his eight years' experience in this court. Another famous trumpeter in this same court was the German known as Simone di Lionardo.[1]

One may be sure these aristocratic trumpeters appeared in all major court festivities. The marriage of Ereditario in Florence, in 1661, included a ceremonial coronation of the new bride by Ferdinando II, a horse ballet, and firing of artillery. Perhaps one sees the duke's personal trumpets in a document which mentions twelve trombetti, dressed in crimson velvet preceding the sergeant general and the 'other' trumpets.[2] A similar scene occurred when Vittorio Amedeo II of Torino returned with his new bride, Anna d'Orleans, niece to Louis XIV, from their wedding in France. They were welcomed on the Beauvoisin bridge by a great number of trumpets and timpani.[3]

The most comprehensive records of Italian courts during the Baroque, with respect to music, seem to be those of the court of the popes, who also had their corps of aristocratic trumpets. This ensemble, called 'concerto de´ 4 trombetti dell'Inclito Popolo Romano,' in 1717, had four principal members, with two alternates called *coadiutori* and *sopranumerari*; the position for a timpani was not made official until 1734, but one surely must have been available on some basis before that time. The Statutes of 1717 reveal many interesting characteristics of this trumpet ensemble. Their first obligation, of course, was always to the pope. Their pay included additional funds for the persons who cared for their horses, their clothes and their barbers.[4] There was a standard payment of six giulii per day (a 'day' is defined here as dawn to the 'Ave Marias' in the evening) for appearances in university or diplomatic ceremonies. On great public occasions, such as horse parades, fireworks, funeral processions, the celebration of cardinals, etc., the trumpets had

[1] Alessandro Vessella, *La Banda* (Milan: Istituto editoriale nazionale, 1935), 94.

[2] Gaetano Imbert, *La vita fiorentina nel '600* (Florence, 1906), 75–76.

12 trombetti vestili di velluto chermisino ...

[3] Luisa Saredo, 'Il Matrimonio di Vittorio Emanuele II su documenti inediti,' in *Nuova Antologia* (Turin, 1885), XLI, fasc. ix.

trombette e timballi sonanti ...

[4] 'che il medesimo concerto deve conseguire da ciascheduno dei padroni de' barberi, cavalli e cavalle.'

to be content with the gifts of money offered by the sponsor; if they complained in this regard they were subject to a fine. The Statutes of 1734 deal in addition with problems of discipline: abusiveness, fighting among themselves, etc.[5]

Another separate papal ensemble was the 'Tamburini del Popolo Romano.' The constitution of 1715 indicates this ensemble consisted of fourteen players, but a lack of funds resulted in only eight principal players together with the same kinds of official alternates.[6] The oldest member became the leader, 'Capo tamburo,' and he carried the flag of the arms of the pope and was responsible for the regulations of the ensemble and the quality of their performance. It was the principal player's duty, in case of illness, to arrange for one of the alternates; attempts at engaging outside players were subject to a fine. This ensemble also performed all public ceremonies, such as the festivals of cardinals, processions for ambassadors, and festivals organized by the mayor. They were paid six giulii per day in addition to a 'tip' of sixty scudi to be divided among those who cared for the horses, their barbers, etc. They were provided their official uniforms, but apparently on an irregular basis. One document of 1758 mentions the new uniform must last for six years.

There was also a wind band under the jurisdiction of the pope. Housed in the *Castel Sant'Angelo*, they are called in documents of ca. 1702, 'musici del concerto di Campidoglio,' in 1702, 'Concerto de tromboni e cornetti del Senato et inclito Popolo Romano,' and apparently 'Concerto Capitolino' in 1705. The constitution of this year calls the leader the 'Priore,' who was elected for a month by the players and was responsible for the selection of the repertoire, their performance, and their pay. Members are cautioned against blasphemy and urged to show the necessary respect toward their colleagues. These eight players, six trombones and two cornetti, performed for the usual papal and civic ceremonies and also for the meals of the Sig. Conservatori.[7]

All of these various ensembles surely participated in the coronations of the popes and surviving documents mention those for Urbano VIII (1623), trumpets on horse and timpani; for Innocenzo X (1644), six tubicines and timpani as well as the papel trombetti; for Clemente IX (1667), ten tamburini in rich velvet crimson cassocks trimmed in gold and the four trom-

[5] Quoted in Vessella, *La Banda*, 115ff.

[6] This is taken from Vessella, *La Banda*, 116–120, where the reader can find sources for numerous contemporary documents.

[7] Vessella, *La Banda*, 103–104, 110–111.

betti del Popolo Romano in red, trimmed in gold; for Clemente X (1670), timpano del Popolo Romano; for Innocenzo XI (1676), various tamburini in rich cassocks and the trombetti del Popolo Romano in red; for Alessandro VIII (1689), ten tamburini and four trumpets; and the same for Innocenzo XII (1691) and Clemente XI (1700).[8]

It is in Italy that one finds the origins of the popular court horse ballets, known as 'Ross Ballet' in the German-speaking countries and as 'Carrousel' in France. These were in part a replacement of the medieval and renaissance tournaments, which no longer made sense after the introduction of firearms, but in Italy they were also the last stage of development of popular horse festivals which can be dated to the fourth century.[9]

There was also an interesting military character mixed in with these great horse ballets. The reason for this seems to lie much deeper than the obvious fact that the military was usually another facet of the court itself. Rather the development, over many centuries, of theories of movement of larger numbers of men and horses in battle had evolved into complicated geometric patterns as the basis of attack and defense. Also, as I have mentioned in the first volume of this series, the ties between the soldier and the dance are very ancient. As a result, Baroque military treatises often chart their formations on choreographic principles rather than purely strategic logic. Möller's *Trilekunst zu Fuss* (Lubeck, 1672), for example, suggests for the defense of Lubeck the placing of the troops in a configuration representing the coat-of-arms of the city![10]

Typically these horse ballets occurred in the central plaza of the city, with great tiers of benches forming a stadium of sorts. There was always a central allegorical theme (one of the earliest being the 'War of Love,' in 1615 Florence), great constructed floats, and military troops arranged in symmetrical formations. The music usually consisted of performances by the aristocratic trumpet and timpani corps, but since their repertoire was memorized (a characteristic of their quasi-secret guilds), little has survived.

In Venice the equivalent of these pageants was, of course, held on water. In 1685, for example, a great naval 'battle' was given in honor of the visiting Duke of Brunswick. This 'battle' was between Venetian and Turkish galleys, with the

[8] Ibid., 125.

[9] Arthur Pougin, *Dictionnaire historique et pittoresque du théâtre* (Paris, 1885), 144, where the author says this kind of festival was introduced to Italy by the Goths. I prefer to believe the origin lay in the Roman circus festivities.

[10] Paul Nettl, 'Equestrian Ballets of the Baroque Period,' *Musical Quarterly* 19, no. 1 (January 1933): 74.

former achieving a glorious victory. The music was supplied by thirty-six singers and twenty-four trumpets, oboes, and drums.[11]

A regular, if less spectacular procession by water occurred on Ascension Day. An eyewitness in 1645 describes it.

> First the Dodge, or Duke in his robes of State (which were very particular & after the Eastern) together with the Senat in their gownes, Imbarked in their gloriously painted, carved & gilded *Bucentoro*, invirond & follow'd by innumerable Gallys, Gundolas, & boates filled with Spectators, some dressed in Masqurade, Trumpets, musique & Canons, filling the whole aire with din.[12]

For the wedding of Prince Cosimo, of the Medici, with the Hapsburg Archduchess Maria Magdalena, another great celebration on the water was given, this time on a river. This spectacle, entitled, 'The Argonauts on the Arno,' included vast numbers of boats decorated as floats, a huge cast representing all the Greek gods, two fire-breathing bulls and a hissing dragon. The music included a group of nymphs and shepherds performing on wind instruments.[13]

Finally, the extant examples of early opera also include some music which must reflect the participation of courtly wind ensembles. The examples of fanfares in *Orfeo* (Monteverde) and *Il pomo d'oro* (Cesti) immediately come to mind, but also the five-part instrumental 'Chiamata alla caccia,' in *Le nozze di Teti e di Peleo* (Cavalli, 1639), for 'Chiamata' was a seventeenth-century Italian term for military fanfare. The *Euridice* by Peri contains a ritornello for flute consort entitled, 'Zinfonia con un Triflauto.'

No doubt there were also occasions when all the available court wind players appeared on stage in great processions, etc. An example perhaps is the opera, *Berenice* (1680), by Giovanni Freschi which included a procession of a chorus of a hundred virgins, several hundred soldiers, two elephants, six trumpeters on horse, six drummers, six trombones, six 'great' (regular?) flutes, six minstrels with 'Turkish' instruments, six with 'octave' flutes, and finally six 'cymbalists.'[14]

[11] Pompeo Molmenti, *Venice* (London, 1908), I, iii, 198.

[12] Evelyn, *The Diary of John Evelyn*, 2:432 (for June, 1645).

[13] A. M. Nagler, *Theatre Festivals of the Medici* (New Haven: Yale University Press, 1964), 115.

[14] John Sainsbury, *Dictionary of Musicians* (London, 1825).

4   Court Wind Bands in Spain

IN TERMS OF LAND, Spain was still the greatest empire of the seventeenth century, but economically she was in trouble. She had lost her naval power, which had controlled her commerce, and she had experienced two important defeats early in the century.

The consequent retrenchments which were necessary can be seen in the organization of the court wind band at Madrid between 1652 and 1655. Spain which had often hired players from the West could no longer afford such a luxury. An extant document[1] orders the head of the court minstrels, Francesco de Baldes (or, Valdes) to begin a school for minstrels so the court could create its own musicians instead of hiring them abroad. He is ordered to form a band of twelve winds, which as we have seen in Germany, seems an obvious imitation of the *Les Grands Hautbois* of Louis XIV in Paris.

[1] Edmond Vander Straeten, *La Musique aux Pays-Bas* (reprinted in New York: Dover, 1969), 7:436–437.

4 soprano shawms
2 tenor shawms
2 'contra altos de shawm'
4 trombones

Still, the aristocracy continued to pretend at greatness as one can see in an eyewitness description of a procession in Madrid, in 1623, with noble after noble competing in luxury of dress and each with the requisite trumpets.

> The honourable TOWNE of Madrid sent forth foure trumpets on horseback, with caparisons of orange-coloured taffats laid with silver lace, and the Trumpeters in cassocks of the same, blacke hats lined with orange-coloured taffata, orange-coloured plumes and silver furniture … There followed the Towne troope, foure Trumpets of the Lord DON DUARTE in a liverie of tawny taffata, with gabardines layd with silver lace, and hats of the same, with tucks of silver, tawny plumes, and brances of silver … it was requisite the Duke of Infantado should follow … He brought with him foure Trumpeters in white freezado mantles; with gabberdines of blacke damaske, edged with silver lace … Presently there entered the ADMIRALL of CASTILE's troup, … There went before his horse foure Trumpetters in long coates of blacke sattin, garded with gold lace, … Four trumpets of the Count de Monterey fol-

lowed, with long coates of white sattin, lacaes and flowers of gold, hats of the same, blacke plumes and golden furniture ... Don Francisco de Sandoval y Roias ... brought four trumpets in four freezado coates, clad in gabberdines of blue sattin, laid with silver lace, blacke hats, wreathes and bands of silver, blue plumes ... The horse were all in number 523, with those of the Trumpets, Kettle-drummes ...[2]

[2] John Nichols, *The Progresses of King James The First* (London, 1828), 892.

5 Court Wind Bands in England

James I

It would be perhaps unfair to expect anyone to look impressive following the reign of the great Elizabeth I, but even with this in mind it is difficult to rank James I very high among English monarchs. His contemporaries describe him as having a rather plump body set on weak, thin legs; eyes which were blue, watery, and rather too large, 'ever rolling after any stranger that came in his presence'; and with a very large tongue, over a small jaw, which caused him to make a distasteful splashing noise when drinking and to dribble gravy into his beard and wine down the side of his cup.[1]

James I was inclined toward books, young men, and extravagance in dress. He considered his ideas as divine imperatives, informing Parliament in 1609,

> For kings are not only God's lieutenants on earth, and sit upon God's throne, but even by God Himself are called gods.

This attitude began the flow of events which would mark that century in England with so much civil unrest and regicide. Still, the Western world remembers two great events from his reign: the flow of his subjects to America, symbolized by the Pilgrims of 1620 who landed in Plymouth, and the 1611 translation of the bible which bears his name.

The reign of James I (1603–1625) began with his coronation in July 1603, with the usual procession postponed until 15 March 1604 due to the fear of plague in London by the aristocracy. The procession began with a gesture toward the queen in the form of a performance of the 'Danish March, her owne-country musicke,' played by nine trumpets and timpani.[2]

There were a number of specially constructed arches to pass under and stages to pass by. An eyewitness describes one of these as a kind of arbor:

[1] Christopher Hibbert, *Charles I* (New York: Harper & Row, 1968), 17–18.

[2] J. S. Shedlock, *Coronation Music*, Proceedings of the Musical Association 28 (1902).

> The whole frome of this somer banqueting house stood upon foure foote; the perpendicular stretching itself to forty-five. We might that day have called it the musicke roome, by reason of the chaunge of tunes that danced around about it; for in one place were heard a noyse of cornets,[3] in a second a consort, a third, which sat in sight, a set of viols …[4]

At St. Paul's Church a student from the grammar school gave an address in Latin, followed, the same observer tells us, by a performance by the church choir with wind instruments.

> … upon whose lower batlements an antheme was sung by the quiristers of the church, to the musicke of loud instruments.[5]

At a place called Fleet Conduit, a great pageant, 'Globe of the World,' was given, featuring the allegorical figures of Envy, Justice, Fortitude, and Temperance. Probably each of these figures was represented by music for another eyewitness described Justice:

> It was super excellent Justice, as I take it, attired in beaten gold, holding a crown in her hand; guarded with shalmes and cornets, whose noise was such as if the Triumph had been endless.[6]

Here also was a singer accompanied by a wind band, for we are told by an eyewitness,[7] 'this song, which went foorth at the sound of haultboyes, and other lowde instruments.' It is possible that this song was written by Ben Jonson, who was one of three men who furnished the official texts for the procession.

> Where are all these honours owing?
> Why are seas of people flowing?
> Tell me, tell me, Rumor,
> Though it be they humor,
> More often to be lying,
> Than from they breath to have trueth flying;
> Yet alter now that fashion,
> And without the streame of passion,
> Let thy voyce swim smooth and cleare,
> When words want gilding, then they are most deere.

---

[3] 'Noyse' was a synonym for 'wind band.'

[4] An account by Thomas Dekker, quoted in John Nichols, *The Progresses of Oueen Elizabeth* (London, 1805), III.

[5] 'loud instruments' was another synonym for wind band.

[6] Gilbert Dugdale, *The Time Triumphant* (London, 1604).

[7] Quoted in Nichols, *The Progresses of Oueen Elizabeth*.

Behold where Jove and all the states of Heav'n, through Heav'ns seaven
    silver gates,
All in glory riding,
Backs of clowds bestriding,
The milky waie do cover,
With starry path being measur'd over,
The Deitie's convent,
In Jove's high Court of Parliament.
Rumor, thou doest loose thine aymes,
This is not Jove, but one as great, King James.

The musical establishment of James I included some forty instrumentalists, of whom at least half represented independent wind bands. Three groups appear consistently: a consort of six recorders, a consort of six flutes, and a consort of nine oboes (the name 'shawm' is now rarely used in England) and trombones, two of which were bass trombones. In addition, there were regular payments to a consort of cornetts, but these players' names appear among those of the previous players—they were, as the English say, 'Double-handed.'[8]

Apart from these musicians there were sixteen or so trumpet players, two 'Dromplayers,' and a 'Phyfe.' These were more functional in character, as one can see in the court tournament of 1619 when both the trumpets of the king and of young Prince Charles were 'richly clad in grene veluet coats laid with gold & silure lace & whie Beruers & fethers.'[9]

The royal trumpets were always present, of course, when a visiting head of state came to London. There are several eyewitness accounts of the visit in 1606 of King Christian of Denmarke. One of these observers, Henry Robart,[10] describes the marvels of the entrance processional, including a 'noyse of trumpets after the sea manner,' and 'other musicall noyse of drums and trumpets.'

After whome followed his Majesties trumpetters, led by their serjeant in a cloake of carnation velvet, bearing the silver mace of his office, and the rest of the company to the number of xiiij in their liverie coates, verrie rich and well mounted. Then followes the King of Denmarkes drume riding upon a horse, with two drums one on each side of the horse necke, whereon hee strooke two little mallets of wood, a thing verie admirable to the common sort, and much admired. Then follow the Denmarke Kinges trumpeters, beeing eleven in all, decently attired

[8] See Thurston Dart, 'The Repertory of the Royal Wind Music,' *The Galpin Society Journal* 11 (May, 1958): 75, and Walter Woodfill, *Musicians in English Society* (Princeton: Princeton University Press, 1953), 179, 296ff.

[9] R. C. Clephan, *The Tournament* (New York: Ungar, 1967), 134ff.

[10] Quoted in Nichols, *The Progresses of Queen Elizabeth*.

Court Wind Bands

The Coronation of James I, engraving by Frans Hogenberg, early seventeenth century.

Detail from bottom center of the Hogenberg engraving showing the nine silver trumpets.

Detail from the middle right of the Hogenberg engraving showing six more trumpeters and two drummers.

after our English fashion, in cloakes of watched, guarded with blacke and striped white; blew velvet white hattes, with bandes imbrodered with gold.

Another observer, in this case Sir John Harington, who attended the court celebrations for the visiting king, leaves one with the impression that the drinking was quite out of control.

> I came here a day or two before the Danish King came, and from the day he did come untill this hour, I have been well nigh overwhelmed with carousal and sports of all kinds ... in such manner and such sorte, as well nigh persuaded me of Mohomets paradise. We had women, and indeed wine too, of such plenty, as would have astonished each sober beholder ... those, whom I never could get to taste good liquor, now follow the fashion, and wallow in beastly delights. The ladies abandon their sobriety, and are seen to roll about in intoxication.

The principal entertainment was the presentation of an allegorical Solomon and his Temple and the coming of the Queen of Sheba. The performers in these roles also seem to have had a few drinks too many. The character of the Queen of Sheba was to carry an armful of 'wine, cream, jelly, beverage, cakes, spices, and other good matters,' up to the King of Denmark to present them to him. In her condition, she forgot the steps before his throne and,

> overset her caskets into his Danish Majesties lap, and fell at his feet, tho I rather think it was in his face. Much was the hurry and confusion; cloths and napkins were at hand, to make all clean. His Majesty then got up and woud dance with the 'Queen of Sheba'; but he fell down and humbled himself before her ... The entertainment and show went forward, and most of the presenters went backward, or fell down; wine did so occupy their upper chambers. Now did appear, in rich dress, Hope, Faith, and Charity: Hope did assay to speak, but wine rendered her endeavours so feeble that she withdrew ... Faith was then all alone, for I am certain she was not joyned with good works, and left the court in a staggering condition: Charity came to the King's feet, and seemed to cover the multitude of sins her sisters had committed; ... She then returned to Hope and Faith, who were both sick and spewing in the lower hall.[11]

One also sees the wind bands participating in one of the family ceremonies, the creation of Henry as Prince of Wales in 1610.

[11] Robert Ashton, *James I* (London: Hutchinson), 242–243.

> By this time the Lord Mayor and Aldermen of London, with the several Companies of the Citie, ... were ready attending, with a great Traine and a sumptuous Shewe to receive his Highness ... Their barges deckt with banners, streamers, ... and sundry sortes of loud-sounding instruments aptly placed amongst them.[12]

[12] Nichols, *James The First*, II.

When the royal family traveled they were given as great a welcome as the local host could afford, often with entertainments which included wind music. An eyewitness describes the entertainments given on a visit to Althorpe in 1603.[13]

[13] Ibid., I, 176–177.

> A Satyr lodged in (the woods) by which her Majesty and the Prince were to come, at the report of certain cornets that were divided in several places of the park ... and began:
> Here! there! and every where!
> Some solemnities are near.

Later in the same entertainment:

> At that the whole wood and place resounded with the noise of cornets, horns, and other hunting music, and a brace of choice deer put out, and as fortunately killed, as they were meant to be, even in the sight of her Majesty.

Another eyewitness describes the entertainment given the queen at Caversham House during her journey to Bath in 1613.[14]

[14] Ibid., II.

> In this space cornets at sundrie places intertaine the time, till the Queene with her Traine is entred into the park. (Following a song and speech by 'Robinshood-men') In the end whereof the two KEEPERS carrie away the CYNICK; and the two ROBINHOOD-MEN the TRAVELLER, when presently cornets begin againe to sound in severall places, and so continue with varietie while the Queen passeth.

The Baroque Masque

One has read, in volume two of this series, of the extensive use of wind bands and wind music in the Elizabethan theater. This tradition continues into the beginning of the seventeenth century as part of the royal entertainments called masques. In previous volumes, I have discussed the primitive mummings of the middle ages and the simple disguisings ('masks') of Henry VIII, all of which used wind bands. Now, in the seventeenth century, the highest development of this entertainment occurs in the extravagant masques of the Stuarts.

Among those masques which are known to have included wind band music, in addition to those discussed below, are several by Ben Johnson, including *Masque of Beauty* [1607–1608]; *Masque of Queens* [1608–1609], ('In the heat of their dance, on the sudden was heard a sound of loud music, as if many instruments had made one blast.'); *Oberon* [1610–1611], ('loud triumphant music'); *Pan's Anniversary* [1624], ('loud music'); and *The Fortunate Isles* [1624–1625], ('loud music,' and later, 'the three cornets play').[15] A masque given in 1610 at Tethys' Festival calls in one place for four-part music by twelve lutes and later, 'at the sound of a loud and fuller musique,' and still later, 'the lowde musique soundes.'[16]

A typical masque usually began with a prologue in verse, with songs and changes of scenery, followed by a dance, actors, and then a main dance in which the maskers invited the royal spectators to dance with them.

Often these masques began with music by the independent wind band. The *Masque of Beauty*, with music composed by Ferrabosco, began with a 'Loud instrudmental overture ...' performed by musicians who were seated in arbors, representing the ghosts of old poets, and attired like priests in habits of crimson and purple.[17]

The *Masque of Blackness* began with a song sung by a triton and two sea maids, accompanied by 'loud music.'

> Sound, sound aloud
> The welcome of the orient flood
> Into the west;
> Fair Niger, son to great Oceanus,
> Now honored thus,
> With all his beauteous race:
> Who, though but black in face,
> Yet are they bright,
> And full of life and light,
> To prove that beauty best
> Which not the color but the feature
> Assures unto the creature.

[15] Nichols, *James the First*, 1:234; 2:383; and 4:988.

[16] Ibid., 2:346.

[17] For additional information on the masques, see Willa Evans, *Ben Jonson and Elizabethan Music* (New York: Da Capo Press, 1965); Edward Naylor, *Shakespeare and Music* (New York: Da Capo Press, 1965), 164; and Gustave Reese, *Music in the Renaissance* (New York: Norton, 1959), 880ff. Extant wind band music thought to have been used in these masques can be seen in John Adson's *Courtly Masquing Ayres* and in compositions found in Cambridge, Fitzwilliam Museum (MS. 24.E.13–17).

Similarly, the *Mercury Vindicated* (1614–1615) began with a 'loud Music' overture, followed by a scene in an alchemist's workshop. Here, Cyclope, tending the fire, sings to an accompaniment of cornetts:

> Soft, subtile fire, thou soul of art,
> Now do thy part
> On weaker nature, that through age is lamed.
> Take but thy time, now she is old,
> And the sun her friend grown cold,
> She will no more in strife with thee be named.

Other masques which began with wind band music were the *The Golden Age Restored* (1615–1616) and *Neptune's Triumph* (1623–1624), both by Ben Jonson, the latter also indicating later in the production, 'three cornets play.'[18]

Sometimes one finds percussion instruments together with the wind bands, as in *Pleasure Reconciled to Virtue* ('wild music of cymbals, flutes and tabors'). In the *Masque of Queens* an 'anti-masque' began with a 'loud instrument' overture and then introduced witches who played on 'spindels, timbrels, rattles, or other veneficial instruments, making a confused noise.'

It appears that the wind band also often performed compositions between the scenes, while the scenery was being changed. They were twice so specified in the last work mentioned and similarly in *Time Vindicated* (after the second 'anti-masque').[19]

In a similar fashion music was perhaps often used during the interval needed for the players to change positions on stage. A stage note in Jonson's *Masque of Queens* reads, 'At which the loud music sounded as before, to give the Masquers time of descending.' Finally, winds may yet have provided dance music after their ancient court tradition. In Jonson's *Time Vindicated* a stage note reads, 'Here to a loud music, they march into their figure, and dance their Entry.'

There are two very interesting eyewitness accounts of masque performances which included independent wind bands. The first of these describes a masque composed for 'Lord Hayes,' for his wedding in 1607, by Thomas Campion. We are told there were three separate ensembles placed around the hall, as if at the points of a triangle. They were a large ensemble of strings and keyboard instruments, a consort of

---

[18] Nichols, *James the First*, 3:124; 4:948.

[19] The use of winds between scenes can also be found in the traditional theater of the day, such as in Marston's *The Wonder of Women* (1605) and *Sophonisba* (1606), both of which call for 'cornetts and organs playing loud full music.' In Beaumont and Fletcher's *The Maids Tragedy* (1610), an oboe band announces the king rather than the more traditional trumpets.

'six chapel voices and six cornetts … in a place raised higher in respect of the piercing sound' of the cornetts, and in a place shadowed by artificial trees, 'those that played on the hautboys at the king's entrance into the hall.'[20]

One 'Chorus' was composed in such a way that all of these ensembles participated, separately, 'in the manner of an echo.' Later, during a procession, 'the six cornetts and six chapel voices sung a solemn motet of six parts.'[21] Nichols[22] gives the text for this motet as follows:

> With spotless mind now mount we to the tree
>   Of single Chastitie.
> The roote is Temperance grounded deepe,
> Which the coldiew'ct earth doth steepe;
>   Water it desires alone,
>   Other drinke it thirsts for none.

The second, and perhaps more valuable, of these eyewitness accounts is by the chaplain to the Venetian Ambassador in London, one Horatio Busino.[23] He describes Ben Jonson's *Pleasure Reconciled to Virtue*, which was given on 6 January 1618.

In his letter to the authorities in Venice, the chaplain first described the extraordinary decorations of the building, and then the six hundred ladies present. The latter, covered with delicate plumes and strings of jewels, looked like so many queens and, he notes, the style of clothes seems designed to hide nature's defects. 'There are no folds so that any deformity, however monstrous, remains hidden.'

At six o'clock in the evening the king finally appears with his court.

> On entering the house, the cornets and trumpets to the number of fifteen or twenty began to play very well a sort of recitative.

This curious reference to a 'sort of recitative,' where centuries of tradition would suggest a fanfare or 'blast,' is one of those rare and valuable clues to performance practice. I believe the word, 'recitative,' here is actually a reference to the new Italian Baroque style which was beginning to replace the old

[20] *The Description of a Maske, presented before the kinges majestie at Whitehall* … (London, 1607).

[21] Dart, 'The Repertory of the Royal Wind Music,' 74, suggests this motet may have been Ferrabosco I's 'Exaudi Deus,' which is found in the wind band manuscript in Cambridge, Fitzwilliam Museum.

[22] Nichols, *James the First*, 2:118.

[23] *Calendar of State Papers and Manuscripts existing in the Archives of Venice, 1617–1619*, 110–114.

Renaissance ones. Ben Jonson used the term, 'Stylo recitativo,' in exactly this meaning in writing about his *Of Lovers Made Men* (1617).[24]

Returning to the account by Busino, the masque, he writes, began with a 'very chubby Bacchus' who sang in an undertone before the king, followed by another stout, drunken figure, 'Bacchus's cupbearer.' The first principal dance was by twelve figures dressed in barrels and wicker-baskets with an accompaniment by the same cornetts and trumpets. Next came a gigantic man representing Hercules with his club and twelve boys in the 'guise of frogs,' who danced and were then driven off by Hercules. An impressive mechanical scene change brought dawn to Mount Atlas, where some high priests and goddesses 'sang some jigs.' Busino was not impressed.

> It is true that, spoiled as we are by the graceful and harmonious music of Italy, the composition did not strike us as very fine.

The final official dance was by twelve masked cavaliers, richly dressed, following which the guests themselves, 'each with his lady,' danced the Spanish Dance. Apparently it was during this dance the weight of the evening's hours and consumption had begun to slow things, for the king became angry and shouted aloud, 'Why don't they dance? What did they make me come here for? Devil take you all, dance!' Whereupon,

> the Marquis of Buckingham, his Majesty's favourite, immediately sprang forward, cutting a score of lofty and very minute capers, with so much grace and agility that he not only appeased the ire of his angry lord, but rendered himself the admiration and delight of everybody.

Our chaplain, 'half disgusted and weary,' left for home at half-past two o'clock in the morning. 'Weary,' indeed, for he had been there for nearly eleven hours!

[24] Ben Jonson, *The Works of Ben Jonson*, ed., C. H. Herford and P. Simpson (125–41), 7:449; also see Reese, *Music in the Renaissance*, 883.

Lesser Lords

With the frequent appearances of the king's wind bands in court, it was socially necessary for the attending lords to imitate this fashion in their own palaces. Thus, for example, in the seventeenth century accounts of the Earl of Cumberland and Lord Howard, one can see many payments to visiting civic wait bands for their performances as part of palace festivities. Of particular interest is an itemized list of costs for a masque given in 1636, found among the accounts of Cumberland. Included here is a payment to 'the waits of York for ther attendance at masque.'[25]

Most lords also maintained, no doubt, some music in their regular households as one of the necessary status symbols. Richard Brathwaite, in his *Some Rules and Orders for the Government of the House of an Earle* (1621), gives interesting illustrations of how these practices followed the royal example. For great banquets there is music to announce the meal, to bring in the food, and to eat it by.

> At great feasts, or in time of great straingers, when it is time for the Ewer to cover the table for the Earle; (the Trumpetter) ... is to sounde to give warning, and the drumme to play till the Ewer is readie to goe up with the service, and then to give place to the Musitians, who are to play ... upon Shagbutte, Cornetts, Shalmes, and other instruments going with winde. In meale times to play upon Violls, Violins, or other broken musicke.[26]

It was impossible to make a journey without the trumpets and drums, for they were the necessary identification of one's status. Brathwaite carefully describes this ritual.

> When the Earle is to ride a journey, (the trumpet) is early every morning to sownde, to give warning, that the Officers may have time to make all things ready for breakfast, and the groomes of the stable to dresse and meate the horses. When it is breakfast time, he is to make his second sounding: breakfast ended, and things in a readiness, he is to sounde the third time, to call to horse. He is to ride foremost, both out and into any towne, sounding his trumpet. Upon the way he may sounde for pleasure. But if he see the day so spent that they are like to bringe late to their lodging, he is to sound the 'Tantara,' to move them to hasten their pace.[27]

[25] Woodfill, *Musicians in English Society*, 260.

[26] Quoted in Paul Jones, *The Household of a Tudor Nobleman* (Urbana: University of Illinois, 1918), 175.

[27] Ibid., 229.

With all this trumpet playing going on while the nobleman was traveling, there was one danger: if the horses were frightened by the trumpets, great danger could come to the royal riders. The solution for this lay in playing for the horses alone, rehearsing with them so to speak, to acclimate them in advance. Surely this must have been the lowest point in the life of the proud court trumpeter.

> ... to goe often into the Stable, to acquainte the horses with the sounde of the trumpet, and the noise of the drumme.[28]

[28] Ibid.

The continuing flow, which began during the sixteenth century, of English publications designed to identify the values and educational goals of the nobleman reflect an unfortunate new trend of thought in society at large. Gradually one sees music fall from its status as one of the distinguishing characteristics of the Renaissance man's education to become only a skill, and thus appropriate to the working class. In James Cleland's *The Institution of a Young Nobleman* (Oxford, 1607) the nobleman is told that it is all right to listen to music, but not to actually play it.

> Delight not also to be in your own person a player upon instruments, especially upon such as commonly men get their living with.[29]

[29] James Cleland, *The Institution of a Young Nobleman* (Oxford, 1607), V, xxv.

Although it may seem ironic to one who values music, this attitude was actually thought of at the time as an argument in raising the culture, not lowering it. This may be understood in the parallel advice by Lord Chesterfield, 'Eat game, but do not be your own butcher and kill it.'[30]

Henry Peacham's *Compleat Gentleman* (1622) goes a bit further and cautions against even listening to too much music; one would not want to 'neglect his more weighty employments.' Interestingly enough, and no doubt related with all of these ideas to the growing puritanical attitudes of seventeenth-century England, this author does encourage singing in the church, which, he says, is 'an enemy to melancholy,' cures some diseases, and helps pronunciation and distinct speaking abilities!

[30] Quoted in Woodfill, *Musicians in English Society*, 220.

Charles I

Charles was a man weak in physique and who also suffered from a speech impediment. His resolute character may be seen not only in his struggle to improve his physical condition, but in his broad education, his ability in several languages, and in his discriminating art collection.

He might have been a great king, if only he had followed the strategies of leadership of Elizabeth I or Henry VIII. Instead, following the blind imperial attitude of his father and no doubt encouraged by his wife, sister to Louis XIII of France, he firmly pursued that course which would lead his country into civil war, bring the monarchy to an end, and result in his own beheading in 1649.

Charles combined his own musical establishment with that of his father's, to create a permanent body of about sixty-five musicians. In the great ceremonies for the funeral of his father, James I, there were payments to an extraordinary group of twenty-one 'Musicians for windy Instruments,' in addition to twenty-one trumpets, four 'Drums and Phife,' and thirteen 'Musitions for Violins.'

Once the reign of Charles himself was underway, the basic wind band seems to have consisted of eighteen players, divided into two rather identical bands of five trombones (one a bass trombone) and four woodwinds (oboes, cornetts, flutes or recorders).[31] After 1630, when the court spent a considerable amount of money on new cornetts, these bands seem to have found a rather stable instrumentation of three cornetts (SST) and three trombones (TTB).[32]

The contract for one of these musicians, hired in 1640, reveals that the members of the wind band were not subject to collections and taxes and were free from arrest. Several extant documents of payments for music prove these musicians were not mere improvising minstrels.

> Warrant for the payment of 23 Pounds to Andrea Lanier, one of his Majesty's musicians for the wind instruments; ie., 20 Pounds for four setts of musique books at 5 Pounds a sett, and 3 Pounds more for two Italian musique cards to compose upon.[33]

---

[31] Dart, 'The Repertory of the Royal Wind Music,' 75; also Woodfill, *Musicians in English Society*, 303ff.

[32] Dart, 'The Repertory of the Royal Wind Music,' believes that after 1630 the oboe falls from favor in England.

[33] London, Lord Chamberlains Accounts, vol. 738, p. 75, for January 10, 1629.

The wind band of Charles I continued to perform in masques and in the theater, until these kinds of entertainments were ended by the government in 1647. The court appearances seem to have become much more functional, centering on music for the king's meals. If the deteriorating economic situation in England, not to mention the civil war, made fewer of the great court entertainments possible, at least at the table Charles could still 'live like a king.' Every year, at Whitehall Palace alone, he and his company consumed three thousand carcasses of beef, fourteen thousand sheep and lambs, twenty-four thousand birds, not to mention vast quantities of pigs, fish, boars and bacon.[34] The musicians were able to work out a rotation system so the same wind players did not have to play for every meal.[35]

In addition to the wind band which played indoors, there was the corps of trumpets, numbering from sixteen to eighteen at this time. They were paid at a higher rate than the other musicians at court and perhaps this was due to the frequent hardships of traveling with one or another of the nobility, their being sent as the king's representative to help assure safe passage. For example, when the Earl of Arundel made a political journey through Germany in 1636, the diary of one who accompanied him notes,

> whilst our trumpeter was allowed to visit ... the castle in order to ask French permission for our further passage.[36]

There were definite risks, of course, and in fact the trumpeter, a Mr. Smith, who began this particular journey was murdered on route.

> This day, after a widespread search, the corpses of His Excellency's Gentleman of Horse and his Trumpeter, together with the corpse of their guide, the Postmaster, were found. They had been barbarously murdered five days before, as they were returning to Regensburg, and their bodies were found tied to separate trees about pistol shot range from the highway, at a point within four miles of Nuringburge (Nürnberg). It appeared that each must have witnessed the death agonies of his companions. The head of the Gentleman of the Horse had been shattered by a pistol shot, the Trumpeter's head had been cut off and the guide's head had been split open.[37]

[34] Christopher Hibbert, *Charles I*, 112.

[35] Henry Lafontaine, *The King's Music* (New York: Da Capo Press, 1973), 72ff.

[36] Francis Springell, *Connoisseur & Diplomat* (London: Maggs Bros, 1936), 89.

[37] Ibid., 80.

Charles II and the Restoration

> This day came in his Majestie Charles the 2d to London after a sad & long Exile, and Calamitous Suffering both of the King & Church: being 17 yeares. This was also his Birthday, and with a Triumph of above 20,000 horse & foote, brandishing their swords and shouting with unexpressable joy: The wayes straw'd with flowers, the bells ringing, the streetes hung with Tapissry, fountaines running with wine: The Mayor, Aldermen, all the Companies in their liver(ie)s, Chaines of Gold, banners; Lords & nobles, Cloth of Silver, gold & velvet every body clad in, the windos & balconies all set with Ladys, Trumpets, Musick ...[38]

[38] *The Diary of John Evelyn*, for May 29, 1660.

Thus wrote a London citizen on the day in 1660 which saw the restoration of the monarchy in England. He also mentions the irony that the army which returned Charles II, 'without a drop of bloud,' was the same army which had been at war for six years to depose his father.

Some call Charles II the 'happy king,' for after fourteen years of wandering, mostly in France, he seemed far more interested in having fun than worrying about government. An Italian diplomat noted,

> his fiercest enemies are diligence and business. He worships comforts, pleasures, and practical jokes, hates implacably all sort of work, and loves with the greatest enthusiasm every kind of play and diversion.[39]

[39] Lorenzo Magalotti, *Relazione d'Inghilterra* (1668).

As a collector of mistresses, he was perhaps without equal for his generation, setting an example for his court and restoration theater. One of the most memorable lines of that century was spoken by one of his ladies when the crowd mistook her for a newly arrived French (and Catholic) mistress. 'Be silent, good people,' she said, 'I am the *Protestant* whore!'[40]

[40] Sir Arthur Bryant, *King Charles II* (London: Collins, 1955), 238.

The coronation of Charles II, which occurred on 22–23 April 1661, included perhaps the largest assemblage of wind bands during the seventeenth century. First came a great procession through London passing the usual triumphal arches, several of which were filled with or surrounded with wind bands. An eyewitness, John Ogilby, wrote that at the first of these, in 'Leaden-Hall Street near Lime Street End,' were thirty trumpets and eighteen drums, playing in the following order:

Drums: Marches of several countries
Trumpets: Several 'Levets'
Drums: Change to a 'Battel'
Trumpets: Sound a 'charge'
Trumpets: Sound pleasant 'Levets'
Drums: Beat a lofty English March

At the second arch were a number of wind bands, probably wait bands from towns throughout the countryside. Ogilby tells us that one consisted of twelve players, two of eight players, and 'the rest' of six players. Here also were a group of seven trumpets and six drums, three groups of six trumpets and three drums, a group of six drums, and his majesty's drum and fife corps.

Still another arch, called the 'Naval' arch, was constructed with two galleries, containing twelve players of 'Winde-Musik,' while outside the arch were two more groups of six winds, one dressed as sailors. Finally, Ogilby wrote that on the towers of the 'great Conduit at the entrance of cheap-side' one heard another group of 'Winde-Musik,' consisting of eight players.[41]

Another eyewitness, John Evelyn, noted that the commercial companies of London also employed wind bands to represent them, as was their custom on great civic occasions.

> The streetes, strew'd with flowers, houses hung with rich Tapissry, Windos & Balconies full of Ladies, The Lond: Militia lining the ways, & the sevrral Companies with their Banners & Loud musique ranked in their orders: The Fountaines runing wine, bells ringing ...[42]

The procession itself included the king's own trumpet players, of course, and they performed again during the coronation ceremony with silver trumpets.

> Warrant to prepare seventeen silver trumpets like that of the sergeant trumpeter's ... so that they may be ready to attend with them at solemnizing his Majesty's coronation, the said trumpets to be held by them as long as they continue in their places, and upon their death ... to be delivered up to the jewel house.[43]

[41] John Ogilby, *The Relation of His Majestic's Entertainment passing through the City of London to His Coronation* (London, 1661), 2–44.

[42] *The Diary of John Evelyn*, for April 22, 1661.

[43] London, Lord Chamberlain Accounts, vol. 741, p. 118.

We also know that the king's wind band performed during the coronation ceremony.

> Warrant for the allowance of liveries to his following musitians for the wind instruments, against his Majesty's Coronation.[44]

Matthew Locke composed at least some of the compositions 'ffor his Majesty's Sagbutts & Cornetts' for these eight players to perform on this occasion.[45]

After the coronation another procession occurred (on 23 April). A wind band of eight players performed on a stage in Crutched Friars and another band of six played from a balcony built for this occasion. At Leadenhall there were several more wait bands and a 'noise of seven trumpets.' At the Exchange in Cornhill a group of singers sang to the accompaniment of wind instruments. Still more wait bands performed at the Stocks, on the Conduit in Cheap, and at the Standard.[46]

Of all the early English rulers, Charles II maintained the most ambitious musical household. He had an orchestra of twenty-four violins, modeled after that which he had come to know in France, and he increased significantly the size of his wind band.

In 1661 one first finds the wind band, called, 'consort, being his Majesty's wind musick,'[47] consisting of thirteen players. By 1663 this band had become sixteen players, who on at least one occasion at Windsor appeared as an ensemble of fourteen, employed together with the twenty-four violins, twenty-two 'lutes & voices,' fourteen trumpets, and seven drummers.[48]

The royal wind band reaches its largest size in 1668 with nineteen members, one of whom was a flute and one of whom was a 'treble Hoboy.'[49] This lone oboist, together with four visiting French 'hoboyes,' was employed to perform a masque at Whitehall in 1675; Dart contends the band was basically a trombone and cornett band by this date.[50]

A document dated 18 June 1669, announced the 'retrenchment of his Majesty's musick' and here one can see the wind band reduced from nineteen to ten; by 1679 there will be only five members.[51]

Another important document[52] announces, 'Mathew Lock in the place of Alphonso Ferabosco (II), composer for the wind music.' The association of these two important English com-

[44] Ibid., vol. 741, p. 160; vol. 817, p. 158.

[45] Grove 11:109.

[46] Alan Warwick, *A Noise of Music* (London: Queen Anne Press, 1968), 27.

[47] London, Lord Chamberlain Accounts, vol. 741, p. 318.

[48] Ibid., vol. 741, p. 375; vol. 742, pp. 380–381.

[49] Ibid., vol. 478, p. 79.

[50] Ibid., vol. 745, p. 197; Dart, 'The Repertory of the Royal Wind Music,' 76.

[51] London, Lord Chamberlain Accounts, vol. 771, p. 239; Lord Chamberlain Papers, Bundle 19.

[52] London, Lord Chamberlain Accounts, vol. 479, pp. 99–100.

posers with the court wind band helps us evaluate the importance of this band in the court and, together with the extant music, confirms, in my opinion, that they did play music of real value.

The quality of their performance was entrusted to Nicholas Lanier, who, as head of the entire musical establishment, had the specific duty of controlling rehearsals.

> Nicholas Lanier ... hath power to order and convocate (his Majesty's musick) at fitt time of practize and service ... if any of them refuse to wayte at such convenient tymes of practize and service ... I shall punish them either in their persons or their wages.[53]

[53] Ibid., vol. 741, p. 316.

Sometimes Charles II was apparently generous enough to loan his players and their instruments out to other lords, no doubt as a political debt to be collected later.

> Warrant to provide and deliver to the earl of Oxford or his assignes, eight cornetts with stands and other necesaries thereunto belonging, seventeen bannerolls for trumpeters with the Jolley Boyes and cordage to them, with tassells, one payre of handerolls for the kettle-drummers.[54]

[54] London, Lord Chamberlain Papers, Bundle 8.

From Pepys' *Diary* it also appears that even individual citizens could, for a price, engage the royal trumpets.

> Up: and called up by the King's trumpets, which cost me 10s.[55]

[55] Entry for December 28, 1668.

One reads again of a trumpet player being killed while on diplomatic duty, in this case, 'John Christmas, who was attending Lawrence Hyde on his embassy to Poland.' This document has as its main concern the consequent loss of one of the king's silver trumpets and, almost as an afterthought, awards 200 Pounds to the widow, 'in regard of the loss of her husband.'[56]

[56] Richard McGrady, 'The Court Trumpeters of Charles I and Charles II,' *The Music Review* 35 (1974): 227.

The royal wind band surely performed at all major state celebrations and we have an eyewitness account of two of these by John Evelyn. First, he describes the celebration of St. George's Day at Whitehall in 1667:

> ... and lastly proceeded to the Banqueting house to a greate feast: The King sate on an elevated Throne at the uper end, at a Table alone: ... at lowere end the Musick: on the balusters above the Wind musique,

> Trumpets & kettle drums ... about the middle of dinner, the Knights drank the Kings health, then the King theirs: Then the trumpets, musique etc: plaied & sounded, the Gunns going off at the Tower ...[57]

[57] *The Diary of John Evelyn*, entry for April 23, 1667.

In 1662, Evelyn observed the arrival of the Russian ambassador.

> ... his retinue being numerous, all clad in vests of several Colours, & with buskins after the Eastern manner: Their Caps of furr, & Tunicks richly embrodrd with gold & pearle, made a glorious shew ... Wind musick playing all the while in the Galleries above.[58]

[58] Ibid., entry for December 29, 1662.

The royal trumpets no doubt joined in all such state occasions, although they functioned as a separate ensemble. Since their repertoire by this date was still memorized and is not extant, one can only guess at its nature. Perhaps a small clue or two can be found in Dryden's *Song for St. Cecilia's Day* (1687), for he was close to the court at this time.

> The TRUMPETS loud Clangor
> Excites us to Arms
> With shrill Notes of Anger
> And mortal Alarms.
> The double double double beat
> Of the thund'ring DRUM
> Cryes, heark the Foes come;
> Charge, Charge, 'tis too late to retreat.

The Court Band after the Retrenchment

We have seen a long and impressive development of the English court wind band, but after the retrenchment late in the reign of Charles II it remains small in character and very little is heard of it.

During the brief reign of James II, England again had a Catholic king, a good man who was prevented success only by his religion. John Evelyn heard only trumpets and drums when his reign was announced.

> The Herauld proclaimed His Majesties Titles to the Imperial Crowne, & succession according to the forme: The Trumpets & Kettle drums having first sounded 3 times.[59]

[59] Ibid., entry for February 6, 1685.

Court Wind Bands in England

An engraving of the coronation itself is extant although its value is limited.[60] It pictures a single fife player; with a banner hanging from his instrument, followed by four drum players and the 'Drum Major,' who carries a walking stick. Next are eight royal trumpeters and among them a pathetic figure bent over under the weight of two timpani on his back, the player walking behind; the 'Sergeant Trumpet,' carries a great mace (see images below). The only illustration of the court wind band is the most interesting, if the most troublesome. One sees three figures entitled, 'Two Sackbuts, and a double Courtal,' who are in fact playing two slide trumpets and a cornett! (see image page 98).

[60] Contained in Francis Sandford, *The History of the Coronation of … James II* (London, 1687).

Engravings of the coronation procession of James II.

Engraving of the coronation procession of James II.

During the reign of William and Mary (1689–1694) an oboe band appears, no doubt modeled after the one in Paris. They first appear in 1690, when a payment is made to six oboes to accompany the king on a visit to Holland.[61] Another interesting reference to them[62] describes four rehearsals and a subsequent performance at a ball for the king's birthday in 1695.

The pay warrants for special dress for the funeral of Queen Mary, in 1695, permit us to see what is probably the entire wind and percussion establishment at that date: six oboes, sixteen trumpets, and twenty-five drums (who are identified as 'military' players).[63] From this ceremony there are no fewer than four extant original compositions. Every wind band enthusiast knows two of these, the beautiful *March* and *Canzona* by Henry Purcell. There remains some doubt what Purcell meant by 'flat Mournfull Trumpets,' but the reaction by one who was present confirms our opinion of these works even today.

> I appeal to all that were present, as well such as understand Music, as those that did not, whither they ever heard any thing so rapturously fine and solemn & So Heavenly in the Operation, which drew tears from all; & yet a plain, Naturall Composition; which shows the pow'r of Music, when 'tis rightly fitted & Adapted to devotional purposes.[64]

The companion works for this ceremony, both entitled, *Queen's Farewell*, by Thomas Tollet and James Paisible, are composed in the several clefs typical of oboe bands of this period.

[61] London, Lord Chamberlain Accounts, vol. 724.

[62] Ibid., vol. 776, p. 31b.

[63] Ibid., vol. 561, pp. 112–119.

[64] Thomas Tudway, London, British Museum (MS. Harl. 7340, fol. 3). The stage works by Purcell also include a great number of brief musical compositions for small numbers of winds.

The basic oboe band and royal trumpets continue into the reign of Anne (1702–1727) and one account speaks of both performing for a state dinner in Bath, during the Winter of 1703–1704.[65]

These same traditions were continued under George I (1714–1727), where a list of the complete musical household includes twenty-four 'musicians,' who are perhaps the violins; twelve trumpets and a 'Sergeant trumpeter'; one timpani; four drummers and four drum majors; and finally the six-member oboe band.[66]

During the reign of George II (1727–1760) the musical establishment appears to decline, at least in so far as winds are concerned. A newspaper notice in 1737 mentions that Frederick, Prince of Wales, was attended by a 'Concert of Trumpets and Horns … on the River,' as he returned to the palace late one evening.[67]

An engraving of 1742 entitled, 'Kings Trumpets &c,' pictures another hunched over person carrying two timpani before the player, two trumpets, and then a small wind band of one bassoon and two oboes (who share four legs!).[68] Such a small royal wind band seems confirmed in the dozen or so works by Handel.[69]

One author suggests that marches in the oratorios and operas by Handel, such as *Rinaldo, Scipione, Deidamia*, and *The Occasional Oratorio*, not to mention the two versions of 'See the Conquering Hero Comes,' from *Joshua* and *Judas Maccabaeus*, can be performed without the doubling string parts, leaving perhaps original marches for oboes and bassoons.[70] I might add that the oratorio, *Deborah* (1733), contains the mention of a 'Military Symphony' as a prelude to act three, which is not in the musical score and may have been a military band work.

How extraordinary in every way then is the greatest wind band composition of the English Baroque, Handel's *Grand Overture of Warlike Instruments*, known today as the 'Fireworks Music.' Scored for three oboes, two bassoons with contrabassoon, three horns, three trumpets, and percussion, although notes in the score indicate the first performance was given by a band of some sixty players.[71]

This masterpiece was composed early in 1749 as part of a celebration held in Green Park, London, on 27 April, commemorating the peace of Aix-la-Chapelle. The music received

[65] David Green, *Queen Anne* (London, 1970), 118.

[66] John Beattie, *The English Court in the Reign of George I* (London: Cambridge University Press, 1967), 279.

[67] James Winston, *Collections relating to Vauxhall Gardens* (Oxford, Bodleian Library [G. A. Surrey C.21-5, I]).

[68] London, British Museum, Anonymous detail from the border on a child's 'Writing Sampler' (1742) (Banks Coll. Mm. 2–97).

[69] I have mentioned above the two extraordinary double concerti by Händel, one for double Hautboisten bands and the other with the addition of horns. Both works contain music also used in the *Messiah*.

[70] Edward Croft-Murray, 'The Wind-Band in England, 1540–1840,' in *Music and Civilisation* (London: Trustees of the British Museum, 1980), 138.

[71] Croft-Murray, ibid.

a public reading at Vauxhall on Friday 21 April 1749, attended by twelve thousand people, causing a tremendous traffic jam on London Bridge. The composition gained the name known today from the fact that the celebration included a fireworks 'machine' (which misfired causing a moment of concern), designed by Chevalier Servandoni.

Finally, we should mention that the music for the well-known 'Pastoral Symphony' in Handel's *Messiah* was based on a performance by an Italian wind band which Handel had heard. He acknowledged this in his autograph score by writing 'pifa' [for *pifferari*] at the beginning of this music.

PART 3

The Origins of Western 'Turkish Music'

The Origins of Western 'Turkish Music'

THE REPEATED BATTLES WITH THE OTTOMAN EMPIRE between 1526 and 1699 made the Turkish nation for a time the primary fear of Western civilization. This empire was a particular source of anxiety for the Viennese for their city lay on the border between East and West and more than once the Turkish armies were at the very gates of the city. There was, of course, a great curiosity about these 'heathen' neighbors and the museums in Vienna today are filled with objects collected outside the city walls after the Turkish troops had left. Every visitor today is told of the discovery, in this manner, of a bag of coffee beans which led to the craze for drinking coffee in Vienna.

This curiosity was shared by musicians and a rare account exists of a musical 'duel' held during a lull in a battle fought in 1683 between the military musicians of East and West. The Turkish musicians were heard playing 'Cymbeln, Glocklein und Schalmeyen,' the Viennese answering with trumpets and timpani.[1] This musical fascination continued in the West, and in Vienna in particular, for a long time. Mozart's first real success in Vienna, for example, was his opera *The Abduction from the Seraglio*, which was the 'hit' of the 1782 season. Similar examples of music 'alla Turca' in works by Haydn, Gluck, and even the Ninth Symphony by Beethoven, are familiar to all musicians.

The Turkish influence on Western military music was much more fundamental, as it helped solve the basic problem of mass movement among the new standing armies. This influence was recognized throughout the Classic and Romantic periods so generally that Western military bands were often called simply, 'Turkische musik.' Ironically, the Sultan Mahmut II ended the indigenous Turkish military band tradition in 1826, when he decided to model his bands after the West and hired the brother to Donizetti to guide this reorganization. What, then, were the Turkish elements which so influenced the military bands of the West and why was this influence so important?

[1] Eugen Brixel, *Das ist Österreichs Militärmusik* (Graz: Edition Kaleidoskop, 1982), 21. It was from this same battle, by the way, that the folksong, 'Prinz-Eugen, das edlen Ritter,' and which is used in the second movement of Hindemith's wind band work, *Konzertmusik*, op. 41, had its origin. (Ibid., 23)

The Turkish Mehter Band

The Turkish wind and percussion band tradition is very old. In volume one of this series, I have discussed their influence on the West during an earlier period, the Crusades, but their history is even more ancient than the modern era. A Chinese chronicle tells of a Chinese general who visited the Turkish city of Balasagun (which no longer exists) in the year 200 BC and was so impressed with the instruments he heard there that he took an entire band back with him to China.[2]

The basic Turkish military band unit was a five-member ensemble called the *Mehter* band, which was doubled and redoubled according to the rank of the person by whom they were employed. The Sultan's band, called *Mehterhane*, was usually the largest and consisted of a nine-fold version of the same basic instruments. For great battles even larger proportions were assembled. The Sultan Selim (1512–1520) took more than two hundred players to the battle of Mercidabik, as did Suleiman the Great (1520–1566) to Vienna. Selim III (1789–1807) also maintained a two hundred piece band.[3]

The instruments included an oboe, conical and wild-sounding like the medieval shawm. Made of plum or apricot wood, it was decorated with precious stones and silver bracelets and called by the Turks, the 'zurna.' There was a primitive trumpet, which seems to have been used more as a rhythmic than a melodic instrument, called the 'boruzen.'

It was the percussion instruments, however, which were the most influential in the West. There were cymbals ('Zil,' the player being called 'Zilzen') very much like the modern ones. There were prototype small timpani, called 'Nekkare,' with leather stretched over twin copper bowls, played in a sitting position on the ground. The final member of the normal Mehter band was a large bass drum, played with a large stick in the right hand and a smaller one, sometimes a branch of a tree, with the left hand.

In larger bands the 'Cevgen' was added, played by a musician who also sang. In English we call this instrument the 'Jingling Jonnie,' or 'Turkish crescent.' It was a high pole surmounted by one or more metal crescents ('Mehter,' itself, is derived from the Persian 'Mahi-ter,' for 'moon'), from which

[2] Much of this material is taken from a publication under the direction of Sabahattin Doras, curator of the Military Museum in Istanbul, *Mehterhane* (Turkiye Turing Ve Otomobil Kurumu, n.d.)

[3] Ibid., 32.

hung many small bells and on each end, horsehair plumes. The contemporary Western bell-lyre is nothing but a surrogate for this instrument.

In one of the multiple Mehter bands, say a five-fold band, there would be a leader for each instrument, called 'Aga,' and the players of each instrument would be grouped together, in this case five oboes, five cymbals, etc. These smaller groups would then be configured into a large half-circle ('moon' again),[4] or in the case of a nine-fold band a full circle. The over-all conductor was called 'MehterbasiAga.'

[4] One writer, Arif Pascha, in *Les anciens costumes de l'Empire Ottoman* (Paris, 1863), suggests that part of the reason for the half-circle formation was that it helped in immediately identifying any player of wrong notes, etc.

Engraving of an Ottoman Mehter band

The royal Mehter band, a nine-fold band attached to the Topkapi Palace, was composed not of Turkish players, oddly enough, but rather of Armenians and Greeks who had been converted to Islam. The viziers, or governors, and commanders of the army troops had seven-fold bands. Civilian organizations, such as trade guilds, were allowed to form Mehter bands for special occasions, processions, etc., but were not allowed to maintain them independently.

The bands dressed in striking uniforms, typically gowns with wide sleeves, turbans wrapped with gauze, leggings, and short, slip-on boots. The conductor, of course, was dressed in colors apart from the musicians.

These bands played at regular times during the day, beginning early in the morning. A Prussian soldier, sent to Constantinople early in the eighteenth century, recalled that the band which marched before his quarters every morning, 'split the ears with its incredible charivari.'[5] On fortresses, these bands also performed a watch duty.

[5] Quoted in *Musikalische Nachrichten und Anmerkungen auf das Jahr 1770* (Leipzig, 1770), vol. 3.

It was in battle that the Mehter band was considered most valuable. Their playing thrilled and excited the soldiers, lifting their morale and driving them into action. Many accounts also remark on the effect of this thundering noise in diminishing the morale and dissipating the enemy. One of the band leaders during the Kara Mustafa Pasha's attack on Vienna, remembered,

> Toward the middle of the afternoon the grand Vizier's mehter band started to play first. Then the bands of the governors of provinces and the bands on the right started to play all together. Thus, after the evening prayer and at dawn, the sound of drums, oboes, kettle-drums, and cymbals joined from every corner the rumble of cannon and gunfire, and the whole countryside echoed with these sounds.[6]

[6] Doras, *Mehterhane*, 27.

The sultan's band performed concerts each afternoon in the palace during peace time as well as during coronations and other ceremonies. During battle, concerts were performed in front of the royal tent. One such concert performed before a guest, Osman Gazi, began a tradition somewhat similar to the curious tradition in the West of audiences standing during the famous chorus in the *Messiah* by Handel. Gazi, out of respect for the Selijuk Sultan, stood during the concert by the Mehter band and for the following two hundred years, until Mohammed II (1451–1481), sultans stood when these bands performed concerts.[7]

[7] Ibid., 32.

There are some interesting eyewitness accounts from the West dating from the seventeenth century, the period in which these Turkish bands began to influence Western military bands. The percussion instruments, while not unknown in the West, caught the attention of Western ears for their use in large numbers combined with fewer melodic instruments. For many this was a shock on first hearing, as in the case of one listener early in the seventeenth century.

> In Turkey there are also many kinds of instruments which they usually play in a confused manner and without the use of consonances, unless these happen to arrive by accident; and the Turks only take satisfaction in hearing loud and confused noise.[8]

[8] Salomon De Caus, *Institution Harmonique* (Frankfurt, 1615), fol. 22v.

Another early writer who gave special attention to the description of the percussion instruments, as heard later during the seventeenth century, was Count Luigi Ferdinando Marsigli. Based on a journey to Constantinople, his account divides the instruments into those which produce shock (the various drums) and those which make musical sounds (oboes and perhaps trumpets). The bass drum he describes as being played on one side with a large wooden mallet ('Gross Baguette de buis') and on the other with a 'Petite Baguette.'[9] This instrument was thus played on both sides alternately, 'with much artistry and solemnity, in a most agreeable manner.' These bass drums, he adds, were played,

9 *Il Sato Militare dell' Imperio Ottomano. Incremento e Decremento Del Medesimo Dell Signore Conte di Marsigli* ... (Hague, 1732), 54ff.

> when the Army is approaching that of its enemies ... and they are beaten around the soldiers guarding the Camp, in order to keep them awake. Meanwhile the drummers cry out *Jegder-Alla*, that is to say, 'the Lord is good!'

He heard this instrument as having the effect of somehow pulling together the sounds of all the other percussion instruments into a more homogeneous effect.

> The different sounds of all these instruments would be harsh to the ear, if they were not corrected by that of the *Grand Caisse*; but when they are reunited the concert that they produce is agreeable enough.

The smaller timpani-type instruments he heard as being played in the Western tradition, with a pair of hard sticks.

> They are reserved for the honor of the Family of the *Bacha*, and serve to signal the march; they enter the concert of Music extremely well, and they are called the *Sadar Nagara*. The *Bachas* march in three lines and have two *Timbalists*, and the *Timbales* are at each side of the procession, and they are beaten in the same way we do in our own army.

Another seventeenth-century observer, Evilya Çelebi, in a manuscript account of travels throughout Turkey,[10] says that the musicians of the Ottoman Empire were organized into more than forty different guilds of builders, players and singers. The Mehter band he heard had nine players, including the

10 Evilya Çelebi, *Narrative of Travels in Europe. Asia, and Africa in the Seventeenth Century* (Joseph von Hammer, trans., London, 1834), 225ff.

conductor who was the oboist. The large bass drum, he wrote, was 'as big as the dome of a Turkish bath. They are played day and night. Their sound is like thunder.'

This same writer gives us an eyewitness account of the daily routine of the royal band.

> The mehters' lodging quarters is an old building at the Demirkapi site of the Palace gates. It has a tall four cornered tower in the middle. Every night after the evening prayer they play three tunes (Fasil) ending in a martial tune and pray for the Sultan. At dawn three hours before morning, they play three very pleasant tunes to invite the members of the court to the assembly, and wake everybody for the morning prayer. If a member of the palace was promoted, the Mehters used to go to his place in order to congratulate him and play for him three tunes. If he were not at home, they played one tune to the people at home. At the palace, the grand council of state which gathered in the council room used to begin their discussions after the mehter band performed.

This account hints at the variety of music, as well as the variety of functions, in the repertoire of these Turkish bands during the seventeenth century. More valuable information regarding the nature of the music itself is given by the same eyewitness, contained in an interesting description of an argument between the conductor of the royal Mehter band and the chief architect of the palace. They had come into conflict over the issue of who should take precedence in a procession during the reign of Murat IV and had taken the issue to the Sultan himself for resolution. The architect spoke first:

> Your Majesty, we are the dancers of Habib Neccar, the mehters are a crowd with no patron-saint, who seem to have embrased the Art of Jamshid. We build palaces, mosques, and, mausoleums for our Sultan. We repair fortresses when they are captured, and we build bridges. We are indispensable for the Islamic Army, and we serve it well. There is no doubt that we should march in front of the mehters.

The conductor of the Mehter band answered,

> Your Majesty, wherever you go, you should walk with the sound of drums and trumpet for the sake of your magnificence, grandeur, and fame toward friend and foe. At the battlefields we are the ones who beat the gigantic drums in order to incite the soldiers to combat. We are the ones who excite the soldiers to a fighting condition. When our Sultan is upset about something, we, entertain him by performing twelve kinds

of mood (Makam), twenty-four kinds of fundamental cadence (Usul), and forty-eight kinds of music (Terkibi musiki). Old wise men have said that music, poetry, and song give joy to the hearts of men. We are the tradespeople who feed the spirit. The workers of the chief architect are Greeks, Armenians, and gipsies. They are cement workers, conduit repairers, plumbers, and even latrine cleaners. We will not allow these tradespeople to march in front of us. Wherever the flag of the Prophet is seen the drums of the Ottoman Dynasty have to be present.

How could any sultan refuse an argument like that?

Another seventeenth-century reference to the music performed by these bands mentions that out of a group of twenty-four tunes heard, six were of a melancholy nature, six were *allegro* and light-spirited, six furious, and six mellifluous or even amorous.[11] He too was impressed by the percussion, for he noted,

[11] Giovanni Battista Donado, *Della Letteratura de' Turchi* (Venice, 1688), 130–134.

> Now, to speak the truth, their universal and ordinary music feels the effect of tumult, since the Turkish Nation is fraught with war.

When one considers how different all this was from the music and practices of the Western military traditions, one can certainly appreciate the curiosity in the exotic and the sense of surprise found in almost all these early encounters.

The Importance of 'Turkish Music' to the West

Because the repeated conflicts between the West and the Ottoman Empire offered numerous points of contact, it is impossible to pinpoint a precise date for the introduction of this 'Türkische musik,' the percussion instruments in particular, in Western military bands. Most sources give this date as the end of the seventeenth century, but I suspect it may have been somewhat earlier. Certainly, for example, it was the new Turkish percussion instruments which Samuel Pepys heard in London in 1661.

> So to the White Hall; where I staid to hear the trumpets and kettle-drums, and then the other drums, which are much cried up, though I think it dull, vulgar musique.[12]

[12] *The Diary of Samuel Pepys* (London, 1924), 3:315, an entry for January 31 – February 3, 1661.

The adoption of these instruments became wide spread near the beginning of the eighteenth century, following a visit to the King of Prussia in Berlin by the Turkish Ambassador, Achmet Effendi. Prussia had apparently been experimenting with these new instruments and in honor of the ambassador's visit arranged a performance with them. The ambassador reacted by exclaiming, 'This isn't Turkish at all!,' meaning, I suspect, that even if the instruments were familiar, the nature of playing them was not. His reaction seems to have shocked the king, who then arranged through the ambassador to acquire actual Turkish musicians to train his own.[13]

[13] Georges Kastner, *Manuel Général de Musique Militaire* (Paris, 1848), 131.

The fact that the King of Prussia had actual Turkish musicians seems to have made such players an instant 'status symbol' among Europe's leading aristocracy. Almost immediately, Augustus II of Poland (d. 1735) acquired a complete Turkish band as a gift from the sultan, the emperor in Austria obtained one, and Anne of Russia sent to Constantinople for a band that included not only the percussion instruments, but oboes in both treble and tenor sizes.[14]

[14] Ibid.; Grove 9:497.

The vital contribution these new percussion instruments made to Western armies must be understood in context with a fundamental change in the nature of these armies during the seventeenth century. It was at this time that the concept of a standing army began to be employed in Western Europe, whereas for centuries earlier when battles were necessary they were conducted by troops hired for that purpose, mercenaries. With a standing army, who could practice marching, the generals could at last successfully introduce coordinated marching. This was a concept which had long been appreciated in theory in the West, but was not practical with short-term mercenaries. Neither the drums, which were still needed for signals, nor the ancient fifes, nor the new oboes and bassoons were sufficient to convey the *beat* necessary for successful coordinated marching by massed troops. It was the addition of all the extra Turkish percussion which had the potential for making the beat audible to the common soldier. Even then, the whole idea of coordinated marching to a beat seems so new and tenuous that even a single beat's rest represented a threat to the order of the feet. The famous German critic, Schubart, wrote that it was here especially that a great clash of percussion helped prevent anyone from getting out of step.[15]

[15] Quoted in Gottfried Veit, *Die Blasmusik* (Innsbruck, 1972), 32:
JederTodstrich wird durch einen mann lichen Schlag so stark conturirt, dass es beynahe unmoglich ist, aus dem Tact zu kommen.

This important association between the new musical instruments and the new concept of the standing army can also be seen in the fact that for a time these newly equipped bands were called *Janissaries*, after the Turkish, 'Yeni cherik,' for 'new troops.'[16]

No contemporary document speaks more earnestly regarding the importance of the musical beat in its potential for moving troops than the *Memoire* of the famous French General, Maurice de Saxe (1696–1750).[17] It was his opinion that the secret of the great military victories of the Greek and Roman generals lay in part in their using music to control both the order and the speed of their troops. This is a concept, he says, which had been completely forgotten by the generations before his own.

> I begin with the *marche*; the necessity to discuss this may seem extravagant to the ignorant.
>
> No one knows what the ancients understood by the word *Tactique*; many soldiers use it- and believe it to mean (only) the movement of troops in battle. The whole world beats a march (battre la marche) without knowing its tradition and everyone thinks this noise is nothing but an ornament of the military.
>
> We should have a better opinion of the ancients and the Romans, who should be our teachers. It is absurd to believe that this war noise served no more unique purpose than to deafen their ears!

The general then pictures for us the army which moves without coordinated steps to a musical beat, 'Every soldier walks according to his own ease, some slow and some fast.' How, he asks, can a commander expect anything from an army that can not even get to the battle in reasonable order? If one is marching and orders the front to quicken the pace, the rear unavoidably loses ground before they perceive the order. Then, the rear runs to catch up, whereupon the front also begins to run, throwing everything into disorder. It would seem impossible, he reflects, to move a body of troops without forsaking all order.

Now he presents his secret, the secret of the Romans as well—music!

[16] The term dates from the fourteenth century when Turkey was the first to institute the modern idea of a permanent, barracked army with regular officers.

[17] Maurice comte de Saxe, *Les Rêveries ou Mémoires sur l'art de guerre* (Hague, 1756), I, vi, 23ff.

> The means to remedy all the problems, as well as others of a similar nature, is very simple, because it is dictated by nature. In one phrase consists the complete secret of this art: *Making them march to a cadence (Faites-les marcher-en cadence)*. There is the whole secret and it is the secret of the Romans as well.
>
> This is why marches were invented and why one beats the drum. It is the word *Tact* which no one understands or pays any attention to.[18]

If one will only march the troops to a musical beat, the general predicts their pace can be controlled at will, the rear will never lag behind, they will be in step, their legs won't get mixed up, and one won't have to stop after every turn to reorganize! Most important, in marching to music the army doesn't get as tired. The general reminds the reader of the 'extraordinary' proof of this.

> There isn't anyone who has not seen people dance all night with continuous energy. But if you have someone dance even two hours *without* music, he will protest! This proves that music (les tons) have a secret power over us which disposes us to exercise our bodies and makes it easy at the same time.

But which tune is most appropriate to play for the purpose of making men march together? The general answers, any tune so long as it is a *march*. It does not matter if it is in two or three beats per bar, although it will be more comfortable if strongly marked. For this reason the tambour and fife are ideal for such tunes. But, what if there are men among the soldiers who are tone-deaf? This has no bearing, the general maintains, because this motion is so natural to all men.

> I have often noticed that in hearing drum rhythms which accompany the flag ceremony (en battant au drapeau), all the soldiers fall into step without realizing it; nature and instinct carry them along. I say more: it is impossible to make a single military movement with a compact order without a beat (tact).

This may all seem superficial, the general accepts, but if one considers that through the cadence one can control the speed of the movement of an army, anyone can see the tremendous advantage. He implies that this was the secret for the Roman's ability to conquer great areas of Europe, for he maintains they could have covered twenty-four miles in five hours, by march-

[18] The reference here to the German *Takt* (beat or measure) seems to be an attempt on the general's part to associate this word with the French *Tactique*; the idea is interesting, if etymologically weak.

ing to a cadence! Just try that with your own troops and see if you can do as well (without music), he challenges his military readers.

> What would one say if I prove that it is impossible to vigorously charge the enemy without this cadence, or without it one always arrives with the ranks out of order? What a monstrous mistake! I believe that for the previous three or four centuries no one has paid any attention to this.

This extraordinary discussion is all the more interesting as it was apparently written before he himself had discovered the advantage offered by the new Turkish instruments. In this text he mentions only the older fife and drums, but it is known that he later added the Turkish percussion during his participation in the War of the Austrian Succession.[19]

These various theories, together with the new Turkish percussion instruments, would all achieve complete acceptance during the eighteenth century; indeed, both the march and the larger percussion sections are still with us today.

[19] Grove 9:497.

PART 4
Military Wind Bands

6 Military Wind Bands in the German-Speaking Countries

FOR MOST OF THE SEVENTEENTH CENTURY, before the introduction of the new oboes, bassoons, etc., the movements of the German army appear to have been controlled by the powerful trumpet guilds which have been discussed above.

These guilds, serving under imperial 'privileges' were sufficiently independent that even while serving the army the trumpeters were subject to guild discipline rather than military codes.[1] Indeed, according to Altenburg, who had first-hand knowledge with this period, one of the imperial 'privileges' goes further and specifically cautions the military officers regarding their treatment of these trumpeters.

[1] Henry Farmer, *Military Music* (London: William Reeves, 1912), 36.

> No colonel, cavalry captain, or commanding officer shall willfully treat a trumpeter or military kettledrummer badly, as unfortunately was in vogue for some time. (He shall not) shame (him), despise (him), prescribe menial labor (for him) without good cause, nor throw him out of the service without pay, but rather, (as has been) the custom as of old, treat him like an honorable officer and let him pass (for one).[2]

[2] Ernst Altenburg, *Versuch einer Anleitung zur heroisch-musikalischen Trompeter- und Pauker-Kunst* (Halle, 1795), 54 [present translation by Edward Tarr].

Altenburg warns the prospective trumpeter that the quality of the uniform varies from regiment to regiment, some having fine cloth trimmed with gold or silver and ostrich feathers on the hat (normally only an officer could wear an ostrich feather), while in other regiments mere dyed cock feathers on the hat and simple ribbons on the coat sufficed. In the latter case, the trumpeter would have to spend some of his own pay to acquire clothes of a better quality—more appropriate to a trumpeter—for it is important that a trumpeter 'shall and must live in grand style, especially when he is young and single.'

For his quarters, the trumpeter was allowed to have extra lodging money which normally only married men received. He received his horse from the nobleman who was paying the costs of his particular regiment, but the trumpeter had to pay the regular cavalryman who fed and groomed the horse, took care of the saddle and boots, etc. To do all of this on a trumpeter's pay requires proper budgeting, warns Altenburg!

The primary role of the army trumpeter in Germany, as elsewhere, was to perform the military signals.[3] Altenburg observes that these, being nothing more than 'artistic variations' on the major triad, must have been invented by someone with talent and intellect to have brought about such diversity from only the six lowest pitches. This possibility of 'artistic variations' was such that Altenburg remembered, and regretted, that the 'old calls' had been gradually abbreviated until they had lost their original meaning and were now so 'capriciously played that their true purpose and Melodiousness have been obscured, especially in the *Feldstücke* played by many instruments together.'[4]

But among them all no *Feldstücke* is more improperly played, by all armies, than the heroic trumpeter march. It should be played slower for the heavy cavalry, in order to express the serious and heroic, and it should be played more briskly for the Hussars because they are the light cavalry.

[3] Numerous icons, as for example the engraving by G. C. Bodenehr (1701–1714), reproduced in Brixel, *Das ist Osterreichs Militarmusik*, 22, demonstrate that this responsibility continued even after the adoption of larger bands (see image reproduced below).

[4] Altenburg, *Versuch einer Anleitung zur heroisch-musikalischen Trompeter- und Pauker-Kunst*, 89.

Engraving by G. C. Bodenehr showing the German army trumpeter performing military signals during battle.

The cause for this loss of the original style of performance, Altenburg attributes to the modern concept of notating the signals. Art, it seems, always is the loser when it is removed from the experiential to the conceptual.[5]

[5] Actual musical examples of seventeenth-century German military signals are quite rare, due to the quasi-secret nature of the trumpet guilds. One extant example, the 'General Caraffa-Fanfare' (1690), is given in Brixel, *Das ist Osterreichs Militarmusik*, 21. An extensive discussion of the development of these signals can be found in Grove, 12:316ff.

Altenburg indicates that the principal military signals known to him at the end of the Baroque Period were the following:

> *Boute-selle*, boots and saddles, sounded two or three hours before riding out of camp, its real importance is to encourage the troops.
> *À Cheval*, to horse. In the field, upon hearing this call the cavalry assembles in order before the commander's quarters.
> *Le Marche*.
> *La Retraite*, retreat, played in the evening after the sun has gone down … and all is calm.
> *À l'Étendart*, to the colors. In the battle it is a signal for the scattered troops to reassemble.
> *Alarme*.
> *Apell blasen*, to signal the retreat.
> *Ban*, for announcements and proclamations.
> *Charge*, the signal to attack.
> *Fanfare*, for days of celebration and gala occasions. It is of two kinds, first, one of an Intrada nature, a short prelude or introduction to a musical piece; this is usually improvised. Second, the *Tusch*, also improvised, as a short fantasy consisting of nothing but arpeggios and runs, played when noblemen drink a toast. Altenburg further observes, 'it makes noise enough, but contains neither art nor order.'
> *Guet*, for changing the guard. Altenburg says the Prussian army trumpeters here played a '*Bicinium* in the clarin register.'

Altenburg says the Germans were superior in playing these field signals because they employed certain embellishments, or 'tricks of the trade'; especially the lowest part, or *Principal*, was very much ornamented or improved. The secret was a system of tonguing based on syllables, following the Renaissance tradition. Altenburg reveals only one for single-tonguing, 'ritiriton,' or 'kitikiton,' together with the observation that either could be turned into double-tonguing by the addition of another 'ti' in front. The military timpani, which were so closely identified with the trumpeters,[6] actually borrowed technical terms from the trumpets to name some of their drum strokes, as for example 'Einfache Zungen' and 'Doppel Zungen,' (single and double tonguing).[7] These military timpanists were apparently just as proud and musical as their trumpeter colleagues. Zedler, in his *Universallexikon* (1735), refers to him as the one 'who knows how to strike the drum elegantly'[8] and

[6] I have shown in volume two of this series that during the sixteenth century the timpani functioned as the harmonic bass of the trumpet choir and not as a rhythmic instrument at all.

[7] Richard Leppert, 'Musical Instruments and Performing Ensembles in Flemish Paintings of the Seventeenth Century' (dissertation, Indiana University, 1973), 206. Curt Sachs, in *The History of Musical Instruments* (New York: Norton, 1940), 330, gives an interesting paragraph about the military timpani.

> Cavalry regiments delighted in the same extravagant parading of their kettledrums, which they used more and more as a special privilege. As late as the twentieth century such a cavalry drummer would wear a full beard, ride on a black horse and throw up the sticks while playing. When, about the middle of the sixteenth century, a German, Baron von Dohna, came to France, his ostentatious entrance annoyed the French so much that the Duke of Guise ordered his kettledrums to be dashed to pieces 'to his great abashment.'

Altenburg mentions their improvision, called *Präambulieren* or *Fantasieren*, and their playing, 'now loud, now soft, now fast, now slow.'⁹

There is one German military signal which had its origin for drums which is particularly interesting, the 'Zapfenstreich.' This term which continues well into the nineteenth century (and appears as the title of a well-known band work by Beethoven) takes its name from the spigot of the wine

⁸ Quoted in Leppert, 'Musical Instruments and Performing Ensembles in Flemish Paintings of the Seventeenth Century', 210.

⁹ Quoted in Ehmann, *Tibilustrium*, 14.

> Das Schlagen ohne Noten nennt man das Präambulieren, oder Fantasieren, welches also gewöhnlich aus eigener Erfindung oder-wie man zu sagen pflegt-aus dem Stegreife geschieht. Hierin zeichnen sich besonders die Deutschen von anderen Nationen sehr vorteilhaft aus. Denn ein geschickter Pauker kann seine Zuhörer, durch die mannichfaltigen Manieren und Kunstschläge, eine ziemliche Zeitlang in der Aufmerksamkeit erhalten. Das, was diesem Instrument in Absicht auf die Anzahl der Töne abgeht, weiss er durch verschiedene Schlagmanieren zu ersetzen. Dies Schlagen, welches bald stark, bald schwach, bald langsam, bald geschwind geschieht, verrichten die Pauker gewöhnlich mit künstlichen Figuren, Wendungen und Bewegungen des Leibes.

Plate 26, *Kaiserlicher Trompeter*, by Christoph Weigel after Caspar Luyken, from *Neu-eröffnete Welt-Galleria*, Nürnberg, 1703.

cask and apparently dates from some remote time when the signal announced the hour for the soldiers to depart from the tavern.[10]

The earliest form of the signal was 'Zapfenschlag' ('to hit or close the spigot') and an edict from 1636, which I paraphrase, tells us its purpose remained the same in the seventeenth century.

[10] Peter Panoff, *Militärmusik* (Berlin: K. Siegismund, 1944), 89ff.

Plate 25, *Kaiserlicher Paucker*, by Christoph Weigel after Caspar Luyken, from *Neu-eröffnete Welt-Galleria*, Nürnberg, 1703.

Moreover We command that as soon as the drum plays, at nine o'clock from our Church of the Holy Trinity (tower?), no tavern, private or public, should pour more wine or beer, but (rather) point out that it is time to go home.[11]

A similar order of 1672 refers specifically to soldiers:

No soldier should go to a tavern after the 'Zapffen Schlag,' or be found in the alley; in addition the Innkeeper should not serve beer after the Zapffen Schlag and if he (does not adhere to this), he will be punished and made an example of.[12]

An edict from the same period is more firm, indicating that any soldier not in his quarters after the Zapffen-Schlage will be punished by running the gauntlet.[13] A similar ordinance is found from the period of Friedrich Wilhelm I (1713–1740) in Berlin.

In the evening after the sun has set, the artillery will fire a shot and at the same time all the drummers of the army will beat a Zapfenstreich. After this there should be no running around and in case a soldier does, he will be required to run the gauntlet thirty times.[14]

It was in his occasional responsibility as an envoy that the military trumpeter held his position of highest trust. Altenburg provides an interesting description[15] of how one should carry out this assignment. First, one takes care to put the message in a safe place, where it will not get dirty. One does not show this message, or disclose his business, with anyone, not even the officers of his own regiment. By merely sounding his trumpet, the trumpeter may pass through the enemy lines, without even the passport that an ambassador needs. Be especially careful, warns Altenburg, to get a receipt from the enemy commander to prove you delivered the message. Be careful not to say anything that might reveal your own army's poor circumstances; but at the same time, discreetly look around for anything that might be welcome information to your own commander. Please, he writes, accept this well-meant advice, 'conduct oneself soberly, moderately, and carefully, since one can otherwise easily run the risk of being shot dead.'

---

[11] *Zur Herstellung der guten Ordnung*, Colln an der Spree, August 29, 1636.

> Ferner gebiethen Wir, dass des Abends, sobald die Trommel geschlagen, welches von nun allemahl, wenn es in Unsern Kirchen zur Heiligen Dreyfaltigkeit 9 Uhr schläget, geschehen soll, in keinem Schenck-Hause, es sey in denen Rath- oder Privat-Kellern oder Häusern, einiger Wein oder Bier mehr, denen Wein- oder Biergästen gezapffet, sondern dieselben nach Hause zu gehen angewiesen werden sollen.

[12] War Article (1672) from Berlin, quoted in Panoff, *Militärmusik*, 90.

> … dann auch kein Soldat sich nach dem Zapffen Schlag in einigen Wirthshause oder auff der Gassen finden, noch der Wirt Ihme nach dem Zapffen Schlag Bier reichen, sondern wann Er betroffen wird, auffgenommen und exemplariter abgestraffet werden soll.

[13] Ibid.

[14] Ibid., 91.

> Des abends nach der Sonnen Untergang wird bey der Artillerie ein Canon-Schuss gethan, worauf alle Tambours von der Armee den Zapfenstreich zugleich schlagen, weshalb selbige bey den Bataillons vorhero par at stehen mussen. Nach dem Zapfenstreich soll keiner schiessen, und im Fall ein gemeiner Soldat es thut, soll selbiger 30. mahl durch die Gassen lauffen.

[15] Altenburg, *Versuch einer Anleitung zur heroisch-musikalischen Trompeter- und Pauker-Kunst*, 42–43.

One final piece of diplomatic tradition is mentioned by Altenburg.[16] After funerals the trumpeter usually was allowed to receive the dead man's boots and dagger, but only after an aristocratic ritual. One removes the boots and dagger from the top of the coffin, where they are placed during the ceremony, and gives them to the captain in charge, offering the captain at the same time a 'tip' appropriate to the rank of the deceased, whereupon the captain is supposed to offer the boots and dagger back to the trumpeter.

Before the advent of standing armies, the free German cities maintained their own militia. When these troops appeared in ceremonies, it was the civic wind band which joined them in a temporary military duty. The basic wind band of shawms now added a few drums, as one can see in the 'Schalmeier, Pfeifer und Trommler,' of 1625 Hamburg and the three musicians of the 'guardia' in 1603 Augsburg.[17]

A particularly valuable account of one of these civic bands participating with the civic militia is found relative to the celebration of the birthday of the Archduke of Austria in Frankfurt in 1716. An eyewitness speaks of the six-member Hautboisten band performing a march by Telemann![18]

Seventeenth-Century Military Shawm Bands

The first true military bands in Germany appear to be found under the Prussian Elector, Friedrich Wilhelm (1640–1688), called 'the Great Elector.' In 1646 the elector founded his Dragoon Life Guards ('Charbrandenburgische Liebguardie'), which consisted of two hundred troops and a band of four 'Schalmeyer' (two discant and an alto shawm with a Dulcian) and four drums which 'concertized' for the troops.[19] Brixel gives an identical instrumentation, but with only two drums, for a regimental band in Austria in 1670[20] and Suppan gives the same four-member shawm band as typical for German regiments in 1674.[21]

Degele also indicates the typical German infantry 'Regimentskapellen' by 1670 was still three shawms and a Dulcian, called 'Feldpfeifer,' but he adds the sound of these ancient shawms was so offensive that the military band was made to march twenty-five to thirty paces in front of the troops![22]

[16] Ibid., 53.

[17] Hans Engel, *Musik und Gesellschaft, Beiträge zu einer Musiksoziologie* (Berlin-Halensee: Max Hesse, 1960), 212, 225.

[18] Caroline Valentin, *Geschichte der Musik in Frankfurt a.M.* (Frankfurt: Volcker, 1906), 240.

... bei dem die 6 Hautbois in ihrer sauberen Montur den Mannschaften voranschritten, die den zu Ehren der Frankfurter Artillerie aufgesetzten Marsch von ... Telemann bliesen.

[19] Johannes Reschke, 'Zur Geschichte der Deutschen Militärmusik des 17. und 18. Jahrhunderts,' *Deutsche Musik-Kultur* 2 (1937): 11. Here the author uses the verb, 'konzertierte.'

[20] Correspondence with the author.

[21] Wolfgang Suppan, *Lexikon des Blasmusikwesens* (Freiburg: Schulz, 1973), 40.

[22] Ludwig Degele, *Die Militärmusik* (Wolfenbuttel: Verlag fur musikalische Kultur und Wissenschaft, 1937), 113.

By 1681 the Elector in Berlin now had a much larger band, consisting of no fewer than twelve shawms.[23] An interesting reference to the military band of the famous general, Leopold von Anhalt-Dessau documents the arrival of the French oboe. His band at about this time had both four 'teutschen Schalmeyern' and a 'französischen hoboisten.'[24] The arrival of the same instruments, here called, 'Hopoen,' can be seen in the military band in Zeitz in 1690, where earlier one found Pfeifers of the Guard (1681), Dragonerpfeifer (1687–1688), and eight Regimentpfeifer (1690).[25]

These shawm, oboe, and bassoon players were not mere ornaments of court military ceremonies, but also apparently saw battle. One record tells of Prince Battalus taking his 'Schalmeier' with him into battle against the Turks in 1691.[26] A very interesting contemporary account says that Grafen von Sparr, a general under the Great Elector, Friedrich Wilhelm, also introduced 'Schalmeyen und Fagotten' into war. This chronicle says that a typical 'Christian' military band at this time (1691) consisted of 'Feldpfeiffen, Trommeln, Trommeten und Pauken' and that the 'French shawm, called Hautbois,' had also been introduced into battle.[27]

I might mention that it was during this period the African blacks begin to appear in European military bands. The first colony of these persons were acquired from the West African coast in 1683 and appear as military timpanists in the Berlin court by 1685.[28]

This became a tradition in Berlin and Friedrich Wilhelm I (1713–1740) had an entire band in his personal regiment composed of fifteen black musicians.[29] A contemporary account relates hearing, as the king sat down to his mid-day meal in the great hall in Potsdam, a procession of twenty-six blacks, playing in the 'Moorish and Turkish' style with cymbals, timpani, and wind instruments.[30]

By the beginning of the eighteenth century these musicians were found in many European regimental bands. Even in Poland, under August der Starke, one finds 29 'Mohren' employed in 1730.[31]

[23] Reschke, ibid.

[24] Ibid.

[25] Werner Braun, 'Entwurf flir eine Typologie der "Hautboisten",' 47.

[26] Herbert Riedel, *Musik und Musikerlebnis in der erzählenden deutschen Dichtung* [Abhandlungen zur Kunst-, Musik- und Literaturwissenschaft XII] (Bonn: H. Bouvie, 1959), 520.

[27] Wolfgang Caspar Printz, *Historische Beschreibung der Edelen Sing- und Klingkunst* (Dresden, 1690).

[28] Panoff, *Militärmusik*, 96.

[29] Ibid., 97.

[30] Quoted in ibid.

Wie nun des Königs Majestät des Mittags an der Tafel sassen, deren zwey in dem grossen Saal zu Potsdam eingerichtet gewesen, hielten 26 Mohren einen Aufzug mit musikalischen Instrumenten, auf denen sie spielten, und zwar nach mohrischer und. tur. kischer Art, Janitscharenmusik mit Becken machten wobei auch Paucken zu hören gewesen und allerhand Instrumente auf welchen geblasen worden.

[31] Johannes Reschke, *Studie zur Geschichte der brandenburgisch-preussischen Heeresmusik* (Berlin: VDI-Verl, 1935), 16.

Period of Friedrich I (1688–1713)

During the reign of the Elector Frederick III (1688–1713) the Hohenzollern family finally succeeded in having their electorate become a kingdom and so, in 1701, Frederick became Frederick I of Prussia. It was during his reign that the new Hautboisten band begins to replace the older shawm band. He maintained a standing army of approximately 31,000 men with each battalion consisting of a grenadier company with two 'pfeifer' and three drums and five musket companies with only three drums in each. His headquarters troops, the Leibgarde zu Fuss, had a regimental drummer and six pfeifer.[32]

This last band was perhaps oboes, and not shawms (pfeifer) as given, for a court record mentions that in 1706 he transferred this military 'Hautboisten' band to the palace musical establishment.[33] There is also some indication that the king provided for the further education of this wind band, for apparently they studied composition for two years under Johann Theile (1646–1724) at about this time.[34]

It was at this time, the end of the seventeenth century, that these military Hautboisten bands begin to appear throughout the German-speaking nations. I have mentioned above the appearance of such a band in Zeitz in 1690. In South Germany as well, one finds in Bavaria, in each infantry regiment under the Elector Maximilian II (1680–1726), a six-member Hautboisten band in 1695[35] and again in 1699.[36]

Also in Austria these new Hautboisten bands appear, Suppan even listing a typical infantry band in 1706 as having two oboes, two clarinets (!), two bassoons, one trumpet, and one trombone.[37] An engraving by Johann Andreas Pfeffel pictures a military Hautboisten band of three oboes and a bassoon performing in Vienna in 1712.[38]

There is no reason to suppose that this first generation of military Hautboisten bands were as musically capable as the wind bands employed by the courts and towns. Indeed one finds the civic wind band in the German town, Stade, complaining, near the end of the seventeenth century, that the nearby garrison Hautboisten, 'have not correctly learned nor do they understand their music.'[39]

---

[32] Panoff, *Militärmusik*, 77.

[33] Sachs, *Musik und Oper*, 66. Now a Hautboisten band of five, they were: Georg Friedrich Hager, Peter Krause, Johann Christian Schultze, Johann Ernst Guldenmeister, and Salomon Lentz.

[34] Frederick Blume, ed., *Die Musik in Geschichte und Gegenwart* (Kassel, 1949–1968), 13:278.

[35] Reschke, 'Zur Geschichte,' 11.

[36] Degele, *Die Militärmusik*, 113.

[37] Suppan, *Lexikon des Blasmusikwesens*, 40. The appearances of clarinets in military bands by 1706 seems to me unlikely, but Kappey, in *A Short History of Military Music* (1894), gives a march for two oboes, 2 clarinets, 2 bassoons, two trumpets, and four horns which he says dates from ca. 1720.

[38] Reproduced in Brixel, *Das ist Osterreichs Militarmusik*, 24–25.

[39] Otto Spreckelsen, 'Der Stader Ratsmusikanten,' in *Stader Archiv* [NF H.14] (Stade, 1924), 32.

 … die Music nicht recht gelernet und verstanden haben.

It was also during this time that the first examples of *türkische musik* begin to appear in this part of Europe.[40] One early exponent was the King of Poland, August der Starke, who by 1699 had an entire *Janitscharen-Bataillon*, including a *Janitscharen-Musikkorps* of twenty-seven: nine shawms, four timpani, four cymbals, and ten drummers (all the players were German).[41] For his coronation in the same year he assembled one hundred and seventy 'Janitscharenleibgarde' members, again with Turkish music as is clear from an eyewitness.

> (They played with) Turkish army music, small oboes, cymbals played by twelve year old boys, large drums and a pair of small copper timpani.[42]

Period of Frederick William I (1713–1740)

Frederick William I was an extraordinary figure who vigorously developed his nation and his court into a strong entity with an emphasis on German, rather than French, qualities. Whereas his father had had a standing army of thirty-one thousand, Frederick William, known as the 'Soldier-King,' increased it to eighty thousand[43] and left it as a highly disciplined bequest to his more famous son, Frederick the Great. Durant[44] gives an excellent picture of this determined man.

> (Frederick William) was short and stout, with a florid face under a cocked hat, eyes penetrating all pretense, voice announcing will, jaws ready to masticate all opposition. A hearty appetite, and no gourmet, he sent the French cook packing, and ate peasant's food; he consumed much in little time with little ceremony, having work to do. He thought of himself as both the master and the servant of the state. He labored dutifully, angrily, at administration, finding much awry and vowing to beat it into shape. He cut in half the number of pompous commissioners whose conflicting authority had obstructed the business of government. He sold the jewels, horses, and fine furniture bequeathed to him, reduced the royal household to the simplicity of a burgher's home, gathered taxes wherever they could be made to grow ...

As I have mentioned, his particular interest was in building the strongest army in Europe and to this end he conscripted the tallest and strongest men he could find, even in one case snatching a man away while he was praying in church.[45] The military officers he created became a ruling caste,

---

[40] Reschke, 'Zur Geschichte,' 12, dates this arrival from ca. 1697.

[41] Panoff, *Militärmusik*, 97.

[42] Quoted in Arnold Schering, *Musikgeschichte Leipzigs* (Leipzig, 1926), 2:297–298.

... mit türkischer Feldmusik, kleinen Schalmeien, messingenen Becken, die von zwölfjahrigen Knaben zusammengeschlagen wurden, dazu mit grossen Trommeln und etlichen paar kleinen kupfernen Pauken.

[43] Panoff, *Militärmusik*, 77.

[44] Will and Ariel Durant, *The Age of Voltaire* (New York: Simon and Schuster, 1965), 437.

[45] *Cambridge Modern History* (New York, 1907), 6:214.

which looked down upon merchants, teachers, clergymen, and the middle classes generally as weakling inferiors, and often treated them with swashbuckling insolence or brutality. Meanwhile they drilled the infantry, artillery, and cavalry in such precise formations and flexible movements as probably no other modern army has ever known.[46]

In each infantry regiment, Frederick William had two battalions and ten companies, totaling forty officers, one hundred and ten 'under-officers,' one hundred and thirty grenadiers and one thousand and eighty muskets. The military music consisted of only three drums in each company, except for the command regiment which had a six-member Hautboisten band (two discant oboes, two tenor oboes, and two bassoons[47]) and six fifes.[48] Frederick seems to have taken keen interest in this Hautboisten band and even used it to replace the usual court 'art' music.[49]

Eventually Frederick added the trumpet to the Hautboisten band and one source[50] says this trumpeter marched in front of the Hautboisten, alternating his fanfares with their music. Brixel quotes an unnamed 1737 source which says the Hautboisten, in turn, took their cue from the drums, beginning to play when they heard the drums begin behind them.[51] The often reproduced engraving by Christoph Weigel (ca. 1720) pictures just such a Hautboisten band of oboes, horns, and bassoon and the trumpeter marching in front. Frederick must have also added timpani, the constant companion to the aristocratic trumpeter, for it is known that he had built a special 'timpani wagon.' One observer of a parade in Prague saw an entire 'türkische musik,' consisting of nine blacks, riding and performing on this wagon.[52]

[46] Durant, *The Age of Voltaire*, 439.

[47] Panoff, *Militärmusik*, 87.

[48] Reschke, *Studie zur Geschichte der brandenburgisch-preussischen Heeresmusik*, 31.

[49] Panoff, *Militärmusik*, 86.

[50] Georg Thouret, *Friedrich der Grosse als Musikfreund und Musiker* (Leipzig, 1898).

[51] Brixel, *Das ist Osterreichs Militarmusik*, 28.

... wann die Tambours aufh8ren, den Marche zu schlagen, sollen die Hautboisten anfangen zu blasen und also wechselweise continuieren.

[52] Panoff, *Militärmusik*, 98.

An engraving by Christoph Weigel (ca. 1720) of a Hautboisten band of oboes, horns, and bassoon and the trumpeter marching in front.

Frederick William's interest in the military and its music is clearly documented in his founding of the Prussian Army Music School in 1724. Unfortunately little is known of the details of this school, especially from its earliest years. It was housed in the Military Orphans Home in Potsdam,[53] a building dating from 1722. In 1740 a new wing was added to this building making possible rooms for the military music students; prior to this they had to stay with the 'gatekeeper.'

The first director of the school was Gottfried Pepusch, who was also the director of the king's Hautboisten. He was paid a thousand Reichstalern for the budget of this school designed to make army Hautboisten of orphans. The number of students may have been small, as one finds only twenty-one in the year 1750. The king seems to have taken a personal interest in the school and in an extant note calls Pepusch's attention to a young boy whom he wanted placed in the school.[54]

The most interesting first-hand account of German military music during the Baroque Period is found in a publication (1726) on the subject by Hans von Fleming.[55] He includes a long discussion of the method of performing the standard drum signals[56] and mentions a player whom I have to this point omitted, the 'Quer-Pfeiffer.' This player, the 'good companion of the drummer,' plays a morning song during Reveille and also plays during marching. He carries both a large and small instrument in a wooden case and, according to Fleming, when he played these instruments, his performance varied considerably with the printed page.[57] Fleming relates seeing these instruments in a procession in Dresden for the changing of the guard.

> In Dresden I have observed that twelve Querpfeiffer and twenty-four drums, six in rank and six in front of the Head Guard, in the New Market Place. As soon as the clock struck twelve, the eldest regimental drummer gave an orderly cadence to the drummers, which was a signal for them to remove their instruments from their shoulder harnesses before preparing to play. Then he commanded them to play the 'Changing of the Guard,' which occurred to their slow beating.[58]

His description of the new oboe, as compared to the old shawm is particularly interesting.

---

[53] A drawing of this building is reproduced in Panoff, *Militärmusik*, 109, from which this material is drawn.

[54] Quoted in ibid., 108.

Se. Majestät befehlen den Directoribus des Potsdamschen grossen Waisenhauses in Gnaden, Dero Hoboisten Fischbach zu verstatten, daraus ein Chor Jungens auszusuchen, und dieselben in der Musik auszulernen.

[55] Hans von Fleming, *Der vollkommene deutsche Soldat* (Leipzig, 1726).

[56] Quoted in Panoff, *Militärmusik*, 79.

[57] Ibid.

Die Methode zu pfeifen und die Stückgen zu componiren ist different.

[58] Ibid., 80.

In Dresden habe ich observirt dass zwölff Querpfeiffer und vierundzwanzig Tambours sechs in einem Gliede sich halb zwölfe vor der Hauptwache auf dem Neumarkte rangiren. Sobald der Zeiger zwölff Uhr schlaget, commandirt der vorstehende älteste Regiments-Tambour nach einem ordentlichen Tempo die Tambours, dass sie ihre Spiele oder Trommeln von den Schultern abnehmen, vor sich halten und zugleich gehörigen Ortes anhängen sollen. Alsdenn commandiret er die Printz Vergatterung zu schlagen, welches in einer langsamschlagenden Vergatterung besteht.

During the time of the shawm there were four players: two discant, an alto, and a Dulcian. After the oboe took their place, one finds six oboes as the oboes were not so strong but had a softer sound. The harmonie was now completed with two discant, two taille, and two bassoons.[59]

This oboe band, he says, marches in front of the troops and generally was attached to the headquarters command; the players carried the rank of corporal.[60]

The most frequently quoted passage from Fleming's work is a passage in which he describes performances by one of the Hautboisten bands which were more in the nature of 'concert' music.

> In the morning, in front of the commander's quarters, the Hautboisten play a Morning Song, a newly composed march, an Intrada, and a pair of minuets, which the commander likes; these are often repeated in the evening (or one might also hear at that time) string instruments, or recorders and other instruments.[61]

Needless to say, almost no 'concert' music of the German military has survived. The one well-known example, however, is the *lustige Feld-Music* (1704) by Johann Philipp Krieger (1649–1725).[62] The composer specified the work for 'four wind instruments,' which in the parts are labeled *Premier Dessus* (three players), *Second Dessus* (two players) *Taille* (one player), and *Basson* (three players). The composer says these (six Overture-suites) may be played by Hautboisten in either the court or in the field and, in the latter case, he hopes that if they are played during a lull in battle, they will be 'like a ray of sun on a stormy day.' In the case of the military Hautboisten, 'who march before the company or perform for the officers,' he notes that almost all the 'Entrées' among these *Partien* can also serve as marches.[63]

One might also mention, as a possible example of 'concert' music for these military bands, the *Parade Sinfonien* for two oboes, taille, and bassoon by Gallo, which was advertised in the 1762 catalog of Breitkopf & Härtel.

These German military Hautboisten bands, small though they were, seem to have had one member who served as a conductor. Several icons from this period seem to picture an oboist–conductor[64] and, as mentioned above, Pepusch served in this role in Berlin. A contemporary account (1740)

---

[59] Ibid., 81.

> Da die Schallmeyen noch Mode waren, hatte man nur 4 Mann, als zwey Discantisten, einen Alt, und einem Dulcian. Nachdem aber die Hautbois an deren Stelle gekommen, so hat man jetzund sechs Hautboisten, weil die Hautbois nicht so stark, sondern viel duocer klingen, als die Schallmeyen. Um die Harmonie desto angenehmer zu completiren, hat man jetzund zwei Discante, zwey Taillen, und zwwy Bassons.

[60] Quoted in Braun, 'Entwurf flir eine Typologie der "Hautboisten",' 53.

[61] Quoted in Ibid., 52.

> Es machen die Hautboisten alle morgen vor des Obristen-Quartier ein Morgen-Liedgen, einen ihm gefälligen March, eine Entree, und ein par Menuetten, davon der Obriste ein Liebhaber ist; Und eben dieses wird auch des Abends wiederholet, oder wenn der Obriste Gastgebothe oder Assembleen anstellt, so lassen sie sich auf Violinen und Violons, wie auch Fleuten doucen und anderen Instrumenten hören …

[62] The remaining extant copy was destroyed during World War II.

[63] Quoted in *Denkmäler Deutscher Tonkunst*, LIII–LIV, lxxiv.

[64] Panoff, *Militärmusik*, plate 41, reproduces an engraving from this period picturing a five-man band with a conductor.

speaks of the Waldeck Kapellmeister not only conducting his twelve-member Hautboisten, but composing for them as well.[65] Johann Graf, who had served the courts at Mainz and Bamberg, used the title, 'Hoboistenmeister,' in referring to a period during which he served in this capacity for six years in Hungary.[66]

A final note regarding these musicians might be made regarding their pay. In Prussia, after 1726, one finds the oboists are the highest paid, at six Taler per month, while the 'Regimentstambour' receives five and the ordinary drummer and fife only three.[67]

It seems to have been during the 1720s that horns appear in the military bands of the German-speaking nations. Fleming speaks of the addition of the horns to the Saxony-Polish army in 1723 as resulting in a 'pleasant harmony.'[68] One finds two horns, together with two oboes and two bassoons,[69] in the oldest extant music of this army, a set of marches dated 1729.[70] Horns also appear at about the same time in Bavaria (1722)[71] and in Austria (1730).[72]

With 1740 the period of Frederick the Great begins in Prussia, which properly belongs to the following volume in this series, however a few additional notes regarding the closing years of the Baroque might be added. A regulation of 1743 gives the personnel of a Prussian Dragoon regiment as thirty-two officers, sixty under-officers, six hundred and sixty dragoons, a four-member Hautboisten band and fifteen drummers.[73] The king himself, however, had a larger band of sixteen members already in 1741.[74]

Degele gives a typical South German regimental band as eight players in 1740[75] and an article in the *Wiener Diarium* for 27 May 1741, describes a parade by a thousand soldiers with music by four 'türkischen Trommeln' and four 'Schalmeyen.'[76]

Finally, the question must be raised, What do we know of the birth of the march form? Unfortunately, little seems to be known of the earliest years of this music or even of the origin of the name. Veit believes the name comes perhaps from 'Marcus' ('hammer') or 'Mark' ('core, heart, essence, strength, vigour,' etc.).[77]

---

[65] Diether Rouvel, 'Zur Geschichte der Musik am Fürstlich Waldeckschen Hof zu Arolsen,' in *Kölner Beiträge zur Musikforschung* (Regensburg: G. Bosse, 1962), 22:102ff.

...Capellmeister bey dem Kaiserl. Fürst Waldeckischen Regiment. Seine Function bestand darin, die zwölf Hautboisten starke Bande zu dirigiren und für sie bisweilen zu componiren.

[66] Peter Gulke, *Musik und Musiker in Rudolstadt* (Rudolstadt: Buchdruckerei F. Mitzloff, 1963), 14ff.

[67] Reschke, *Studie zur Geschichte der brandenburgisch-preussischen Heeresmusik*, 31.

[68] Quoted in Braun, 'Entwurf flir eine Typologie der "Hautboisten",' 52.

... welches eine recht angenehme Harmonie verursacht.

[69] Panoff, *Militärmusik*, 88–89, refers to this as the 'second period' of the Hautboisten era; I refer to the instrumentation as the 'Harmoniemusik' instrumentation.

[70] *Die Infanterie Märsche der vormaligen Churfürstl. Sächsischen Armee 1729* (Dresden, Sächsische Landesbibliothek [Aktenband Loc. 10945]).

[71] Reschke, 'Zur Geschichte,' 15, gives two horns in the Leibregiment for 1722 and six 'oboes' and two horns for the 'Kurprinz' regiment in 1728.

[72] Brixel, in correspondence with the author, gives a typical Austrian military band for 1730 as two oboes, two clarinets, two bassoons, two horns, trumpet, and bass drum.

The oldest Baroque example of wind band music I am familiar with which uses this name is a work by Johann Störl, dated 1711, for two oboes, two horns, and bassoon. Other extant wind band marches from the Baroque include those by Grafe, Graun, Heinrich, and Hertel. It is possible that 'serious' composers did not yet look in favor on this new form, for one finds when Franz Benda made a gift of some marches to a dragoon regiment, he specified that his name not be used![78] The generals, however, must have had greater appreciation for this new form. Kastner quotes an unnamed Prussian general as boasting,

> With a good march and my oboes, it is a true pleasure to speak to Europe with the punctuation of the cannon.[79]

[73] Panoff, *Militärmusik*, 83.

[74] Reschke, 'Zur Geschichte,' 14.

[75] Degele, *Die Militärmusik*, 113.

[76] Brixel, *Das ist Osterreichs Militarmusik*, 30.

[77] Veit, *Die Blasmusik*, 40.

[78] G. Kerber, 'Musikalisches aus dem Nachlasse des Generals C. H. v. Czettritz,' in *Monatshefte für Musikgeschichte*, vol. 32, p. 161.

[79] Georges Kastner, *Manuel général de musique militaire* (Paris, 1848), 124.

7   *Military Wind Bands in France*

DURING THE SEVENTEENTH CENTURY IN FRANCE, as in Germany, one finds the prevalence of the military trumpet, especially with the mounted cavalry. Documents from this period indicate that most companies maintained only two trumpets, with companies of two hundred men having three.[1] Each regiment maintained a Trumpet-Major, who trained new members and was the keeper of the repertoire during this age when the music was still memorized.

During parades the trumpets rode three or four paces in front of the commander, in front of the troops. In battle, however, both the trumpets and the commander stood safely at the rear, with the trumpets conveying the various orders for movement.[2] In addition to this purely practical function, these military signals had a psychological value as well, as pointed out by Mersenne in 1636.

> As to the usage of the trumpets, they serve in time of peace and war for all sorts of public celebrations and solemnities, as is seen in marriages, banquets, tragedies, and carrousels. But its principal usage is destined for war ... it is easy to conclude ... how they would prepare the heart and mind of the soldier for going to war, for attacking, and engaging in combat.[3]

Mersenne gives a summary of the seventeenth-century French military trumpet signals:

> The first is called the *cavalcade*, used when the army or one of its regiments approaches towns, through which it passes going to a siege or places of combat, to warn the inhabitants and make them participants in the cheerfulness and expectation of winning the victory. The second is named *to the saddle*, used for breaking up camp, and then follows the *call to saddle*. In the third place is sounded *on horseback*; and then *to the standard*, and *the charge*. Further is sounded the *watch*; but all these ways of sounding are most often distinct only through the interval of meter, for the fourth is performed almost always ... Thus two or more trumpets are easily heard a quarter league away and make many discourses which can take the place of speech. Still there is nothing particular in that, except that they can be heard from further away than the other instruments, which can be similarly used to hold some desired discourse.[4]

[1] Paris, National Archives (MS 01/715, fol. 171, 173, 179, 181–187).

[2] Georges Kastner, *Manuel général de musique militaire* (Paris, 1838), 107ff.

[3] Marin Mersenne, *Harmonie Universelle* (Paris, 1636), 331.

[4] Ibid., 332.

To this list of signals, Kastner adds 'la sourdine,' which he says was an order to march 'with little noise.'[5]

These trumpeters, if few in number, were in a position of responsibility in the cavalry and no doubt were carefully chosen for this position. A famous French military treatise of 1691 describes the character of the man needed for this role.

[5] Kastner, *Manuel général de musique militaire*, 107–108.

> The trumpet must be a man of patience and vigilance, to be ready at all hours to execute the orders of the calls (military signals) … the trumpet must be a discreet man, primarily when he is used in the negotia-

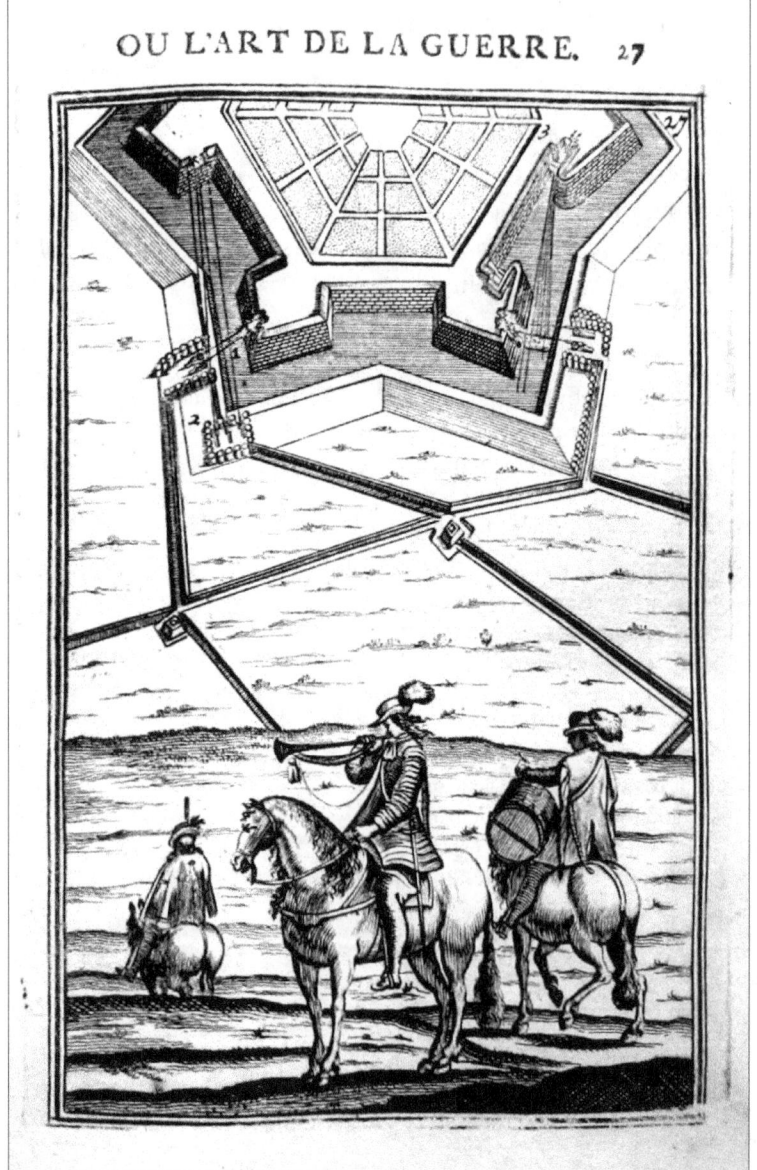

Alain Manesson-Mallet (1630-1706), *Trompette et Tambour à cheval*, from *Les Travaux de Mars ou l'art de la guerre*, 1696.

tions, where he must never use other terms than those he is instructed with, never interfere by giving counsel, in order that in conferences and treaties there will be no ambiguity or statements contrary to those proposed.[6]

[6] Alain Manesson Mallet, *Les Travaux de Mars ou l'Art de la guerre* (Paris, 1691), 3:96.

In spite of such testimonials to the importance of the cavalry trumpeter, a contemporary officer[7] testifies that he often had the experience of finding, in an army of twelve or fifteen thousand men, ten trumpets who did not know their signals.

[7] Lieutenant-Colonel Lecoq Madeleine, in *Le service ordinaire et journalier de la cavalerie*, quoted in Kastner, *Manuel général de musique militaire*, 117.

Alain Manesson-Mallet, *Du Trompette, & de la Trompette*, from *Les Travaux de Mars ou l'art de la guerre*, 1696.

In the normal cavalry service, one assumes the signals were not harmonized, but they may have been doubled for strength.[8] On the other hand, mutes were known and used, as in the case of the 'la sourdine' signal mentioned above. A treatise of 1631 adds some details of this use.

> The mute is used when there is a risk of being discovered by the enemy or when it is wished to surprise them, as also when it is desired to decamp or secretly withdraw.[9]

Finally, one contemporary writer mentions the special relationship which he presumed to have existed between the trumpeter and his horse.

> The trumpets are the instruments best to use for horse dancing because they (the horses) can (learn) to breathe when the trumpets breathe. There is no instrument more agreeable to the horse, because it is martial, and the horse which is naturally generous, likes to be animated by its sound.[10]

French cavalry units began to use the timpani at about the time of the reign of Louis XIV. The first use of the instruments were actually instruments captured from German troops and at first only those troops who had acquired them in this manner had the right to use them.[11] In view of this tradition, one can understand how timpani became prized emblems of a regiment's honor and why, when the troops were in foreign countries, the timpani were always preceded by four Cavaliers with guns to prevent the instruments from falling into the hands of the enemy. Even with such protection, it was left to the responsibility of the player, in the last resort, to prevent this.

> The timpanist must be a man of heart, preferring to perish in combat rather than surrendering his timpani. He must have good arm movement and an accurate ear, and be able to divert his master with agreeable tunes (in peace time). There is no other instrument which gives a more martial sound than the timpani, especially when it is accompanied by trumpets.[12]

---

[8] Smithers, *The Music and History of the Baroque Trumpet* (London: Dent, 1973), 231ff., says they were often doubled as many as four to the part.

[9] Pierre Trichet, *Traité des instruments de Musique* (Bourdelois, 1631) [a copy can be found in Paris, Bibliotheque Sainte-Genevieve, MS. 1070].

[10] Claude Ménestrier, *Des Ballets anciens et modernes selon les règles du Théâtre* (Paris, 1682), 238.

> Les trompettes sont les instrumens les plus propres pour faire dancer les chevaux, parce qu'ils ont loisir de reprendre haleine quand les trompettes la reprennent. Il n'est point aussi d'instrument qui leur soit plus agréable, parce qu'il est martial et que le cheval, qui est naturellement genereux, aime ce bruit qui l'anime.

[11] Kastner, *Manuel général de musique militaire*, 106.

[12] Mallet, *Les Travaux de Mars ou l'Art de la guerre*, 3:98.

Like the trumpeter, the timpanist rode (the instruments were carried just to the front of the saddle) in front of the commander during parades and to the rear of the action in war time.

According to Titcomb, the timpanist usually performed as part of an ensemble with two or three trumpets, improvising with their signals, but at the same time forming the harmonic bass to their parts.

Alain Manesson-Mallet, *Du Timbalier & des Timbales*, from *Les Travaux de Mars ou l'art de la guerre*, 1696.

The 'Charge' for the kettledrum is nothing but a very great noise produced by animated rolls, which go from the right timpani to the left and from the left to the right, with some detached strokes; as this noise constitutes exactly the underlying bass for the trumpets, it suffices that the kettledrummer must have a good ear to fulfill this air.[13]

The technique of the timpanist even included certain special effects, such as simulated echoes.[14]

The tambour performed the same role for the foot soldiers, the infantry and dragoons, that the trumpet performed for the mounted cavalry. In the case of the troops which performed both on horse and on foot, such as the Mousquetaires and the archers, they used accordingly either the trumpet or the tambour.

The tambour, according to Mersenne (1636),[15] was made of oak, but sometimes brass or a different wood. Iconography shows the instrument played in a near vertical position by the left leg.

[13] Caldwell Titcomb, 'Baroque Court and Military Trumpets and Kettledrums,' *Galpin Society Journal* 9 (June, 1956): 61ff. One of the most interesting manuscripts in Paris, Bibliotheque Nationale, is a huge volume, 'Airs Propres pour le Timpanon,' consisting of nothing but pages of exercises, 'airs,' and signals for the timpanist.

[14] Titcomb, 'Baroque Court and Military Trumpets and Kettledrums,' 71, 75–76.

[15] Quoted in Michel Brenet, 'French Military Music in the Reign of Louis XIV,' *Musical Quarterly* 3, no. 3 (July, 1917): 344.

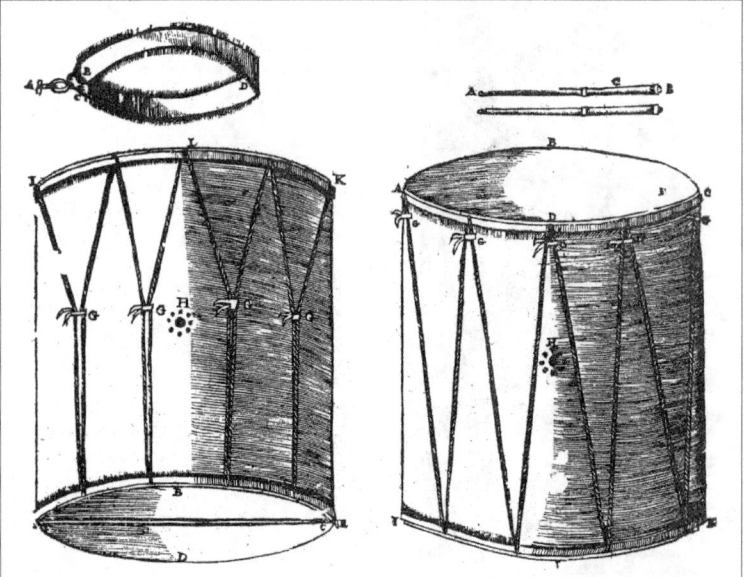

Marin Mersenne (1588–1648), *Les Tambours*, from *Harmonie universelle*, 1636.

When on parade, the tambours—rather like sheep dogs— were placed before and after the troops in an effort to keep them together.[16] This was probably also necessary in order for each soldier to be able to hear clearly the beat. Apparently by the seventeenth century the soldiers generally did march to a beat, a practice in France which we know from Arbeau (1588) dates at least from the sixteenth century.

[16] Kastner, *Manuel général de musique militaire*, 111.

Were it not for these, the men would march confusedly and without order, which would cause them to be in danger of being overthrown and defeated; that is why our French soldiers are commanded to make ranks and squads march to certain rhythms.[17]

[17] Thoinot Arbeau, *Orchésographie* [1588], trans., Peter Warlock (New York, 1925), 26.

A late seventeenth-century French chronicle gives an interesting and detailed explanation for the coordination of feet and drums.

Alain Manesson-Mallet, *Du Tambour*, from *Les Travaux de Mars ou l'art de la guerre*, 1696.

> A company of soldiers marches to the beating of the drums who give seven beats; some are given by the drums and others are rests. They pick up one foot on one, suspend it on two; on three they put that foot down and begin to lift the other. On four they suspend it, on five they put it down and on six they affirm it. The seventh is a rest, after which they begin again.[18]

[18] Claude Ménestrier, *Des représentations en musique, anciennes et modernes* (Paris, 1681). 124.

The same writer tells us that the manner of marching to tambours differed from country to country. The Swiss, for example,

> who are much more weighty in their marching, the French being more agile, will move first on four *breves* and push on a *longue*, afterwards they have two pauses, which the *Pata pata pan* ... expresses. The *longues* are the *Pan*, the breves (les brefs) are *Pata* and the very brief are *Frrr*.[19]

[19] Almost all early percussion notation symbols are graphic or expressed in syntax.

The basic tambour signals for battle are given by another contemporary, Mallet, in 1671.

> In each company, it is mandatory to have two, or at the very least one Tambour player. The duty of the player is to beat the *Marche* for entering a campaign, the *Allarme* for running to take arms, the *Chamade* for calling the Soldiers, and the *Blanc* for warning them. In each Regiment there is a Tambour player who commands all the others of the same Corps and this Drummer is called the Tambour Major.[20]

[20] Mallet, *Les Travaux de Mars ou l'Art de la guerre*, 3:6. Susan Sandman, in 'Wind Band Music Under Louis XIV' (Dissertation, Stanford, 1974) reproduces from the Philidor Collection of 1705 (Paris, Bibliotheque Nationale [Res.F.671]) the notation for the *le ban francais* (for reading of a public proclamation), *l'assemblée, la diane* (reveille), *la chamade*, and *l'alarm*.

Some confusion on the battle field regarding the intent when the commander called for the tambours to beat the *l'assemblée* led to a clarification in 1670, by which the king himself created a new signal, the *la générale*.

> His Majesty—wishing to see to it no confusion arises among his infantry troops because of different drum beats, and that when one regiment is to begin fighting, everyone knows if the entire army or the whole infantry corps should march or only the regiment which is to fight—His Majesty has ordained and ordains, wishes and means that, when in the army there is an order for the entire infantry to march, the first begins to fight because of the beat newly ordained by His Majesty, which is called *la générale*; for the second the usual *l'assemblée* and then in the time that the soldiers are coming out of their tents the beat that was ordained for the entrance and the exit from the camp; and when it is only one regiment and not the whole infantry corps which has orders to

march, then the drums beat, for the first, *aux champs*; for the second, the former *l'assemblée*, then the exit from the camp (which is followed by an) *en marche*.[21]

[21] Quoted in Kastner, *Manuel général de musique militaire*, 393–395; English translation is from Sandman, 'Wind Band Music Under Louis XIV', 79.

Some years later, in 1725, this new signal, together with some additional new ones, was mentioned by Guignard.

> *La Générale* which is played when the entire infantry corps is to take up arms; *l'assemblée* to give notice to assemble and get ready to take up arms; *le Drapeau* to get the flags and get ready for battle, and to lay down arms in a pile in the *Corps de Garde* or in quarters; *aux champs* to march, or to show the first group to march when the entire infantry is not to take up arms; *la Retraite* to retreat into camp or into quarters or to cease combat; *la Fassine* or *Breloque* to give notice to the workers to go to work, and the hour at which they stop working to eat or leave—this drum beat serves also to give notice that mass is going to begin; *appeller* to assemble the officers and soldiers and to instruct them to gather in an assigned place; *le Ban* to introduce and receive an officer, and to read the prohibitions or publications of rules from the King or General; and *la Diane* for reveille.[22]

[22] Claude Guignard, *L'École de Mars* (Paris, 1725), 695.

As in the case of the trumpet, these signals not only gave directions for movement, but provided last-minute inspiration for the soldiers. A contemporary observed,

> The tambour is not only a great help in the armies for the marching of the infantry, serving as a sign for moving on, marching, retiring, for assembly and the other orders which would (otherwise) be difficult to carry about at the same time, and to make as many people hear, but they also animate the soldiers and give them heart when they must crush the enemy in combat. The trumpets, timpani and oboes have nearly the same effect. The beating of the timpani, which controls the stamping and the marching of the horses, also insures that these animals march with the most noble pride.[23]

[23] Ménestrier, *Des représentations en musique, anciennes et modernes*.

In addition to the use of tambours for military movement, and the field related uses discussed above, they were also used as a means of giving peaceful salutes from one troop to another.[24] They could also perform quasi-diplomatic roles, carrying on a dialog with the drummer of the enemy. An eyewitness to the surrender of Luxembourg, in 1684, mentions the use of tambour in this regard.

[24] Marcelle Benoit, *Versailles et les Musiciens du Roi* (Paris: Picard, 1971), 238.

> ... as he was coming back at dawn, the drummer of the besieged beat a *petite Diane* and an *Appelle*. As soon as he was finished an officer appeared on the bastion and cried that he was sent from the Prince de Chimay and that he wished to send envoy—officers to speak with the General to arrange the surrender and that he would send hostages ... None of this was of any use, the drummers dispersed, our fire continued for a while and then diminished a little ... The drummers came and cried, after having played, that they had come to call for capitulation.[25]

[25] Charles Sévin, marquis de Quincy, *Histoire militaire du règne de Louis le Grand* (Paris, 1726), 2:81, 83.

Finally, there are a few contemporary accounts which offer insights into the actual technique of the drummers, apart from the descriptions of the nature of the signals. First, a rather early seventeenth-century account (1626), implies variation in touch and even muting.

> The French *batterie* is the finest of all, and the *Marche* sounds better, and the Tambour gives a clearer cadence than in the practice of any other nation; because the drum gives distinct mark to the fundamental step of the soldier. For the *allarmes*, the Tambour Colonel himself should give a more compact batterie with a light touch and a rather tight play. When it is necessary to dislodge secretly, the Tambour must be covered with a small cloth in order to deafen its sound. After sounding the *allarem*, the Tambour player should raise his hand, for it is a mistake to say that the sound continues to live, even though it ceases to be commanded. Therefore, the player should stop promptly and cut short without refrain, omitting the customary ramble (ballade), which drags on for a long time.[26]

[26] René François, *Essay des Merveilles de Nature, et des Plus Nobles Artifices* (Rouen, 1626), 140ff.

At about the same time, Mersenne mentions the stick technique.

> If I had some musical characters at my command, I should have placed here all the ways of beating of the French drum ... and I should have explained what the *baton rond*, the *baton rompu*, and the *baton meslé* are; I can only say that the beat of the *baton rond* is made when the two sticks strike each blow one after the other; that of the *baton rompu*, when each hand strikes twice in succession; and the beat of the *baton meslé* when each beats sometimes once with each hand and sometimes twice. As to retreat, the two sticks beat all together.[27]

[27] Mersenne, *Harmonie Universelle*, 556.

Kastner adds that the Mousquetaires used drums which were much smaller than those of the infantry, and that they beat 'in a very different way, which was much more gay.' Unfortunately he provided no further details.[28]

[28] Kastner, *Manuel général de musique militaire*, 111.

As in the case of the other countries in Western Europe, the most interesting turning point in the history of modern military bands comes with the adoption of the oboes.

According to Farmer,[29] this occurred in France before 1643, whereas a more recent authority[30] points to the year 1665, when three oboes were added to each of two companies of Mousquetaires to replace a single fife; the five tambours remained. By 1667 a fourth oboe had been added and for some reason this seems to have inspired the need for yet another tambour.[31] According to Grove,[32] these four 'oboes' were two treble, a tenor (taille des hautbois), and a bassoon, which corresponds with what this term also meant in the Écurie division of this court.

As we have seen above, these Mousquetaire 'oboe bands' were very active in performing as independent ensembles before the court. It is no surprise, therefore, that other commanders, even infantry commanders, sought to add the double reeds to their music. This had become a concern of the king and in 1683 he issued the following edict:

> His Majesty, knowing that in most of his infantry companies there are several tambours, (and) even fifres and hautbois in some whose service is not only useless, but also causes an expense for the captains to maintain them, and His Majesty, wishing, therefore, to limit the number of said tambours that he henceforth wants to be maintained in his French infantry troops, and to eliminate completely the hautbois, His Majesty has ordained and ordains, wishes and means that henceforth, in each French infantry company, there can be only a single tambour and in a regiment a single fifre which will be attached to the colonel's company, with no hautbois, and without the number of tambours being permitted to be increased for whatever reason or for any pretext whatsoever.[33]

Brenet has expressed the viewpoint that it was not the king's actual intent to eliminate the oboes, however the edict reads, but rather only to limit the excess in expanding the musical units due to cost considerations.[34] Indeed, an account of the Battle of Mons, a few years later in 1691, still mentions the oboes in the artillery. This reference is a valuable one as a rare example of seventeenth-century military band concerts.

> One day, during the siege of Mons, after the tragic spectacle which had offered murderous hostilities, the artillery became silent suddenly around 11 a.m. and the frightful sound of bombs was replaced by an oboe concert which the officers of the King's regiment were giving

[29] Henry Farmer, *Handel's Kettledrums* (London: Hinrichsen, 1965), 43.

[30] Benoit, *Versailles et les Musiciens du Roi*, 236.

[31] The reader may recall Kastner's remark that the tambour of the Mousquetaires was smaller than the one in the infantry.

[32] Grove 12:311.

[33] Quoted in Kastner, *Manuel général de musique militaire*, 394–395.

[34] Brenet, 'French Military Music in the Reign of Louis XIV,' 355.

for the women of the city. The musicians had installed themselves on the still burning remains of the city which our troops had just taken possession of. It seems that the women of the city were sensitive to this homage, because they rushed up to the ramparts to hear the concert, and returned only after it had ceased.[35]

35 Quoted in Kastner, *Manuel général de musique militaire*, 103, n.1; translation from Sandman, 'Wind Band Music Under Louis XIV,' 87–88.

The following year, on 21 May 1692, a military concert was given which must have been extraordinary in its scope. This concert, held during the Siege of Namur, was given in the field under a tent before the king, his officers, and a number of ladies invited for the occasion. The music was taken from the works of Lully.

The king having invited the ladies to dinner the next day treated them to a war-like concert, composed of 120 tambours of the Gardes, 40 tambours of the Swiss Guards, with trumpets and timpani of the Gardes du Corps, the Light-Guard, to the number of 36; and all the oboes of the Mousquetaires and the Regiment of the king. Altogether they played a French march, and then the Swiss march. The trumpets and timpani gave separately the pleasure of a march on horseback. Mr. Philidor, whom the king had put in charge of the concert, had arranged a great finale for the entire ensemble. The oboes played airs from La Grotte de Versailles and Mr. Philidor played with them. The trumpets and timpani then gave a divertimento of the old airs de guerre, which they did in two choirs, interspersed with menuets played by the oboes. All the tambours, timpani and trumpets then played *la charge* at the same time and the king had them repeat it three times. After that one heard the three last arias from Psiché. One then played *la Generale, l'Assemblée, la Retraite Francaise, et les Dianes*. All of these airs were well played, nicely orchestrated, and played by all of these excellent men, each (of whom was) outstanding in his profession.[36]

36 'Siège de Namur,' in *Mercure Galant* for May, 1692.

Two final things regarding the French military music of the Baroque should be mentioned. First, there apparently was some form of military music on French ships; the Trichet treatise of 1631 mentions trumpets on 'war-ships.' Second, one of the strangest moments in the annals of the military in the Baroque must be the reappearance, after ages beyond number, of the conch in the French army in 1689. For some reason, these were instituted especially for the campaign against the bandits of Catalan, who were fighting for the Spanish. According to Guignard, in each company there was a man who played this 'instrument,' which was used in place of the tambour. He describes, it as 'a great snail-shell from the sea played by a hundred men.' The sound was 'surprisingly rustic and at the same time martial.'[37]

37 Guignard, *L'École de Mars*, 1:722.

8 *Military Wind Bands in England*

> Farewell the plumed troop, and the big wars,
> That make ambition virtue! O, farewell!
> Farewell the neighing steed, and the shrill trump,
> The spirit-stirring drum, th´ear-piercing fife,
> The royal banner, and all quality,
> Pride, pomp, and circumstance of glorious war!

This speech by Othello,[1] first spoken in 1604, describes the English military music as it would remain for most of the seventeenth century—the trumpet and the traditional fife and drum.

It was the drum which presumably had the principal responsibility for the control of the troops through its rudimentary signals. The success of this system depended first of all on the ability of the drummers to produce clear and unvaried signals. If the drummers were to improvise on the pattern, for example, it might go unrecognized by the ordinary foot soldier. This seems to have happened from time to time and a royal edict intended to correct this problem is extant from 1610.

[1] Shakespeare, *Othello*, act 3, scene 3.

> Whereas the ancient custome of nations hath ever bene to use one certaine and constant forme of March in the warres, whereby to be distinguished one from another. And the March of this our nation, so famous in all the honourable achievements and glorious warres of this our kingdom in forraigne parts (being by the approbation of strangers themselves confest and acknowledged the best of all marches) was through the negligence and carelessness of drummers, and by long discontinuance so altered and changed from the ancient gravity and majestie thereof, as it was in danger utterly to have bene lost and forgotten. It pleased our late deare brother prince Henry to revive and rectifie the same by ordayning an establishment of one certaine measure, which was beaten in his presence at Greenwich, anno 1610. In confirmation whereof wee are graciously pleased, at the instance and humble sute of our right trusty and right well-beloved cousin and counsellor Edward Viscount Wimbledon, to set down and ordaine this present establishment hereunder expressed. Willing and commanding all drummers within our kingdome of England and principalitie of Wales exactly and precisely to observe the same, as well in this our kingdome, as abroad in the service of any forraigne

prince or state, without any addition or alteration whatsoever. To the end that so ancient, famous, and commendable a custome may be preserved as a patterne and precedent to all posterite.[2]

The success of this system also depended on the soldiers' ability to recognize these signals. An often quoted phrase from Markham[3] cautions, 'It is to the voice of the Drum the Souldier should wholly attend, and not to the aire of the whistle.' Similarly, the Earl of Arundel and Surrey issued an edict in 1639, stating,

Every souldier shall diligently observe and learne the distinct and different sounds of Drums, Fifes, and Trumpets, that he may know to answer and obey each of them in time of service.[4]

A chapter in the Markham book gives an interesting description of the numerous functions of the drummers' signals.

First in the morning the discharge or breaking up of the *Watch*, then a preparation or Summons to make them repaire to their colours; then a beating away before they begin to march; after that a *March* according to the nature and custom of the country (for diuers countries have diuers Marches), then a *Charge*, then a *Retrait*, then a *Troupe*, and lastly a *Battalion* or a *Battery*, besides other sounds which depending on the phantasttikenes of forain nations are not so useful.[5]

The drummer had a very responsible role as one can see and Markham added that he should be considered 'rather a man of peace than of the sword, and it is most dishonourable in any man wittingly and out of knowledge to strike him or wound him.'[6]

The responsible role of the drummers, together with the need to oversee their accuracy, as mentioned above, no doubt led to the creation of the position of 'Drum-major.' One of the earliest (1590) references to this position calls for a man 'of great perfection in his science.'[7] Seventeenth-century treatises illuminate the many facets of this position: he was responsible for the provisions of the 'dromes and phifes'[8]; he was responsible for discipline and should 'with his staff correct the drums which fail in their duty'[9]; and he 'must likewise be well skill'd in several languages and tongues.'[10]

[2] Horace Walpole, *Catalogue of Royal and Noble Authors* (London, 1758).

[3] Francis Markham, *Five Decades of Epistles of Warre* (London, 1622).

[4] *Lawes and Ordinances of Warre*, quoted in Grove 12:316.

[5] Markham, 'Of Drummes and Phiphes,' in *Five Decades of Epistles of Warre*, I, v.

[6] Quoted in Henry Farmer, *Military Music* (London: William Reeves, 1912), 40.

[7] Thomas Digges, *An Arithmetical Warlike Treatise* (London, 1590).

[8] Gerat Barry, *A Discourse of Military Discipline* (Brussels, 1634).

[9] John Du Praissac, *The Art of Warre* (Cambridge, 1639).

[10] Richard Elton, *The Compleat Body of the Art Military* (London, 1650).

The trumpet player held much the same role as the drummer for most of the seventeenth century, and indeed Markham equates them, 'The Trumpet is the same which the Drum and Phiph is, only differing in the tearmes and sounds of the Instrument.' The trumpeter too was carefully chosen. Elton recommended, 'a politic, discreet and cunning person,'[11] and Sir James Turner agreed:

> (The trumpeter should be) witty and discreet, and must drink little, so that they may be rather apt to circumvent others, than be circumvented; they should be cunning, and wherever they are sent, they should … observe warily the works, guards, and sentinels of an enemy, and give an account of them.[12]

A publication of 1635 says the trumpeter was given a sword, but with a broken point to demonstrate that he was a non-combatant![13]

The terms given in a seventeenth-century description of the military trumpet signals reminds us of their Italian origin.

> The first point of Warre is *Butte sella*, clap on your saddles; *Mounte Cauallo*, mount on horseback; *Tucquet*, march; *Carga, carga*, an Alarme to charge; *A la Standardo*, a retrait, or retire to your colours; *Auquet*, to the Watch, or a discharge for the watch, besides diuers other points, as Proclamations, Cals, Summons, all which are most necessary for euery Souldier both to know.[14]

Two other instruments are found in the seventeenth-century English military music tradition before the arrival of the oboes. First, with the restoration of the monarchy in 1660, one begins to find the timpani used with the trumpets in the Royal Life Guard, each troop having four trumpets and one timpani; these players were paid somewhat better than most due to their association with the king. They played silver trumpets and wore velvet coats, trimmed with silk and silver lace, embroidered with the royal arms on front and back.[15]

When the timpani was later permitted to regular horse guards, it was nevertheless restricted to higher ranking officers, reflecting its ancient association with the aristocrats. During the early years of the eighteenth century, the artillery units were also allowed to have timpani. Not wanting to carry their timpani on horse, as the horse guards, they constructed large

[11] Elton, *The Compleat Body of the Art Military*.

[12] Sir James Turner, *Pallas Armata* (London, 1683).

[13] *Souldier's Accidence*, quoted in Farmer, *Military Music*, 40.

[14] Markham, *Five Decades of Epistles of Warre*, III, i.

[15] Farmer, *Military Music*, 38.

and elaborate wagons to carry them, drawn by six white horses. They appear, wagon and all, first during the Irish Rebellion of 1689, the tradition disappearing by the end of the Baroque. A surviving war order, from the Flanders Campaign of 1747, instructs the timpani player to 'mount the kettledrum carriage every night half-an-hour before the sunset, and beat until gun-firing.'[16] Was it to make the enemy think the guns were still firing, all through the night?

Finally, the bagpipe was a wind instrument which had been popular with the aristocracy in England during the Medieval period, but had gradually been losing ground. A pay warrent survives from 1674 for teaching one person in each company of the King's Regiment of Foot Guards how to play the bagpipe,[17] however, a document which more accurately reflects the diminished status of the instrument is quoted by Turner (1683).

> In some places a piper is allowed to each company: the *Germans* have him, and I look upon their pipe as a warlike instrument. The bagpipe is good enough musick for them who love it; but sure it is not so good as the Almain Whistle. With us any captain may keep a piper in his company, and maintain him too, for no pay is allowed him, perhaps just as much as he deserveth.[18]

Again it is the addition of the oboes which brings a major turning point to the development of military bands. In England one sees them first in 1678, with the creation of the new Horse Grenadiers, the first English troops who served both mounted and dismounted. Six 'hoboys,' which is to say, four oboes and two bassoons,[19] were added at this time and were clearly a reflection of the influence of the French court on Charles II. Shortly thereafter there were ten 'hautboys' and four drummers wearing 'velvet coats trimmed with silver and silk buttons and loops.'[20] A pay record for new uniforms for 1691 lists the musicians of one troop of the 'Granadeers' as 'three trumpeters, a kettledrummer and four hautboyes, and two drummers.'[21]

Shortly after the introduction of oboes into the new Grenadiers, they were also authorized (ca. 1685) in the Foot Guards. Farmer says these bands never exceeded six players,[22] but Panoff says the band was twelve in 1685.[23]

[16] Henry Farmer, *Memoirs of the Royal Artillery Band* (London: Boosey, 1904).

[17] Farmer, *Military Music*, 28.

[18] Turner, *Pallas Armata*.

[19] Peter Panoff, *Militärmusik*, 130.

[20] Farmer, *Handel's Kettledrums*, 43; and Harold Hind, *The British Wind Band* (London: Hinrichsen, 1952), 184.

[21] London, Lord Chamberlain Accounts, vol. 754, p. 256.

[22] Farmer, *Military Music*, 48.

[23] Panoff, *Militärmusik*, 131.

Similarly, the Horse Guards acquired four oboes and two drummers for each troop beginning in 1686.[24] Another pay record, of 1691, shows a fewer number of oboes for the ordinary troop, but four oboes, two drummers, three trumpets, and a timpani for the Horse Guards under the Earl of Marleborough.[25]

Some companies were limited to very small musical components. The Dragoons, created in 1689, were allowed only one 'hoboy' and two drums for each company.[26] In 1731 it was ordered that the music of the Grenadier Company of the Honourable Artillery Company of London should have 'one curtail three hautboys and no more!'[27]

A letter from Popham to Blake in 1650 requests not only four additional trumpets for the fleet, but a 'complete noise,' a full band, for his own ship.[28] It appears, therefore, that there was some use of naval bands in England during the Baroque. No doubt the wind players serving on the ships were civilians as they usually were on shore, but in this case probably 'impressed,' or kidnapped.[29] Drum-majors and Sergeant-trumpeters appear to have had the power to 'recruit' musicians in this fashion. When one, John Digges, challenged a sergent-trumpeter to a fight in 1637, the latter arranged to have Mr. Digges abducted and impressed into military service![30]

With civilian musicians serving in the military, not to mention the abducted ones, one can understand that discipline may not have always been of the highest order. A newspaper notice of 1724 gives a tantalizing hint of such a problem.

> We hear that the Musick belonging to the 2d Regiment of Guards have been this Week at Richmond to beg their Royal Highnesses (George, Prince of Wales) Pardon for their ill Conduct on the Thames some Days ago at Richmond, when attending a certain Person of Distinction, and were generously forgiven, the Misdemeanour, as we are inform'd appearing to be undesign'd and involuntary.[31]

[24] Lord Chamberlain Accounts, vol. 751, p. 180.

[25] Ibid., vol. 209, p. 26; vol. 754, p. 268.

[26] Farmer, *Handel's Kettledrums*, 43.

[27] Ibid.

[28] Farmer, *Military Music*, 16, fn. 2.

[29] A forebearer of the present writer was so 'impressed' in service on an English ship during the eighteenth century.

[30] Farmer, *Military Music*, 37.

[31] Quoted in Edward Croft-Murray, 'The Wind-Band in England,' in *Music & Civilisation* (London: Trustees of the British Museum, 1980), 142.

9   *Military Wind Bands in Italy*

In the civic militia of Rome, each military leader, 'Capitano Generale,' had a personal ensemble of trumpets and drums, very much like that in the court of a lesser prince. One sees such a person, Giovanni Francesco Aldobrandini, with his four trumpets and 'tamburo generale' during his campaign in Hungary in 1601. In addition, each company had two or more tamburi and sometimes a fife.[1]

During the seventeenth century, the cavalry, which was also divided into companies, had two or more trumpets in each; timpani were added ca. 1650.[2] The dragoons, founded during the middle of the seventeenth century, had one tambour for each company of fifty to one hundred horses.

The first military 'oboe bands' in Rome appear in 1708 as 'piccolo concerti,' consisting of oboes, bassoons, and sometimes timpani. These seem at first to have been organized privately, independent of the civic government.[3]

From Naples there is documentation, but only from the eighteenth century, of large numbers of fifes and drums. The Swiss Guards in 1735 was organized into seven companies with eight fifes and fourteen tambours under a leader, growing by 1743 to nine fifes and twenty-nine drums for ten companies.

The regiment of the royal Bourbon infantry in 1741 had six companies with fourteen tamburi and a 'tamburo maggiore.'[4]

The military bands in Piemonte during the second half of the seventeenth century are more interesting, due to more international influence. One influence was French, as Vittorio Amadeo II had married a niece to Louis XIV in 1684, as one can see in the change of his court band's name from 'banda di tromboni' to 'banda di hautbois.' In 1694 an additional small oboe band was formed in the Guards to help with larger court celebrations, again an imitation of the French court.[5]

There was also a strong German influence in this area of Italy, due to the presence of Austrian and German troops with their bands. When Charles II, the King of Spain, died a semi-idiot in 1699, a will which had been extorted from him deeded the crown of Spain to the French Prince, Philip of Anjou,

[1] Alessandro Vessella, *La Banda* (Milano: Istituto editoriale nazionale, 1935), 123–124.

[2] Ibid.

[3] Ibid.

[4] Ibid., 126.

[5] Ibid., 130–131.

grandson to his sister, under the title of Philip v. However, according to the laws of hereditary descent, the crown should have gone to an Austrian, and so in Vienna the son of Leopold I was crowned King of Spain as Charles III. Thus the War of the Spanish Succession occurred, which made Italy one of the great battlefields for some fourteen years.[6]

Consequently one finds many names of German musicians in the military bands of this area, in particular Giorgio Cristoforo Albmeyer, who was the leader of the 'Hautbois' of the Reggimento Rhebinder until 1722.[7] One finds additional military oboe bands formed in the Reggimento di Piemonte (1737) and the Reggimento di Saluzzo (1750).[8]

[6] John S. C. Abbott, *Italy* (New York, 1871), 473–474.

[7] Vessella, *La Banda*, 131, 168.

[8] Ibid., 168.

10 *Military Wind Bands in the Low Countries*

THREE INTERESTING PAINTINGS FROM THE LOW COUNTRIES during the seventeenth century show typical military instruments, but unfortunately not the oboe bands. First, the *Procession of the Military Guilds*, by Denis van Alsloot (early seventeenth century) pictures a total of twenty-eight fife and drum players, some with visible snares. They are grouped one fife for each two drums.

In the *Triumph of Isabella*, by the same artist, at the head of a group of 'Turkish' cavalrymen, one sees a single trumpeter accompanied by a black, mounted timpanist (see image on following page).

A group of seven trumpeters and three timpanists can also be seen in Frans Duchatel's *Inaugural Celebration of Charles II, King of Spain, as Count of Flanders at Ghent, May 2, 1666.*[1]

Denis van Alsloot, *Procession of the Military Guilds*, shows twenty-eight fife and drum players.

[1] David Leppert, 'Musical Instruments and Performing. Ensembles in Flemish Paintings of the Seventeenth Century' (Dissertation, Indiana University, 1973).

154 Military Wind Bands

Detail from Denis van Alsloot's *Triumph of Isabella*, showing a single trumpeter (upper left) accompanied by a black, mounted timpanist.

11 *Military Wind Bands in Russia*

During the middle part of the seventeenth century military music was central to the development of musical culture in Moscow, with military instruments performing for both state and folk festivals. Schools to train wind players for the military also date from the seventeenth century.[1]

The development of truly Western military bands began with Peter the Great (1682–1725) who made extensive travels throughout the West for the purpose of learning first-hand everything he could to bring Russia up-to-date. His particular interest in military music was perhaps due in part to the fact that he had been a drum player in his youth.[2]

Peter imported German players of oboe, bassoon, trumpet, horn and timpani[3] and established additional military music schools in the garrisons themselves in order to train the children of the soldiers.[4] One can say the great Russian tradition of military bands, which continues to the present day, began at this time.

Under Peter the Great the artillery had an oboe band with timpani.[5] The dragoons had trumpets and percussion, one such regiment in 1741 having twelve trumpets, twelve drums, and one timpani. The husars and cavalry had trumpets, but only the headquarters company had a timpani. The Panduren Regiment had fifes and drums and an oboe band with horns in the headquarters company by 1750.

[1] Peter Panoff, *Militärmusik*, 116, provides early examples of military music in Russia, including trumpets by the sixth century, trumpets and timpani in the Siege of Kiews in 1151, and the addition of shawms in the war against Bulgaria in 1220.

[2] Ibid., 123.

[3] Alessandro Vessella, *La banda*, 134.

[4] Grove 12:602.

[5] The following descriptions are taken from Panoff, *Militärmusik*, 120ff.

PART 5
Civic Wind Bands

12 Civic Wind Bands in the German-Speaking Countries

CIVIC WIND BANDS ATTAINED THEIR GREATEST STATURE, before the modern era, during the seventeenth century and their importance in German culture can be seen in the fact that they were the training ground for virtually every career in music.[1]

In seventeenth-century Germany and Austria one would have found many small towns with four civic bandsmen, as for example in Marburg, Radkersburg, and Graz.[2] In the larger, more prosperous cities these groups were larger: Augsburg began the century with six, but soon added a seventh; Nürnberg had six; Leipzig had seven; and Hamburg had eight in its principal wind band, but had also seven bands of five each organized as associated civic bands which could help out in great celebrations.[3] Also on great festival days, such as the seventeenth-century 'band days,' one would often find the local civic wind band joined by bands from surrounding towns. Such an example can be seen when the emperor visited Dresden in 1662 when the civic wind band was joined by those from Meissen, Pirna and Freiberg.[4]

Evidence of the highly organized nature of these civic wind bands, and perhaps a clue to their quality in many cases, can be seen in the careful audition process and the demands on prospective members. The modern reader might at first be surprised by the expectation that these players be proficient on so many different instruments, but in reality this had been part of the craft of the professional musician for centuries. As pointed out in earlier volumes in this series, it was the change of instruments from composition to composition which provided variety in instrumental color, rather than the 'orchestration' by the composer. One can see this expectation, as well as some of the personal qualities sought by the civic bands, in a very interesting letter by a father, and Stadtpfeifer in Stralsund, recommending the consideration of his son for a tower music position in Stettin in 1607.

> My son has arrived at a point in his art where he has studied and learned diligently all the musical instruments. First he is a good trumpeter and secondly a good cornett player and plays well the discant violin,

[1] Werner Braun, 'Entwurf für eine Typologie der "Hautboisten",' in *Der Sozialstatus des Berufsmusikers vom 17. bis 19. Jahrhundert* (Kassel: Barenreiter-Verlag, 1971), 57.

[2] Eugen Brixel and Wolfgang Suppan, *Das Grosse Steirische Blasmusikbuch* (Wien: Molden, 1981), 36.

[3] Liselotte Krüger, *Die Hamburgische Musikorganisation im XVII Jahrhundert* (Leipzig: Heitz, 1933), 188–189; and Wilhelm Ehmann, *Tibilustrium* (Kassel: Barenreiter-Verlag, 1950), 21.

[4] Grove 5:615.

Querpfiefe, Dulcian, quart-, tenor-, and alto-trombone. In summary: all perfect instruments, although without proclaiming his fame—for as one says, 'Self praise stinks.' But he can prove himself where it matters, in what the ear hears and the eye sees. To cover the subject, he doesn't quarrel or criticize, has good friends, takes care of things quickly, and can use the instruments I have given him in praise of God: trombones, cornetts, a good quart-trombone; a Dulcian consort; a large and small bombard consort; a large cornett consort; a crumhorn consort; a Querpfeiffen consort; a flute consort; and a violin consort. He can play all parts and use the fifth, sixth, or eighth voices (read all the various clefs), comes from a good home ... and is twenty-six years old.[5]

To test an applicant's ability in performing on a variety of instruments, the town council would often commission compositions to be used in the audition. When, for example, in 1743 the Zeitz civic wind band had an opening, they paid Johann Gorner, music director of Leipzig University, twelve Thalers to compose works for trumpet, trombone, cornett, horn, and two each for strings and oboe.[6] Similarly there is an interesting extant document by Bach, relative to the audition for such a position in Leipzig in 1745. Bach wrote that the audition was held before the entire group of the civic musicians and that the applicant, one Carl Pfaffe, performed to general applause on 'all the instruments that are customarily employed by the Stadtpfeifers, Violine, Hautbois, Flute Travers, Trompette, Waldhorn and the "Bass" instruments.'[7]

[5] Letter by Jonas Degensee quoted in Ehmann, *Tibilustrium*, 22.

> Was nun meinen Sohn anlangt und seine Kunst, die er mit allem Fleiss gestudieret und geiernt hat auf allerlei musikalischen Instrumenten, erstlich ist er ein guter Trompeter, zum and ern ein guter Zinkenbläser, zum dritten geiget er einen guten Discant, pfeift eine gute Querpfeife, auf Duīcian, auf der Quartposaune, Tenor- und Altposaune, in Summa auf allerlei Instrumenten perfekt, doch ohne Ruhm zu melden, wie man saget: Eigenlob stinket, aber er kan es beweisen, darauf stehet alles, was die ohren hören, die augen sehen, die bezeugen das werck, ist ein sitzsamer mensch ist kein haderer oder zencker, weis sich bei guten leuten wol zu halten, wartet seines dings mit fleiss darzu er bestallt ist die instrumente die ich ihme mitgebe kan er Godt lob alle gebrauchen, posaunen und zinken dar bei eine gute quart posaune zum 2. ein stimmwerck dulcian zum dritten ein stimmwerck grosse und kleine bomhart zum vierten ein stimmwerck grobe zinken zum fünften ein Stimmwerck krumphörner zum sechsten ein stimmwerck querpfeiffen, zum siebenden ein stimmwerck flöten zum achten ein stimmwerck geigen, das er mit achterley ahrt stimmen der instrument verendern kan und gebrauchen quin und Sex vocum oder octo vocum dis habe ich dem Herrn aus guter woimeinung wollen vermelden, wenn ich nun wuste was zu rahten were so wolte ich sampt meinem sohn andreas mit seinen gesellen und die vorbenannten instrumente genn Stettin bringen und sich hören lassen was ihm unser Herrgott verliehen hat, von der instrumentalischen music er ist seines alters in des 26 jahr, hir mit ins gotts almacht sampt alle den eweren befohlen.

[6] Arnold Schering, *Musikgeschichte Leipzigs* (Leipzig, 1941), 3:151.

[7] Quoted in Arnold Schering, 'Die Leipziger Ratsmusik von 1650 bis 1775,' in *Archiv für Musikwissenschaft* (1921), 44.

> ... er auf jedem Instrumente, so von denen Stadt Pfeifern pfleget gebraucht zu werden ...

This article also quotes in entirety the adjudicator's evaluation of two candidates in 1769, discussing in detail their performance on horn, violine, slide trumpet, tenor and bass trombone, and violin.

Many towns maintained large collections of instruments for these players to use. One can see in the town accounts of Nürnberg, for example, as late as 1620, payment for the restoration of the town's consort of Renaissance crumhorns.

> Paid to Friderich Lang, town player, for use for his private practice as ordered, one of the council's crumhorns in a case, of which there are nine together, for having cleaned it like new, repaired its keys, and made new reeds for them.[8]

One extant description which pictures the Nürnberg civic musicians performing on a variety of instruments, is an account of a pageant-concert given in 1643. Here, in addition to performing on strings, they performed a work on 'silver trumpets and clarions'; a 'Greek military composition' with trumpets, drums, and timpani, but with four bassoons and two bombards accompanying the chorus; a motet accompanied by (unnamed) winds; and a funeral composition for male chorus and four trombones.[9]

One must quickly add, however, that in the day to day performance by the German civic musicians there was a definite hierarchy of instruments. The most frequently used instruments, and the highest ranking in this hierarchy, were the cornetts and trombones, followed by strings, and then the lowly bagpipe and percussion.[10]

Ordinarily, the one instrument the Stadtpfeifers were not supposed to use was the trumpet, which, as the reader has seen above, the strong aristocratic trumpet guilds attempted to reserve for themselves. One finds, for example, that the city council in Leipzig had to make a formal report to the elector explaining why their music director, J.H. Schein, used trumpets in a performance in St. Thomas Church. Schein was directed to use the cornett in the future![11] Perhaps one famous incident can speak for the seriousness of this issue.

> At the end of the seventeenth century in Hanhover, the Elector's trumpeters once broke into the house of the chief Stadtpfeifer, with whom they were at loggerheads, took his trumpet on which he was practicing and knocked out several of his front teeth with it. And what is more, these worthy Kameraden contended that they had only asserted their just right—and escaped all punishment.[12]

---

[8] Quoted in Ekkehart Nickel, *Der Holzblasinstrumentenbau in der Freien Reichsstadt Nürnberg* (Munich: Musikverlag Katzbichler, 1971), 86, 420.

> Zalt Friderich Langen, Stadtpfeiffern, so zu anbefollenen privato exercitio eines E. Raths Krumhörner in ein Futeral, deren 9 beysammen, auffdas Neu wiederumb verseubert, die Schlösser daran aufgebessert und zu denselben neue Rohr machen lassen ...

See also Altmann Kellner, *Musikgeschichte des Stifes Kremsmünster* (Kassel: Barenreiter-Verlag, 1956) regarding the town instrument collection in Halle, and Jean Lobstein, *Beiträge zur Geschichte der Musik im Elsass und besonders in Strassburg, von den ältesten bis auf die neueste Zeit* (Strassburg, 1840) regarding Strassburg.

[9] Elisabeth Krückeberg, 'Ein historisches Konzert zu Nürnberg im Jahre 1643,' in *Archiv für Musikwissenschaft* (1918–1919): 590ff.

[10] Ehmann, *Tibilustrium*, 23, 30.

[11] Gottfried Viet, *Die Blasmusik* (Innsbruck, 1972), 24.

[12] Werner Menke, *History of the Trumpet of Bach and Händel* (London: W. Reeves, 1934), 26–27.

I believe the quality of these German civic wind players was as high as any instrumentalist of this period. To be sure, from individual to individual or from town to town, there must have been some who did not 'measure up.' Kuhnau, Bach's predecessor at St. Thomas in Leipzig, commented, certainly with considerable exaggeration, that out of a hundred Stadtpfeifers there was scarcely one who could write ten words on paper, even if his life depended on it.[13] When Bach himself arrived in Leipzig, some forty years later, he too, found some of the civic musicians at his disposal somewhat lacking.

[13] *Musicus vexatus* (1690).

> Discretion forbids me to speak of their quality and musical knowledge, but it should be mentioned that some of them are *emeriti* and others are not in as good *exercitio* as they should be.[14]

[14] Quoted in E. H. Müller von Asow, *Johann Sebastian Bach Briefe* (Regensburg: Bosse, 1950), 112.

One may be sure that in some cases it was the bureaucratic interference by the town council that resulted in the hiring of musicians who were not as distinguished as their colleagues. In one such case, early in the eighteenth century in Altenburg, the mayor hired a Stadtpfiefer named Rosselt without the proper audition, and apparently without even consulting the chief Stadtpfiefer Stöckel. Stöckel was therefore in an unenviable position of having to sustain the decision of the mayor as a loyal employee, yet had to suffer the contempt of his colleagues for allowing this 'bungler' to be hired. Apparently this case attracted wide attention among musicians and a former member of the Altenburg civic wind band, Hans Christian Biedermann, who had gone on to become a court trumpeter in Weimar, wrote a letter of condemnation to Stöckel for his part in this affair.

> Parenthetically I must, Mr. Stöckeln, although unhappily, report that a bad *Aestim* of you and your *collegen* has resulted even so far away as Leipzig, Jena, and here in Weimar ... (as a result of your actions) all bunglers will now travel to Altenburg (and the word will go out) that all bunglers and 'fellows of the road' who have been cut off (from other employment) can be engaged in Altenburg ... I have strong misgivings (in writing this letter) for to be sure I am no kunstpfeifer, a profession I have called *finis*, but (as a former member of the Altenburg guild) I am indebted to you and yours and I hope honest men will direct toward me more praise than reproach for my making this warning. (I am considered an honest man) and so I say freely, that you have bound yourself to his

Rosselt and you must look out for evil. You should not have let him draw a single stroke on a violin before consulting with the guild ... and formalizing the contract with a *Notario*.[15]

Most Stadtpfeifers must have been more capable; to begin with, it was the ability to read music which set them apart from the 'Beer fiddler.'[16] Among them must have been many who were outstanding musicians in every sense and I mention as representative of those Gottfried Reiche, the senior Stadtpfeifer in Leipzig during the time of Bach. A contemporary[17] says that one can see in an engraving of this musician that 'he resembles an honest man as closely as one drop of water does another.' A measure of Reiche's reputation can be seen in the fact that during the year-long period of mourning in 1694, when musical performances were not permitted, the city council voted a special monetary 'Gratifikation' to Reiche to make sure he was not tempted to leave town.[18]

This faithful civic wind player, by the way, died playing his trumpet in the service of the city! In October 1734, the Elector of Saxony, Friedrich Augustus II, came to Leipzig for celebrations relative to his succession to the Polish throne. Bach composed his 'Preise dein Gluck, gesegnetes Sachsen' for the occasion and it was sung in the Marktplatz by the students of the Collegium Musicum. An eyewitness suggests that Reiche's death the following day was the direct result of his performance in this evening serenade.

---

[15] The entire letter is quoted in Arno Werner, *Städtische und fürstliche musikpflege in Zeitz* (Buckeburg, 1922), 41–42.

> Beyläufig muss sich Herrn Stöckeln, wiewohl ungern, berichten, dass ein schlecht aestim von ibm und seinen collegen in der Frembde gemacht wird, massen nich nur die Leipziger, der Jenische und hier in Weimar Herr Balthasar aufs schmpflichste von dessen Person und Zugegebenen reden, dass sie nemblich alle Kunst manir hindansetzten, alle verdorbene Pfuscher sich accompagnirten und folglich die Kunst in Altenburg zu einer offenbahren Pfufcheren machten, wodurch manchem ehrlichen Kerl der Weg abgeschnitten wäre, in Altenburg engagiret zu werden. Ja, sie trohn, sie wollten ehest gegen ihn und seine Collegen den Process und ihn zu Frankfurt von der Kunst ausschliessen, seine Jungen vor infam erklähren und in den Catalogum der Pfuscher einschreiben, welches ich zu verschweigen hohes Bedencken trage, denn ob ich wohl ist kein Kunstpfeifer und es mit mir heisst finis, so bin ich doch Herr Stöckeln und seinen Zugegebenen so sehr verbunden, dass ich selbige warnen muss, und ich hoffe ein ehrlicher Mann werde mich disshalber mehr lob en als schelten. Ich rede mit ihm als ein ehrlicher Biedermann und honnet Homm und sage frey heraus: Herr Stöckelt hat sich mit diesem Rosselt recht eine Ruthe gebunden und sich sehr übel vorgesehen, er hätte ihn nicht einen Strich gigen lassen sollen, bevor er sich mit der Kunst verglichen und in tractaten sich eingelassen. Seinen Vergleich hätte er nicht nur in Gegenwart einiger von der Kunst von einem Notario förmlich zu Papier bringen sollen ...

[16] Arno Werner, *Vier Jahrhunderte im Dienste der Kirchenmusik* (Leipzig: Merseburger, 1933), 264.

[17] Mattheson, *Ehren-Pforte* (1740).

[18] Don Smithers, *The Music and History of the Baroque Trumpet* (London: Dent, 1973), 126–127.

On October 6th the skilled and experienced musician and Stadtpfeifer, Gottfried Reiche, ... and senior member of the local musician's guild suffered a stroke not far from his lodging in the Stadtpfeifergasschen, as he was on his way home, so that he collapsed and was brought dead into the house. And this is said to have occurred because on the previous day he had been greatly fatigued by playing in the royal music and had suffered severely from the smoke of the torches.[19]

The official duties of the baroque Stadtpfeifer were as varied as those of civic wind players during the fifteenth and sixteenth centuries, but the most frequently remembered today are those we call 'tower music.' The historic duties and responsibilities of the tower musicians are no where so eloquently recalled as in the 1679 poem by Jacob Lottich.

> When Titan's high course is about to bring midday, the clock strikes ten;
> Then the musicians meet with all their odds and ends,
> Form a group and let us have a tune for lunch on their trombones.
> The midday music can be heard from the town hall tower,
> Almost high up in the open air; it sounds for the honour of God and to inform the people,
> So that everyone knows each day at this time it is the tenth hour.
> When Latous has departed from us with his never tiring horses
> And when we no longer see any light or any rays from him on earth,
> Then a bell is rung so that its sweet sound entices us to vespers.
> A cornettist then takes the best of his Zinken,
> Chooses a psalm which he considers just suitable, and he pipes in an artful manner;
> He does his duty, stays on the church tower and remains awake for the rest of the night.
> In the streets guards who have been appointed for this purpose walk up and down and see
> To it that the streets are safe; they seize the trespasser against law and order;
> They prevent fire and turmoil so that everyone shall be safe while they rest.
> As often as the clock strikes the hours are called out.
> There is no shortage of clocks: hardly anywhere would you find such ingenious clock works.
> Anyone who does not believe this should come here and see for himself that one weight alone propels two big clocks.
> As soon as Aurora gleams in gold and roscate hues the watchman still awake takes his trumpet, alerts and wakes up the town with a morning song.
> After that he retires and makes up for his lost sleep.[20]

[19] The original German text is quoted in Gustav Wustmann, *Quellen zur Geschichte Leipzig* (Leipzig, 1889), 1:436.

[20] Quoted, with the original German, in Smithers, *The Music and History of the Baroque Trumpet*, 121–122.

These varied duties can be seen in various extant contracts from this period, as for example one for Christoph Schumann in 1726.

> He should at 3:00 A.M., 9:00 A.M. and 9:00 P.M. play (Abblasen) with diligence a spiritual Psalm, to the honor of the Almighty God and to inspire Christian prayer and to sustain the goodwill of the citizens and the entire community. Further, at night he should faithfuly watch and take heed that with his assistant the horn player they mark every quarter hour with the usual horn playing. He should keep his quarters in the tower clean. He must volunteer to play in church with his instrument and assist the civic musicians with weddings, operas, and official banquets, although not permit himself, though helping, to actually take part in the ceremonies.[21]

One sees here the role as surrogate clock. In Hamburg such a signal was also given every hour; in Nürnberg the signal was given each hour, echoing back and forth from tower to tower.[22]

Musically the most important of the tower musicians functions was the above mentioned 'Abblasen,' the playing of spiritual music. Far from mere chorales, these also included chorale canzonas, chorale fantasies, free canzonas, sonatas and suites.[23] There was also a certain 'public relations' aspect to this music, in so far as these musicians were representatives of the town. An ordinance from Zeitz in 1701 speaks of the performance of Abblasen to 'better ornament the town for visitors.'[24]

Examples of this tradition, 'a friendly and peaceful sound' as Pezel called it,[25] can be found throughout Germany, in cities of all sizes. In Greiz, in 1619, the Stadtpfeifers played spiritual songs on trombones at 3:00 A.M., 9:00 A.M., and at 7:00 P.M.; at 9:00 A.M. and 4:00 P.M. they played on trumpets. In the free Reich city of Nordhausen one heard the Abblasen morning, afternoon, and evening, and in Altenburg twice a day in 1661.[26] In Nürnberg, three verses of 'an appropriate song' were played, with the final verse echoed from tower to tower, as in the case of the time signal. This tradition lasted in Nürnberg until 1806.[27]

The spiritual and psychological impact of this music on the citizen on the street should not be underestimated. The trombones, on which the Abblasen were most frequently performed, had themselves become symbols of God and Christian

---

[21] Quoted in Ehmann, *Tibilustrium*, 32.

> Er soll morgens 3 Uhr vormittags 10 Uhr und abends 9 Uhr, Gatt dem Allmächtigen zu Ehren, wie zur Erweckung christlicher Andacht einen geistlichen Psalm mit allem Fleisse abblassen, und sich allerwege dermassen hören lassen, dass Herren wie Geschworene, auch ganze Gemeinde und übrige Bürgerschaft, ihr aufrichtiges Wohlgefallen daran haben mögen. Er soll ferner Nachts getreue Wachtund Acht haben mit seinem Adjuncto dem Tüter und alle Viertelstunde das gewöhnliche Tützeichen vernehmen lassen. Er soll auch sein Logiement auf dem Turme reinlich halten, und bei einfallenden Kirchenmusiken soll er mit seinem Instrument gratis aufwarten. Übrigens gönnt man ihm gern Tagsüber einige Nebenaccidentien durch Assistenz der Ratsmusikanten, bei Hochzeiten, Opernspielen und vornehmen Gastereien, doch darf er sich nich förmlich dabei enrollieren lassen.

[22] Ibid., 31. Regarding Nürnberg, in 1620:

> Die Thurmer sollen auch allweg, alsbaldt es Zwai gehn tag geschlagen und nachts, umb ainz der grössern uhr, blasen, auch sonst bey nacht, uff der hörnlein wechter blasen, dass sie denselben jedesmal mit derm Horn widerantworten, ihr fleissig auffmercken haben.

[23] Ibid., 34.

[24] Werner, *Kirchenmusik*, 218.

> ... zu besserer Zierde der Stadt bei denen Fremden.

[25] Werner, *Kirchenmusik*, 217.

[26] Ibid., 217.

[27] Ehmann, *Tibilustrium*, 34–35.

music, as the fiddle had become the symbol of the Beer hall. Kuhnau, Bach's predecessor in Leipzig reflected, 'When our civic musicians at Festival time blow a spiritual song on the loud trombones, every measure stirs the image of angels singing.' No other instruments, but wind instruments, he says are played in Heaven by the angels![28] One can imagine the effect of this spiritual music, floating down several times a day from on high, played by instruments which were themselves symbols of God, on the ordinary man.

The poem by Lottich, quoted above, speaks of the midday concert at 10:00 A.M.:

> When Titan's high course is about to bring midday, the clock strikes ten;
> Then the musicians meet with all their odds and ends,
> Form a group and let us have a tune for lunch on their trombones.

It was for this tradition of a 'mini-concert' each work day at ten o'clock in the morning (the beginning of the 'noon' break in a society which began work at dawn) in Leipzig that we have today the extraordinary *Hora decima*, a collection of forty sonatas by Johann Pezel. This tradition began in Leipzig in 1599, when a new balcony was added to the tower of the city hall, or *Rathaus*. During the first years of the seventeenth century Leipzig suffered six sieges as part of the Thirty Years War and was even occupied by the enemy on several occasions. However, after the war the city entered into a period of rapid economic and artistic growth. With this resumption of normal civic life, the town council ordered the performance of a chorale or other dignified composition from the tower every work day at 10:00 A.M. During the second half of the seventeenth century it was the custom of the Stadtpfeifers to perform this music with an ensemble of two cornetts and three trombones, a fifth member being hired to perform with the four regular civic wind players.[29]

The *Hora decima* was published in 1670 and dates from the period when Pezel first became a Stadtpfeifer in Leipzig, having earlier been a Kunstgeiger. Born in lower Silesia (now Poland) in 1639, he seems to have had a better education than the usual civic wind player, for he apparently was educated in Latin, judging from the titles of his music and his subsequent literary publications.[30] In addition to his duties as a Stadtp-

[28] Quoted in ibid., 55–56.

Wenn unsere Stadtpfeifer etwa zur Festzeit ein geistliches Lied mit lauter Posaunen vom Turme blasen, so werden wir über alle Massen darüber beweget und bilden uns ein, als hören wir die Engel singen ... Die ewige und himmlische Instrumentalmusik wird aus lauter Pfeifen bestehen ... die engelischen Musikanten sich keiner and ern Instrumente als der Pfeifen bedienen.

[29] Smithers, *The Music and History of the Baroque Trumpet*, 123–124; Mary Rasmussen, 'Historical Notes,' together with Sonata (North Easton, MA, 1962); and Anneliese Downs, 'The Tower Music of a Seventeenth Century Stadtpfeifer: Johann Pezel's *Hora decima* and *Fünff-stimmigte blasende Music*,' in *Brass Quarterly* 7, no. i (1965): 4, 7.

[30] *Inflex musicus*, *Musica politico-practice*, and *Observationes musicae*.

feifer, he was also the musical director of the Collegium Musicum of the University of Leipzig from 1673 to 1682. In 1677 he applied for the position of cantor of St. Thomas Church (the position Bach would later hold) but was not acceptable as he had been a Catholic. His death occurred in 1694.[31]

There is, of course, another extant work by Pezel composed for his colleagues in the Leipzig civic wind band, the *Fünffstimmigte blasende Music* which dates from after 1670. This is a massive collection of seventy-six compositions, mostly dance movements. The only other extant wind composition by Pezel is the *Bicinia*,[32] consisting of one hundred and ten compositions probably intended as two-part recreational music for the tower musicians to play during their long and lonely hours on duty. Among the lost works of Pezel were the two Intrada collections (Leipzig, 1669 and 1676) for cornett and three trombones and a collection of six-part compositions for two cornetts and four trombones, the *Decas Sonatarum* (Leipzig, 1669).

Some readers may perhaps take exception to my use of the word 'concert' for the ten o'clock Abblasen performances as not conforming to the present day understanding of the term. But if one defines 'concert' as music listened to, as opposed to 'background music,' and agrees that a formal concert hall may or may not a concert make, then who can say these were not concerts? Certainly all would agree that their importance is documented in their regularity and consistency throughout Germany.

In addition to the morning Abblasen 'concerts,' one reads also of evening concerts, which are usually associated with the city hall building and clearly imply performing for the public. Even in so small a town as Duben, an order for the regulation of the Stadtpfeifers in 1725 requires such concerts by the civic wind band as required by the city council.[33] There were also late evening performances by the tower musicians, after midnight, called *Aubaden* or *Nachtmusiken*.[34]

Compositions which may have been used for such 'concerts,' such as the above mentioned sonatas of Pezel, exist in great numbers from the German Baroque, but perhaps a few of the composers should be singled out at this time.[35]

A well-known collection is the *Vier und zwantzig Neue Quatricinia* by Gottfried Reiche, works, as the title page explains, which were intended to be performed from the city

[31] For further information on Pezel see Downes, 'The Tower Music of a Seventeenth Century Stadtpfeifer,' 8–9ff., which includes an analysis of his compositions for winds, and Grove 14:607ff.

[32] *Bicinia variorum instrumentorum, ut a Violinis, Cornettis, Flautis, Clarinis et Fagottis com apprendice a 2 Bombardinis vulgo Schalmeyen* (Leipzig, 1675).

[33] The entire ordinance (October 25, 1725) is quoted Werner, *Kirchenmusik*, 228–229.

> Item 6. Endlich sind die Herren Stadtpfeifer auch schuldig, zum wenigsten dem Herrn Präsidi des Abends vor dessen hause ein Ständchen mit blasenden Instrumenten zu machen, damit die Kantorei um desto mehr ein Ansehen gewinne.

[34] Ibid., 231.

[35] Volume seven in this series lists sources for more than nine hundred original compositions for wind band from the German-speaking countries during this period.

hall. The dedication reminds us that this was no mere tedious duty, but rather an important event in the daily musical lives of the citizens.

> Nothing in all art can claim finer qualities than Noble Music. My pen is much too weak either to repeat here, or to say better what professional and highly-learned men have affirmed so competently. As this matchless art spreads its charms in many ways, we find in most cities the praise-worthy custom of having the so-called 'Abblasen' sounded from churches and town halls. This is always a sign of joy and peace; because, wherever such music must be discontinued there must be national mourning, war, or other misfortune. In the same spirit I have contrived the present Quatricinia and respectfully request, dear music-loving reader, that you will allow yourself to be pleased by this work. In my own small way, I am also willing, For the honor of God and the useful pleasure of my fellow men, to publish some five-part pieces. I have already written forty five-part Sonatas for the musicians here in Leipzig, with whom I have now been associated for eight years, but because of the difficulties their appearance presents to the technique of printing, I have had to put them aside. I have taken care with the Quatricinia to make them easy on the eyes and to write something using slower notes. One more thing must be understood: the Alle breve is performed with a fast moving beat. Although this reminder is not for the musically enlightened, it is added for the benefit of those who know less about the art.[36]

[36] The original German text is given in Mary Rasmussen, 'Gottfried Reiche ...,' *Brass Quarterly* 4, no. i (1960): 10, fn. 30, which also contains a musical analysis of this collection.

The five-part sonatas he refers to are unfortunately lost and are the greater loss by his suggestion that there was something so unusual about them that publication was impossible in Leipzig. In view of his comment regarding the present work being rather easy in nature, perhaps they required greater numbers of ligatures than was customary. His estate, after his death in 1734, listed five books of chorales for the tower musicians which are also lost.

Daniel Speer is another composer who has left a rich literature composed for civic wind bands, probably dating from his service as a civic musician in Breslau before 1680. The best known of his collections is his *Neugebachene Taffel-Schnitz* (1685), meaning something like 'newly baked table goodies,' containing seven sonatas for wind ensemble. This collection is followed by another, the *Musicalisch-Türckischer Eulen-Spiegel* (1688), which contains the six five-part sonatas for wind band and is dedicated to several civic wind band musicians.

To those well-honored and highly regarded ones who so well practice and perform the noble free art of music; Herr Johann Gotthard Heinrich Strenz, well-deserving instrumentalist of the Holy Roman Imperial city of Heilbronn; and Herr Georg Gottfried Blinzing, commissioned city musicians at the princely Württemberg capital city, Tübingen; his especially highly honored, worthy and well-loved gentlemen and friends.[37]

After Speer became associated with the Latin School in Göppingen-Württemberg, he published an educational treatise on various instruments called, *Musicalisches Kleeblatt*. This work contains a number of smaller wind ensemble compositions, such as sonatas for three trombones, etc. Two additional publications of Speer are now lost, but almost certainly were part of the civic wind band literature of the seventeenth century. There were a dance collection, *Joco-seria* (after 1688) and another 'Klee-Blatt' volume with five-part instrumental compositions published after 1697.

Original sonatas, intradas, etc., exist in great number and include many of the distinguished composers of the German Baroque, including Kindermann, Schmelzer, Biber, Graun, Hassler, Schein, etc.

The Stadtpfeifers also participated in the ceremonies of those institutions which were virtually inseparable from the town itself, the church (which I shall discuss below) and the university.

Our American commencement ceremonies, usually the only occasion for which the faculty don their regalia, are only a pale reminder of the rich and more numerous ceremonies of the early universities. The annual celebration of the founding of Leipzig University in 1709 began early in the morning with twenty cannon shots followed by ringing of bells from throughout the city. From the two main towers of the city one heard the tower musicians performing both sacred and secular music.[38] During a banquet, celebrating the two hundredth anniversary of the founding of Marburg University, held in 1727, one heard a band of oboes and horns performing in alternation with an ensemble of trumpets and timpani.[39]

During the ceremony for the awarding of the doctorate at the university in Mainz, in 1663, one heard trumpet fanfares and also music by a wind band of oboes, shawms, and bassoons.[40] A similar ceremony honoring the new doctorates at

[37] Quoted in Mitchel Sirman, 'The Wind Sonatas in Daniel Speer's Musicalisch-Türkischer Eulen-Spiegel' (Dissertation, University of Wisconsin, 1972), 32.

[38] Schering, *Musikgeschichte Leipzigs*, 2:41–42.

[39] Heinz Oepen, *Beiträge zur Geschichte des Kölner Musiklebens, 1760–1840* (Cologne: Arno Volk-Verlag, 1955), 27.

[40] Adam Gottron, *Mainzer Musikgeschichte von 1500 bis 1800* (Mainz: Auslieferung durch die Stadtbibliothek, 1959), 64–65.

the University of Köln, in 1600, included a performance by four 'Herren Spilleuth' (Spielleute: here wind players) who were paid in food and drink.[41]

As official representatives of the town, the Stadtpfeifers performed in any ceremony involving a visiting dignitary and in fact one reads of a Stadtpfeifer losing his job for refusing to play when the elector rode through Eilenburg in 1624.[42]

The Stadtpfeifers also played for the townspeople, of course, in all of their important festivals and celebrations. I have mentioned above the 1731 procession of the Nürnberg carpenters, which included three wind bands, each of three oboes, two horns, and bassoon.[43] For a festival procession in Halle in 1616, the 'Procession of Savages' (Aufzug der wilder Männer), one sees a large wind band of four crumhorns, shawms, and cornetts.[44]

For the civic shooting match in Bitterfeld, in October 1734, the civic wind band (oboes and trumpets) played before the 'Capitains' house, at eight o'clock in the morning, a chorale and a special 'Riflemen's March.' This was followed by performance in a procession to the shooting grounds and the playing of trumpets and timpani throughout the match itself.[45]

In addition to their official appearances for civic events, in the church, for the universities, etc., the Stadtpfeifers were sometimes required to participate in court activities, in those cases where a nearby court did not have its own complete musical establishment.[46]

One can believe these civic wind band musicians must have often felt over-worked, but over-work is always better than no work. In this regard, death was a special enemy of the seventeenth-century German civic bandsman for following the death of any nobleman, not to mention the occasional plague, periods of public mourning were declared during which there could be no public festivities, not even weddings. For a minor nobleman's death such periods could last as long as two-months; two months with no outside income! In the case of the death of a higher nobleman, such as the death of an elector, this period could last an entire year, spelling near disaster for a Stadtpfeifer. No wonder Kuhnau observed, 'Nobody will pray more devoutly for the long life of his sovereign than the instrumentalists!'[47]

[41] Nan Cooke Carpenter, *Music in the Medieval and Renaissance Universities* (Norman: University of Oklahoma Press, 1954), 243.

[42] Werner, *Kirchenmusik*, 216.

... weil er bei der Kurfürstlichen Durchreise nicht abgeblasen ...

[43] Braun, 'Entwurf für eine Typologie der "Hautboisten",' 54.

[44] W. Gerauth, *Musikgeschichte der Stadt Halle* (Halle, 1931), II/I, 17–19.

[45] Werner, *Kirchenmusik*, 230.

[46] Ibid., 223.

[47] Manfred Bukofzer, *Music in the Baroque Era* (New York: Norton, 1947), 406.

All things considered, these civic wind band players were probably better off than most musicians of this time.[48] The Kapellemeister of the Weissenfel court, Johann Beer, writes of his envy of the civic musician.

> … many princely musicians long for the city, because the service in the court is so insecure and he must be ready to move if the support for music by the noble fails or if he decides to cut back. What good are riches without stability? I say continued poverty could be called better luck than irregular riches, where one may go from a horse to an ass and from the ass even to sit in the dust.
>
> …
>
> (In the city one can hope for quicker advancement) … this has the civic musician, but at court even if he had a doctorate in all three faculties he waits without hope. The more excellent he is, the more he will remain in his station which he once accepted, to remain used, all feathers plucked from his wings so he can not hope to soar higher.[49]

The civic wind bands organized themselves into strong guilds, primarily to control competition and to establish and maintain their 'rights.'[50] Indeed, in the years immediately after the Thirty Years War, one see an extraordinary gathering of forty such guilds from upper and lower Saxony, in an instrumental music 'Collegium,' through which they hoped to strengthen these rights.[51]

In Leipzig, the civic band guild also controlled the rights of the regular Stadtpfeifers as opposed to their adjunct, and lesser esteemed, colleagues, the Kunstgeigers. Even so famous a player as Reiche had to wait in Leipzig for eighteen years before being admitted as a Stadtpfeifer. Once admitted, the Stadtpfeifer seems to have held his position for life, as the average tenure in the eighteenth century was thirty-three years!

The Stadtpfeifers were a proud ensemble and were contemptuous of the lower Kunstgeigers, even though most of them had been Kunstgeigers earlier in their careers. The Stadtpfeifers reserved for themselves all the important weddings and civic affairs, leaving to the Kunstgeigers an endless round of minor weddings and civic functions.[52]

[48] A comparison of pay for civic and court players can be found in Werner, *Kirchenmusik*, 241ff.

[49] *Musikalischen Diskursen* (1719), quoted in Werner, *Kirchenmusik*, 223.

> Viele fürstliche Musiker sehnen sich nach den Städten weil der Dienst an den höfen so unsicher ist und er den Wanderstab ergreifen muss, sobald man aus der Gunst der herren fällt oder die Musik am hofe eingeschränkt wird. Was ist aber Reichtum ohne Bestand? Ich sage: Die beständige Armut könne glückseliger geheissen werden, als ein unbeständiger Reichtum, da man vom Pferd auf den Esel und von dem Esel gar in den Staub sitzen muss.
>
> ……
>
> … dessen hat sich ein Musikus, und ob er in allen dreien Fakultäten Doktor wäre, bei hofe nicht zu getrösten. Je erzellenter er ist, je mehr wird er eben bei der Station, dazu er einmal angenommen, zu bleiben genötigt und ihm alle Federn aus den Flügeln gerupft, damit er sich nicht hoher aufschwingen möge.

[50] Arno Werner, *Städtische und fürstliche musikpflege in Weissenfels* (Leipzig, 1911), 6S.

[51] Werner, *Städtische und fürstliche musikpflege in Zeitz*, 40

[52] Rasmussen, *Historical notes to Sonata*.

Most of the extant regulations of these guilds deal with the arrangements for performing at private weddings, which seem to have been an important source of extra income. Some of these weddings employed numerous wind and percussion players, as for example one in Danzig in 1670.

> ... with the drums which first played on their own for a while, after which the trumpets joined in, and then the sackbuts, Storten and cornetts.[53]

No doubt the Stadtpfeifers wanted to guarantee that they were central to such large productions. The guild ordinances in Zeitz allowed a bride and groom to bring in outside musicians, but only after they had 'come to terms' with the local Stadtpfeifers.[54]

I would like to summarize the guild regulations for a large instrumental guild[55] in the Alsace region for these ordinances of 1606[56] are probably typical of all such guild regulations. This guild was formed under the House of Ribeaupierre and led by a 'king' (König or Pfeifferkönig).

1. No wind player, string player or other musician may play by day or night, in the street or in a house for dances or dinners, nor may he receive money or gifts, unless he is first admitted to the fraternity of musicians of Alsace, under penalty of confiscation of his instrument; the same is true for minstrels ...
2. Each new member must swear to be obedient to the king and the brotherhood statutes.
3. Each member when in uniform must wear a silver medal showing the Queen Mother of God.
4. Upon entering the fraternity he must show his birth certificate and have a signed authorization by the noble of the area he comes from.
5. To be admitted a player in the city, a minstrel must have served two years apprenticeship.
6. The right to join as an apprentice, or to resign an apprenticeship, costs 12 Strasbourg 'schellings.'
7. To become a fraternity member, or to resign, costs two 'écus d'Empire.'
8. All the members will assist with the annual musicians day festival (Pfeiffertag) and are exempt from annual taxes.
9. On the day of this celebration, the entire fraternity must meet at the church, then to the castle to give hommage to the noble. Each of them has to take part in the fraternity meal and take his turn at

[53] Hermann Rausching, *Geschichte der Musik und Musikpflege in Danzig* (Danzig, 1931), 87.
... mit den Heerpauken welche erstlich eine weile allein gespielet, darnach die Trompeten dazugestossen, darauff die posaunen Storten und Cornetten folgeten ...

[54] Werner, *Städtische und fürstliche musikpflege in Zeitz*.

[55] This is perhaps the guild in Strassburg, mentioned by Ehmann, *Tibilustrium*, 28, which he says had seven hundred and fifty-one members in 1745.

[56] The original text is given in M. B. Bernhard, 'Notice sur la Confrèrie des Joueurs d'Instruments d'Alsace,' in *La Revue historique de la Noblesse* (Paris, 1844), 8ff.

the dance which the king will have arranged with the host. The king is exempt from (playing for the dance) along with two colleagues; the four masters, or jurists, do only half.

10. If a member, through illness or by order of the noble, can not take part in this festival, he must justify it with good evidence and send his annual tax.
11. Each member has to pay to the sergeant who announces him.
12. Each year, at the time of this festival, the members must renew their certification that they are on the roles of the fraternity. Without this certificate they are prevented from playing their instruments …
13. If a member leaves the fraternity and wishes to return he must pay one 'écu d'Empire.'
14. Upon the death of a member, his best musical instrument and his medal belong to the king of the fraternity.
15. A member does not have to have apprentices.
16. None will play instruments at dinners, dances, festivals day or night, indoors or out without being contracted through the fraternity.
17. If someone makes a contract with a musician after he has made a contract with a first one, the former does not have to play unless the latter receives a salary equal as if he had played.
18. No musician has to play with a musician who is not a member of the fraternity.
19. One does not play instruments for the wedding of a Jew who has not paid a golden gulden, which must be given to the king.
20. All difficulties relative to the profession, contracts contrary to the statutes and injuries between members, etc., are settled by a tribunal of the fraternity and the king.
21. On the day of the annual festival no player has to play elsewhere than the place of the festival.
22. All infractions of the statutes are judged by the king or in combination with a tribunal of the fraternity. Fines, according to the nature of the infraction, will be paid in money which goes to the chapelle de Notre-Dame …
23. A member can appeal the judgement of the king or the tribunal to the court.
24. This fraternity having been founded in the glory of God and in particular in honor of his very saintly mother, each member must annually say a Mass, and not just to help with the annual festival, to help honor all the festivities of Notre-Dame …
25. The Noble reserves the right to change these ordinances according to the needs of the time.

In spite of these strong civic wind band organizations and the fine literature they inspired, the seventeenth century was the last chapter of German civic wind bands in the development which began in the Middle Ages. Some activity would continue into the Classic Period, and of course an entirely new kind of civic music appears in the nineteenth century, but the kind of civic wind bands seen thus far in these volumes seem to have lost their momentum.[57] By 1750 they were in general decline and one sees the musicians taking other work.[58]

But if the wind bands died, their heritage as civic musical institutions did not. It was these same wind players and their string colleagues, often in cooperation between town and court musicians,[59] who performed in the first civic orchestras of the modern tradition.

The civic wind players were also active in the civic Collegium Musicum groups throughout Germany. There were student organizations which met, sometimes in coffee houses, for the performance and enjoyment of music. One of the most famous of these was the one in Leipzig, sometimes conducted by Bach, from which one can trace an almost direct line of development to the establishment of the Gewandhaus in the late eighteenth century.[60]

While traditional scholars in writing on the subject of the development of the symphony have focused primarily on the development of the form, there was also an independent development of the medium itself. I believe that when this subject receives further study it will be seen that the civic wind bands were present at the birth and passed on their heritage of organization and musical discipline.

---

[57] Werner, *Städtische und fürstliche musikpflege in Zeitz*, 40, points to the Thirty Years War as slowing down the progress of these institutions.

[58] Braun, 'Entwurf für eine Typologie der "Hautboisten",' 55, cites several oboists who became organists at this time.

[59] Smithers, *The Music and History of the Baroque Trumpet*, 129–130, cites examples of such cooperation by musicians in Neuburg, Ansbach, Bremen, Hannover, and Halle.

[60] Grove 10:637.

13 Civic Wind Bands in England

The usual size of English civic wind bands during the seventeenth century was five players. In many cases the fifth player was only added early in the century, as one can see in Bristol where the town council decided in 1619 that the band needed strengthening and voted funds 'to a fifth man to play with the other musitions of the City on the saggebutt to make up a fifth part.'[1]

As during the sixteenth century, these bands continued to wear uniforms of bright colors. One could see the band from Morpeth (1632) in green coats, drab knee breeches, each with a silver badge on his right arm; or in Pontefract (1657) in 'Coates of blew clothe and fac'd with white taffity'; or in London (1660) in gowns and silver chains, 'with one quartermaster and one conductor.'[2]

However, in general, the seventeenth century, while rich in references to English wait (wind) bands, represents as in Germany the final chapter of their extraordinary Medieval and Renaissance traditions. In England one sees the wind tradition diluted by the demands for the players to learn the new string instruments and even to be proficient in singing. Thus a famous description of the Norwich Waits, in 1600:

> Passing the gate ... where ... stood the Citty Waytes ... such Waytes (under *Benedicite* be it spoken) fewe Cities in our Realme have the like, none better; who beside their excellency in wind instruments, their rare cunning on the Vyoll and Violin, theyr voices be admirable, everie one of them able to serve in any Cathedral Church in Christendoome for Quiristers.[3]

The gradual breakdown of these old traditions also resulted in a breakdown of the normal professional disciplines, as one can see in numerous examples of various civic wait bands being reprimanded or even discharged by their civic governments. In Canterbury, in 1640, an escutcheon painted for the waits to wear was withdrawn, 'on accounts of disorders and misbehaviour.'[4] In Durham, in 1684, the Consistory Court

---

[1] Bridge, 'Town Waits and their Tunes,' *Proceedings of the Musical Association* 54 (1927–1928): 75.

[2] Lyndesay G. Langwill, *The Waits* (Hinrichsen, 1952), 175; and Bridge, 'Town Waits and their Tunes,' 75.

[3] The Morris Dancer, Kemp, quoted in Bridge, 'Town Waits and their Tunes,' 85.

[4] Ibid., 73.

took note of the fact that one of the waits had been discharged and ordered no longer to play in the city or the suburbs, for 'indecent expression' toward the mayor of the city.[5]

[5] Ibid., 72.

A drawing of a group of town waits (attributed to Marcellus Laroon), ca. 1680

Sometimes the entire band was fired, as was the case in Leicester (1602), Manchester (1620), and Coventry (1635).[6] In one rather unique case, the Chester wind band seems to have vanished entirely in 1612 with no explanation.

[6] Walter Woodfill, *Musicians in English Society* (Princeton: Princeton University Press, 1953), 88.

> Geo. Musitian exhibiteth his petician desiring that he and his fellow musitians may be admitted Waytes of this Cittie instead of the waytes now absent, finding instruments of his own charge to perform the service; which is deferred to be graunted untill it may be understode what are become of the ould waytes.[7]

[7] Bridge, 'Town Waits and their Tunes,' 73.

The well-known Norwich Waits also seem to have been discharged in 1622 and a civic order relative to this provides an interesting inventory of the instruments which the city had provided them.

The Waytes discharged and desired to deliver their instruments several of which they had sold, but delivered as follows: Three Sackbuts, four Hoboyes and an old one broken, two tenor Cornetts, one Treble recorder, two Counter-Tenor Recorders, five Chaynes and five Flaggs.[8]

By 1676 only three members of this band survived. They and the widows of the two deceased members had among them five sackbuts, three cornetts, three hautboys, together with the same five sets of chains and flags.[9]

Even the proud London waits seem to have experienced the general decline in the fortunes of the seventeenth century waits, or so it would seem in the evident loss of esprit de corps reflected in the following 1625 edict by the civic government:

> … through the contentions and ill dispositions of some particular persons of this society (of waits) the whole company suffereth often in their credits and reputations by uncivil and retorting of bitter and unsavory jests and calumnious aspersions upon one or other of them; which only nourish the discord and confusion amongst them with continual quarreling and heart burning yea especially in the times of their service to his honorable city.[10]

By the beginning of the eighteenth century the decline of the London Waits was such that now they were the object of cruel humor in contemporary literature, a sad contrast with their earlier role as representatives of civic pride.

> We blundered on in pursuit of our felicity, but scarce had walked the length of a horse's tether, ere we heard a noise so dreadful and surprising, that we thought the devil was riding on hunting through the City, with a pack of deep-mouthed hell-hounds, to catch a brace of tallymen for breakfast. At last bolted out fro the corner of the street, with an ignis fatuus dancing before them, a parcel of strange hobgoblins covered with long frieze rugs and blankets, hooped round with leather girdles from their cruppers to their shoulders, and their noddles buttoned up into caps of martial figure, like a knight-errant at tilt and tournament with his wooden head locked in an iron helmet.
>
> One was armed, as I thought, with a faggot-bat, and the rest with strange wooden weapons in their hands in the shape of clyster pipes, but as long, almost, as speaking-trumpets. Of a sudden they raised them to their mouths, and made such a frightful yelling, that I thought the world had been dissolving and the terrible sounds of the last trumpet to be within an inch of my ears.

[8] Ibid., 79.

[9] Grove 13:329. A sale of wait instruments by the city of Leicester in 1636 included 'Two horns, two clarionets' (clarions?), four piccaloes, and a bassoon.' (Bridge, 'Town Waits and their Tunes,' 79)

[10] Woodfill, *Musicians in English Society*, 43–44.

Under these amazing apprehensions I asked my friend what was the meaning of this infernal outcry? 'Prithee,' says he, 'what's the matter with thee? Why these are the City waits, who play every winter's night through the streets.'

'Lord bless me!' said I, 'I am very glad it's no worse. Prithee let us make haste out of the hearing of them.'

At this my friend laughed at me. 'Why, what,' says he, 'don't you love music? These are the topping tooters of the town, and have gowns, silver chains, and salaries, for playing *Lillabolaro* to my Lord Mayor's Horse through the City.'

'Marry,' said I, 'if his horse liked their music no better than I do, he would soon fling his rider for hiring such bugbears to affront his ambleship.'[11]

[11] Ned Ward, *The London Spy*, ed. Arthur Hayward (New York: Doran, 1927), 29–30.

The border of a writing sampler, issued by James Cole in 1742 illustrates 'The Procession of the Lord Mayor.' By this date the civic waits, called here, 'City Musick,' are no longer playing the instruments of the Renaissance, but the pre-Harmoniemusik instruments of the Classic Period (here, three oboes and two bassoons).[12]

There are several accounts of massed bassoon ensemble performances in England at the end of the Baroque. A concert given at Stationers' Hall in London, on 22 February 1713, advertised,

[12] The engraving is reproduced in Edward Croft-Murray, 'The Wind-Band in England, 1540–1840,' in *Music and Civilisation*, plate 109.

Among other choice Compositions, a celebrated Song of Mr. Hendel's by a Gentlewoman from Abroad, who hath never before exposed her Voice publickly in this kingdom. To which will be added an uncommon piece of Musick by Bassoons only.[13]

[13] Quoted in John Ashton, *Social Life in the Reign of Queen Anne* (London: Chatto & Windus, 1911), 277.

An even more extraordinary advertisement for a concert at Lincoln's Inn Theatre, in 1744, promised a,

new concerto grosso of 24 bassoons, accompanied by Signor Caporale on the violoncello, intermixed with Duettos by 4 doublebassoons, accompanied by a German flute, the whole blended with numbers of violins, hautboys, fifes, tombany's, French horns, trumpets, drums and kettle-drums.[14]

[14] *General Advertiser* (London, October 21, 1744).

One would be tempted to read this advertisement as merely a humorous one were it not for evidence of another performance by the twenty-four bassoons (surely after the famous 'Twenty-Four Violins' of Louis XIV) the following year.

According to Stephen, Johann Ernst Galliard (1687–1749) composed a work for twenty-four bassoons and four string basses for a benefit performance in 1745.[15]

[15] Leslie Stephen, *Biographie National* (London, 1885)

The English civic wind bands of the Baroque performed a wide variety of services for the public. Of these, the appearances one would wish to know more about today are the ones for which the least information is extant: the concerts. We know that both the Norwich and London wait bands, at least, gave regular performances of a concert nature.[16] In London this was already an old tradition and an interesting dramatic entertainment staged in 1656 by Davenant, 'after the manner of the ancients,' included a 'Concert of music imitating the Waits of London.'[17] An edict by the London Court of Aldermen in 1625 renewed the demand for concerts from the turret of the Royal Exchange, 'upon such days and at such times as have been anciently observed.'[18] This refers to the traditional concerts began by the London Waits in 1571 and given every Sunday and holiday evening from seven to eight o'clock in the evening. It is one of the many contributions which the wind band has made to our culture which one fails to find in the standard histories on music. In this case, as Woodfill observes,

[16] Woodfill, *Musicians in English Society*, 81; and Mary Ede, *Arts and Society in England under William and Mary* (London: Stainer and Bell), 94–95.

[17] Bridge, 'Town Waits and their Tunes,' 67.

[18] Woodfill, *Musicians in English Society*, 50.

> It places the earliest public concerts in England a century before the concerts begun by John Banister in 1672, the accepted date for the first public concerts in England. Banister's concerts stand as the first commercial venture of the kind in London, but take second place to the waits' concerts for antiquity and continuity of existence.[19]

[19] Ibid.

It was for these concerts, in part, that the London Waits held regular rehearsals on Monday mornings from eight o'clock until noon.[20]

Far more ancient than concerts, of course, was the watch duty from a city tower. By the seventeenth century in London two kinds of watch were known, the tower watch and a more ceremonial, processional one which was something like a military review. A description from 1618 pictures the latter.

[20] Ibid., 44.

> Then had yee besides the standing watches, all in bright harnesse, in every Ward and streete of this Citie and Suburbs, a marching watch, that passed through the principal streets thereof ... The marching watch

contained in number 2000 men, part of them being old Souldiers, of skill to bee Captaines, Lieutenants, Serieants, Corporals, etc., Riflers, Drummers, and Fifes ... Sword-players, Trumpeters on horsebacke ...[21]

[21] Quoted in Don Smithers, *The Music and History of the Baroque Trumpet*, 117.

The older original form of watch also continued, as one can see in the appointment of two new waits in Rochester in 1640.

Edward Rolfe and John Aleworth, Musicians, were sworne this day Freemen of this Citty, and in regard their freedoms were given them freely by the Citty, they do promise in lieue thereof to play through the Citty every morning upon their lowed musicke[22] called the weightes between Hollantide and Candlemas as usually done in the Cittyes of London and Canterbury.[23]

[22] 'Loud Music' was a synonym for wind music.

[23] Bridge, 'Town Waits and their Tunes,' 74.

In London this wait tradition was carried on by groups of four wind players, performing a more musical or entertainment function than a real watch.[24] In fact, there is some evidence that the citizens had become tired of this nightly performance, as in Aberdeen, where this role was performed by a bagpiper, one reads that the magistrates decided to discharge,

[24] Woodfill, *Musicians in English Society*, 46–47.

the common piper of all going through the town at nycht, or in the morning, in tyme coming, with his pype—it being an incivill forme to be usit within sic a famous burghe, and being often found fault with, als weill by sundrie nichtbouris of the toune as by strangers.[25]

[25] Francis Collinson, *The Bagpipe* (London: Routledge, 1975), 98.

A civic edict from 1677 in London sought to limit the number of musicians in the streets during the night. Edicts of this nature during earlier centuries were given from a sincere concern that extraneous musical sounds might be confused with real watch alarms. Here, on the other hand, perhaps the sleepy citizens were concerned more about the noise of a now much larger city.

Foreign musicians, Swiss fiddlers, pipers, waits and others do frequently play up and down in all parts of this City, expressly contrary to divers good orders of the Common Council. On this the Court ordered and strictly enjoined that no manner of person or persons not being free of this city do use or exercise singing or playing upon any instrument in any common Hall, Tavern, Inn, Alehouse, or any other like place within this City or liberties. And Likewise that no manner of person (other than the Common Waits of this City) do play upon any instrument in any open Street or public passage within this City ... between the hours of ten o'clock in the evening and five in the morning. And the Master and Wardens of the Company of Musicians and also the Waits of this City are to take care that this order be duly complied with.[26]

In London, every great public celebration included performances by the civic waits. Among these were the annual Saint Bartholomew's Fair and the Vigil of St. John the Baptist. An eyewitness of the latter in 1618 describes the houses, each with green birch boughs on the doors, and 'Lamps of glasse, with Oyle burning in them all the night.'

> Then had yee besides the standing watches, all in bright harnesse, in every Ward and street of this Citie and Suburbs, a marching watch, that passed through the principal streets thereof … There werd also diuers Pageants, Morris dancers, Constables … The Waytes of the City.[27]

A visit by royalty was always cause for great public gatherings and an appearance by the waits. When the new King James arrived in London after the death of Elizabeth, the waits had to first perform as he entered the gate of the city, and then hurry ahead to 'Bowthome Barr,' where they would be waiting on a scaffold to perform once again when the king's procession passed.[28] In 1613, the city of Canterbury paid their five waits 'for playing the loud music, on the top of All Saint's Church,' when Prince Charles visited.[29]

The published order of the procession in Chester, in honor of the king's visit in 1610, included as the twelfth group in the parade, 'a noise of cornetts.'[30] In another reference, an eyewitness suggests that these appearances were not all 'noise' but some perhaps were musically satisfying. Describing the celebration of the king's return from Richmond in 1610, he remembers,

> bardges upon the water, with their streamers and ensignes gloriously displayed, drommes, trumpets, fifes, and other musikes attending on them, to awaite the Lord Maior and Aldermens' comming. No sooner had his honor and the rest taken bardge, but on they rowed, with such chearefull noyse of harmonie … as made the beholders and hearers not meanely delighted.[31]

[26] Quoted in an unsigned article in H. A. F. Crewdson, *The Worshipful Company of Musicians* (London: Charles Knight, 1971), 168.

[27] Alan Warwick, *A Noise of Music* (London: Queen Anne Press, 1968), 26.

[28] Woodfill, *Musicians in English Society*, 80.

[29] Ibid.

[30] John Nichols, *The Progresses of King James The First* (London, 1828), 294.

[31] Ibid., 318.

In seventeenth-century England, as in Germany, there were traditional university ceremonies celebrated with great pomp, including of course music. John Evelyn, who attended the dedication of the theater building at Oxford in 1669, mentions a wind band's participation and at the same time gives us the flavor of these ceremonies. The dedication, he writes, was conducted,

> with the greatest splendor & formalitie that might be, & therefore drew a world of strangers & other Companie to the University from all parts of the Nation: The Vice-Chancelor then, Heads of Houses, & Doctors being seated in magisterial seates, the Vice-Chancellors Chaire & Deske, Proctors &c: covered with Brocatell & Cloth of Gold: The Universitie Register read the Founders Grant & gift of it to the Universitie ... Then follow'd Dr. South the Universities Orators Eloquent Speech upon it; it was very long, & not without some malicious & undecent reflections on the Royal Society as underminers of the University, which was very foolish and untrue, as well as unseasonable ... the rest was in praise of the Arch Bish: and the ingenious Architect: This Ended, after loud Musique, from the Corridor above ... all of which lasted from 11 in the morning til 7 at night, which was likewise concluded with Bells ringing, & universal joy & feasting.[32]

[32] *The Diary of John Evelyn* (Oxford, 1955), 3:531–532, for July 9–10, 1669.

A similar ceremony at Oxford in 1634, for the laying of the cornerstone of what is now the Bodleian Library, included music by what was apparently a wind band in residence at the university itself. An eyewitness wrote that after all the officials were seated, 'the University Musicians who stood upon the leads at the west end of the Library sounded a lesson on their wind music.' At the conclusion of this particular ceremony, a scaffold broke and a hundred or so people, 'namely the Proctors, Principals of Hall, Masters, and some Bachelaurs fell down all together one upon another into the foundation.'[33]

A student at St. John's College in Cambridge has left a description in his diary of the celebration of the John Port Latin Day in 1618, including yet another mention of a wind band.

[33] Quoted in Nan Cooke Carpenter, *Music in the Medieval and Renaissance Universities*, 176–177.

> And after the feast in hall was ended, all the fellow-commoners and bachelors of the house, according to their annuary custom, went down the river to a pretty green near Chesterton, accompanied by a band of loud music.[34]

[34] Quoted in ibid., 196.

One wonders if they were the Cambridge Waits. Pepys, in his famous diary, recalls having heard them fifty years later, in 1667, when he was not impressed. 'But Lord!,' said he of the Cambridge Waits, 'what sad music they made.'[35]

[35] Quoted in Langwill, *The Waits*, 174.

There is also an eyewitness account of a student wind band, consisting perhaps of younger students, who performed before the queen when she visited in 1613. Returning from Bath, her route took her,

> over the downes at Wenskyke within the parish of Bishop's Cannings; of which Ferebe having timely notice, he composed a song in four parts, and instructed his scholars to sing it very perfectly, as also to play a lesson or two (which he had composed) on their wind instruments.[36]

[36] Quoted in Nichols, *The Progresses of King James The First*, 668.

As during the sixteenth century, the civic wait bands were hired to supply music for the theaters in London. An extraordinary testimonial to one of these performances comes to us from Samuel Pepys. The play, *The Virgin Martyr*, was pleasant, but not worth much, he wrote.

> But that which did please me beyond any thing in the whole world was the wind-musique when the angel comes down, which is so sweet that it ravished me, and indeed, in a word, did wrap up my soul so that it made me really sick, just as I have formerly been when in love with my wife; that neither then, nor all the evening going home, and at home, I was able to think of any thing, but remained all night transported, so as I could not believe that ever any musick hath that real command over the soul of a man as this did upon me: and makes me resolve to practice wind-musique, and to make my wife do the like.[37]

[37] *The Diary of Samuel Pepys* (London, 1924), 7:319–320, for February 25–27, 1668.

Pepys' choice of words reminds one of another reference to additional income available to the wait bands. The newspaper, *Tatler*, for 9 September 1710, notes,

> as the custom prevails at present, there is scarce a young man of any fashion in a Corporation who does not make love with the town music; the waits often help him through his courtship.[38]

[38] Quoted in Bridge, 'Town Waits and their Tunes,' 66.

The waits could also gain extra income by visiting and performing in other towns. The Chamberlains' accounts for 1615 in Coventry include payments on a single day (30 March) to the wait bands from Leicester, Nottingham, Sowtham, and

Shrewsbury.[39] All these forms of extra income for the civic wind players must have spelled the difference between life and death during a time when the salaries were meager and often late in coming. Sometimes the city council would withhold payment of wages as a form of punishment, as happened in 1637 to the London Waits when they sent substitutes instead of appearing themselves on a festival day.[40]

Yet another source of income for both the civic and the court wind players were the celebrations, especially the masques, given by the law schools, known collectively as the Inns of Court.[41] Eyewitnesses report a number of wind band appearances at these law schools during the 1612–1613 season, citing 'Loud musick' in masques by Chapman and Beaumont given at Lincoln's Inn and Gray's Inn, among others. The Beaumont masque began with a procession by water to the theater, 'with all variety of loud musick.' An earlier procession, on land, included burning torches and 'many trumpets sounding melodiously, which was a sight both to eye and eare, of exceeding glorie.'[42] The following year, *The Masque of Flowers* was given at Gray's Inn and an observer wrote, 'The Daunce ended, the lowd musicke sounded.'[43]

A final use of civic musicians in London might be of interest. A note in the autobiographical materials of John Eyelyn, relative to a discussion of London weather, mentions,

> At the Thames they beate drumms, to direct the Watermen to make the shore, no lights being bright enough to penetrat the fogg.[44]

Unfortunately, while there is a fair amount of extant musical literature which was composed for court wind bands and may have also been used by the civic wind bands, virtually no music has survived which was composed directly for these wait bands. There are a few surviving melodies, called 'Wait Tunes,' with names like 'London Waits,' which must have some relationship with the early waits.[45]

Finally, a few notes on the last chapter of the ancient minstrels in London. The guild of independent minstrels had reached a low ebb at the end of the sixteenth century, but seems to have attempted a restoration of their fortunes early during the seventeenth century by gaining a new charter in 1604. Now called 'Master Wardens and Commonalty of the

---

[39] Woodfill, *Musicians in English Society*, 284.

[40] Ibid.

[41] Many of the individual wind players are identified in Robert Wienphal, *Music at the Inns of Court* (Ann Arbor: California State Univeristy Northridge, 1979).

[42] Nichols, *The Progresses of King James The First*, 592ff., 579, 550–551.

[43] Ibid., 742.

[44] Evelyn, *The Diary of John Evelyn*, 5:363, for November 5, 1699.

[45] For further information on ten of these tunes, see Langwill, *The Waits*, 178.

Art or Science of the Musicians of London,' their charter includes many familiar regulations, such as restricting members from performing with non-members and reserving all weddings for members of the guild. Two new regulations are interesting, one stating that the wind players must not play in fewer numbers than four, 'in consort with violins.' Another provision rules against going about the city with an instrument uncased or uncovered.[46] This was no doubt intended to distinguish themselves from the poor wandering minstrel, playing in the streets with no case.

Unfortunately, the new zeal of this guild caused a sense of alarm on the part of the royal musicians, who refused to consider themselves related to minstrels or their guild. They set out in 1634 to deliberately destroy the independent minstrel guild by asserting in court that the recent charter had been obtained on the basis of fraudulent application; this view prevailed and the guild died.

Without the protection of a guild the musicians who were not regularly employed, the true minstrels, were once again classed with the lowest persons. In a debate on a 'Bill touching rouges, vagabonds and sturdy beggars,' during Cromwell's Parliament of 1656, a Mr. Robinson hoped that 'fiddlers and minstrels would be included, as they did corrupt the manners of the people and inflame their debauchery by lewd and obscene songs.' The Alderman Hooke responded, 'I hope you intend not to include the *waits* of the city of London which are a great preservation of men's houses in the night.'[47]

Under such increasing pressures from royal and civic ordinances, the minstrel who carried on the medieval tradition of wandering freely from town to town did not survive the seventeenth century in England.

[46] This discussion is taken from Crewdson, *The Worshipful Company of Musicians*, 40.

[47] Quoted in Bridge, 'Town Waits and their Tunes,' 67–68.

14 Civic Wind Bands in the Low Countries

WHEN ONE THINKS of the civic wind bands of the Low Countries during the seventeenth century, one thinks of the *ommegang* processions in which participated civic officials, religious and military organizations, and guilds. There were decorated wagons depicting historical and religious themes together with the more fantastic and allegorical. What had begun centuries before as a purely religious event was, by the seventeenth century, a much broader civic celebration.

In May 1615, the Archduchess Isabella visited Brussels resulting in a great celebration which began with the traditional 'Shooting of the Popinjay,' an ancient ceremony still observed in the Netherlands. In this ceremony crossbowmen shot at the figure of a parrot, made of wood, mounted on top of a high pole—something like a May pole. The visiting Archduchess was invited to try her hand with the crossbow and of course everything was arranged so that she would appear to hit the target on her first try. Her 'success' in this event led to her being crowned 'Queen of the Festival,' which followed for a period of thirteen days.

To capture all these events for posterity, Isabella commissioned the painter, Anthonis Sallaert, to paint a large pictorial record of the festival. In the painting of the opening event we see the Brussels civic band, a six-member band with cornett, trombone, curtal, and three shawms of at least two sizes. The

Archduchess Isabelle and Archduke Albert at the Procession of the Maids of the Sablon, Anthonis Sallaert, 1615

trombonist appears to be holding a piece of music in his hand, which has led to the suggestion that perhaps he played the cantus firmus above which the other musicians improvised.[1]

Following the ceremony with the crossbows, a procession on a fairly small scale occurred, the 'Procession of the Maids of Sablon,' which celebrated Isabella's donation of a large sum of money, the interest of which was to be divided each year among six girls of poor, but honest parents. In Sallaert's painting of this procession we see the same town band just ahead of the statue of the Virgin, which is being held high in the air. A second painting of the procession, seen in a different part of town, pictures the band but with the cornett player missing and the trombonist with a full head of hair, whereas he was bald in the first painting![2]

On 15 May, the *ommegang* took place and because this was the greatest event of her visit, Isabella commissioned the court painter, Dennis van Alsloot, to paint six canvases as a record of the procession. The sixth of these paintings shows the civic wind band of six players, marching in front of the statue of the Virgin again. Alsloot painted the same band the following year in his 'Procession of the Religious Orders of Antwerp on the Feast Day of the Rosary.'[3]

[1] Richard Leppert, 'Musical Instruments and Performing Ensembles in Flemish Paintings of the Seventeenth Century', 165ff.

[2] Leppert, ibid., 168.

[3] Now in the Museo del Prado, Madrid.

Denis van Alsloot, *Procession en l'honneur de Notre-Dame du Sablon a Bruxelles le 31 mai*

An account of an *ommegang* in Ieper in 1617 includes among the musicians in the procession a player of the 'clockspeelder,' which I take to be a glockenspiel.[4] In Gand, in 1697, a civic timpani player appears.[5]

A description of an *ommegang* at the end of the Baroque is quite different, for in this procession, in Grammont in 1718, one sees the town band using the Hautboisten instruments, oboes and bassoons.[6]

Concerts by the civic wind bands of the Low Countries continued during the seventeenth century. A civic edict from Mechlin (1606) describes very carefully several characteristics of these concerts. They were to occur every Sunday and feast day, for one half-hour, from eleven to eleven thirty o'clock in the morning. The musicians were to play the concert, 'for the honor of the city,' on 'schalmayen, trompettes et autres instruments.' To prepare these concerts the band was ordered to rehearse at least twice per week.[7]

Another civic document which speaks of concerts for the reputation and honor of the city comes from Gand in 1620. Here one reads that the six members of the civic wind band performed from the civic bell tower for the entire summer season.[8] Vander Straeten also documents a concert by the new Hautboisten band of oboes and bassoons in Audenarde, in 1700, where this instrumentation is found at least two years earlier.[9]

The movement of Italian styles into the northern countries hastened the decline of the old guilds, which had always fought to restrict musical performances in a particular city to themselves. In Brussels there were civic edicts in 1606, 1651, 1662, 1665, 1682, 1685, 1699, and 1721, all intended to support the wind guild's attempt to protect their territory. But because of the entertainment offered so many people by opera, comedies, and public balls, the city informed the civic wind guild that these events were now exempt from the ban on foreign players. In no time at all, one sees the names of many foreigners in the lists of performers for opera here.[10]

---

[4] Comptes de la ville d'Ypres, quoted in Edmond Vander Straeten, *La Musique aux Pays-Bas* (Brussels, 1867), 2:317.

[5] Ibid., 4:129.

[6] Ibid., 4:74.

[7] Raymond Van Aerde, *Ménéstrels communaux ... á Malines, de 1311 à 1790* (Malines, 1911), 40–41.

[8] Comptes de la ville de Gand, quoted in Vander Straeten, *La Musique aux Pays-Bas*, 4:128.

> Betaelt de ses scalmeyers deser stede, over ende ter causer dat sy ghespeelt hebben up den belfort, tot reputaetie ende erre deser stede, alleenelick binnen de somer saisoene van den jaer deser rekenynghe ... xxvijen martij 1620.

[9] Ibid., 4:74.

[10] Ibid., 1:135ff.

15 Civic Wind Bands in France

ONE MIGHT ASSUME that the civic wind band tradition of sixteenth-century France continued into the seventeenth century, but because of the interest in court music, which reaches such a great height during this century, there seems to have been little research done in the field of civic musical institutions.

There is an eyewitness description of civic wind music in Bordeaux, in 1631, but it mentions only trumpets.

> At Bordeaux our public administrators, known as jurats or aldermen, have two officers each of them whom carries before them a long, straight silver trumpet with a banner attached bearing the arms of the city. But this takes place only on the occasion of city processions, bonfires or other public ceremonies. The same officers are employed with their trumpets to make public proclamations and are obliged to be present at executions of criminals condemned to undergo some punishment for their crimes as an example to their fellow men.[1]

[1] Trichet, *Traité des Instruments de Musique* [1631], quoted in Don Smithers, *The Music and History of the Baroque Trumpet*, 231.

There are also some interesting descriptions of wind ensembles in a more popular sense. In Paris, there were several annual fairs which created wide public interest and also made an important contribution to art, for here were performed the 'comédie en vaudevilles,' which grew into opéra comique. The most famous of these fairs, the Foire St. Germain, lasted from 3 February until Palm Sunday. Here one could see popular farces, acrobatic displays, animal shows, marionette plays, and hear music.[2] A contemporary poem, Scarron's 'La Foire St Germain' (1643), suggests that perhaps wind instruments were the primary music.

[2] Grove 18:728.

> The noise of the penetrating whistles,
> The flutes and the flageolets,
> The cornetts, oboes and musettes,
> The sellers and the buyers,
> These mingle with the acrobats,
> And the tambours with bells,
> Marionette players,
> That the people cry singers![3]

[3] Quoted in Clifford Barnes, 'Instruments and Instrumental Music at the "Théatres de la Foire",' in *Recherches sur la Musique francaise Classique* (1965), 5:142.

The *Mémoires* of the abbé de Marolles give an extended description of the Touraine countryside in the earliest years of the seventeenth century. Of particular interest is his description of a small village wedding which was not complete without a wind band concert.

> When our good people celebrated their children's marriages it was a delight to see how they dressed; for beside the bride's finery, never less than a red gown and a head-dress trimmed with tinsel and glass beads, the parents were clad in their own pleated blue dresses which they had taken from chests scented with lavender, dried roses and rosemary. I speak of men as much as of women for they too had their pleated cloaks which they wore over their shoulders with high stiff collars like those of certain monks. Peasant girls, their hair neatly arranged, flaunted parti-colored petticoats. Nor were wedding favors lacking; everyone wore them at his belt or on his shoulder. Then there was a concert with bagpipes, flutes and hautboys and, after a sumptuous banquet, country dancing which lasted until nightfall.[4]

[4] Michel de Marolles, *Les Mémoires de Michel de Marolles, abbé de Villeloin* (Paris, 1656–1657).

Finally, it may surprise the reader to learn that slave galleys were still common in southern Europe during the seventeenth century. John Evelyn visited Marseilles in 1644 and left an eyewitness account of his visit to the port where he saw more than twenty of these galleys at anchor. Some of these slaves were musicians and were allowed to play when the boat was at rest. Evelyn reports that in the case of the boat he visited they played mostly as a wind band (loud music) and only rarely as a 'soft musique.'

> The Captaine of the Gally royal gave us most courteous entertinment in his Cabine, the Slaves in the interim playing both on loud & soft musique very rarely: Then he shew'd us how he commanded their motions with a nod, & his Wistle, making them row out; which was to me the newest spectacle I could imagine, beholding so many hundreds of miserably naked Persons, having their heads shaven cloose, ... a payre of Course canvas drawers, their whole backs & leggs starke naked, doubly chained about their middle, & leggs, in Cupples, & made fast to their seates: and all Commanded ... by an Imperious & cruell seaman ... Their rising forwards, & falling back at their Oare, is a miserable spectacle, and the noyse of their Chaines with the roaring of the beaten Waters has something of strange & fearfull in it, to one unaccostom'd. They are ruld, & chastiz'd with a bullspizle dry's upon their backs & soles of their feete upon the least dissorder, & without the least humanity ... after we had bestow'd something amongst the Slaves, the Cap: sent a band of them to give us musique at dinner where we lodged.[5]

[5] *The Diary of John Evelyn*, 2:164–165, for October 7, 1644.

16 Civic Wind Bands in Italy

REFERENCES TO THE INSTRUMENTATION of civic wind bands in Italy during the seventeenth century vary with the location. In Modena, one reads of the performance of three cornetti and five trombones, conducted by Paolo Bravusi, given in celebration of the visit of Isabella of Savoy in 1608.[1] Another city which may have had a band with trombones was Siena, for the leader of this band, called the 'Cappella e del Concerto della Signoria,' was Alberto Gregori, who was considered the first trombonist of all Italy.[2] In Palermo, a civic document of 1619 speaks of the 'trombe et pifari' of the 'musica di citta.'[3]

Regarding Bologna, another city with a rich wind band tradition, an eyewitness in 1602 describes the two civic ensembles of the ruling city council.

> When they appear in public, these 'Signori' are dressed in rich robes of silk, and during the winter they are muffled up with very precious furs as well. They are accompanied by a very respectable household of eight trumpeters, with a drummer, or player of the nakers, who with these trumpets play certain Morish drums. To both the drums and trumpets are attached banners with the arms of liberty; also eight excellent musicians with trombones and cornettos.[4]

Another reference speaks of concerts played by the last mentioned civic wind band.

> The main piazzas of the city are the great piazza, called the 'Piazza del Comune,' where the 'Legato' and the governor and his 'Auditori' live; also the 'Gonfaloniere di Giustizia' with his 'Signori Antiani'; There the city government meets, and the 'Gonfalonieri del Popolo,' and a company of Italian light cavalry. Above the door of this Palace is placed a very beautiful bronze statue of Pope Gregory XIII, who came from Bologna, which was made by the Bolognese smith, Alessandro Mengati ... and there is a very beautiful arch or balcony of stone, where trumpets are played every evening. And after the trumpets have finished, very pleasant music is played on trombones and cornettos at the same Piazza as well as the great building of the church of St. Petronio.[5]

[1] Grove 3:221.

[2] Alessandro Vessella, *La Banda*, 96.

[3] G. Di Marzo, *Diario della città di Palermo*, 2:94.

[4] Vizani (1602), quoted in Don Smithers, *The Music and History of the Baroque Trumpet*, 77–78.

[5] Ibid.

Extant musical literature suggests such bands existed in both Rome and Venice, for there is a manuscript in Berlin composed in ca. 1700 for the 'Sonatori di fiato' by Francesso Magini, a professor at the conservatory of Rome, and the sonatas of Gussaghi (1608) are dedicated to the 'Excellent Virtuosi' of Venice, specifically the cornettist, Lodouico Cornale.

One must also mention the *Sonate/Symphonie* (1626) and *Sonate e sinfonie* (1629) of Biagio Marini, although neither is extant in a complete form. The latter was for two cornetti and three trombones, with one composition for four cornetts and four trombones.

17 Civic Wind Bands in Russia

ALTHOUGH RUSSIA is beyond the confines of this study, the reference found in *The New Grove Dictionary of Music and Musicians* to civic wind music there during the Baroque must be cited in the hope that some reader will investigate this topic further.

In Leningrad (St. Petersburg), the celebration of various military victories between 1702 and 1709 'required new forms of community music making: trumpets and kettledrums and large ensembles of wind instruments were used for open air festivals.'[1]

[1] Grove 10:659.

In another place one finds,

> In early 17th century Moscow there were many instrumentalists among whom the trumpeters enjoyed special respect, although ... it is impossible to determine exactly what instrument was played. A particularly large number of trumpeters appeared in 1660, suggesting an increased public interest in music. Their performing skill was prized and they were sufficiently highly paid for almost every trumpeter to purchase his own courtyard. In 1660 special teachers, 'mastera trubnovo ucheniya' (masters of trumpet teaching), like S. Burakov, appeared among the trumpeters. During this period the first state school for wind players, the S'ezhey Dvor Trubnovo Ucheniya (Assembly Court of Trumpet Teaching), was opened.[2]

[2] Ibid., 12:601.

PART 6
Church Wind Bands

18 Church Wind Bands in the Low Countries

BY THE SEVENTEENTH CENTURY, churches in the Low Countries had long been familiar with the use of wind instruments. Their influence can be seen in the multi-textured *Pieces d'orgue* by Lambert Chaumont (ca. 1630–1712), of Liège, where the composer includes contrapuntal movements with titles such as 'récits de cornet, tierces en taille, basses de trompettes, and basses de cromorne.'[1]

[1] Grove 4:181.

It is somewhat of a surprise, then, to find a voice questioning the propriety of instrumental music in the church. Libert Froidmont (d.1653), doctor of theology at the University of Louvain, wrote a treatise entitled, 'Is it necessary to hear the music of the Princes?,' where he complains the instruments only tend to obscure the voices. In the church, he says, one hears 'luths, lyres frémissantes, des clairons, des flutes, des cornets, des trompettes,' joined together with the sounds of the organ, to 'gargle' the praises of the noble.[2] Where such a view in England was the voice of Puritanism, here one wonders if it were not rather anti-monarchical in nature.

[2] Edmond Vander Straeten, *La Musique aux Pays Bas*, 1:186.

The bassoon appears frequently in church records of the Low Countries, no doubt used to strengthen the continuo as in the extant six-part Mass by Pierre Lamalle (1672), of Liège, which calls for obbligato bassoon and continuo.[3] Among these records are a few names of bassoon players: the parish church records of Alost mention in 1603–1605 'Hans Goderick … spelen op de fagotte';[4] Philippe Van Ranst was the 'premier fagotiste de la chapelle' of Albert and Isabelle in 1619 and a note relative to his retirement mentions thirty-five years of continuous service;[5] and accounts in the Cathedral in Antwerp mention the death of a church bassoonist, 'Elvigius, fagotista, obiit decembris 1639.'[6]

[3] Grove 10:390.

[4] Vander Straeten, *La Musique aux Pays Bas*, 4:74.

[5] Ibid., 4:75.

[6] Ibid., 4:73, fn. 2.

But there is evidence of a greater variety of winds used in the church, particularly in the town of Ieper. Here, in 1683, for the three hundredth anniversary of Notre-Dame de Thuin, one heard organ, trumpets, shawms, flutes, and even timpani.[7] The Church of Saint-Martin in the same town has extant documents which mention a variety of instruments. In

[7] Ibid., 4:135, fn. 3.

1618 one finds payment to a trumpet player (tubicen), Chrétien Pureur, for performing in both the vespers and the masses. In 1631 there is the first mention of a bassoonist (fagotum pro choro) in this church. During the early years of the eighteenth century one reads of payment to a 'serpentiste,' in 1730; the purchase of a bassoon in Brussels in 1735; and the purchase of an oboe, again in Brussels, in 1740.[8]

Finally, there are a few references to the use of wind instruments in the church dramas of the seventeenth century in the Low Countries. In Liège, in 1695, a prototype opera was given by the College of Jesuits in which the libretto is interspersed with instrumental interludes called 'Symphonie des Hautbois' and 'Symphonie de Flûte douces.'[9] In Brussels, in the same year, there was a 'biblical tragedy' during which the Brussels civic wind band, the 'Joueurs de hautbois de Bruxelles,' performed.[10]

[8] Ibid., 4:272–273, 289.

[9] Ibid., 3:52ff.

[10] Ibid., 4:184.

19   *Church Wind Bands in England*

FOR MOST OF THE SEVENTEENTH CENTURY, until after the restoration of Charles II, whenever instrumental music, other than the organ, was used in English cathedrals it seems to have been almost exclusively wind bands.

One sees them for the christening of Princess Mary at Greenwich in 1605,[1] for the visit of King James to Oxford in the same year,[2] and for the funeral of Prince Henry in 1612.[3] An eyewitness to the latter ceremony in the Chapel of St. James' Palace, wrote,

> the Gentlemen of the Kings' Chapel, with the Children thereof, sung divers excellent Anthems, together with the Organs and other wind Instruments.[4]

When King James visited St. Paul's Cathedral in 1620, another eyewitness recalled,

> it was being then three of the clocke, they began to celebrate Divine Service, which was solemnly performed with organs, cornets, and sagbots.[5]

Regular service in the church may have been required for the king's wind band, as suggested by a pay account for twelve wind players in 1633, under the title,

> Order to be observed throughout the year by his Majesty's musitions for the wind instruments for waiting in the Chappell.[6]

Following this practice of wind bands in the Service in London, the major cathedrals throughout England also employed them, including those of York, Norwich, Exeter, Winchester, Worcester, Salisbury, Durham, and Lincoln.[7] Furthermore, others came to England to hire the necessary wind players to participate in this tradition. One, Edward Kellie, Master of the Chapel Royal in Scotland, came to London in 1632 and,

[1] Edward F. Rimbault, *The Old Cheque-Book* (London, 1872), 168.

[2] Carpenter, *Music in the Medieval and Renaissance Universities*, 176.

[3] Thomas Birch, *The Life of Henry Prince of Wales* (London, 1760), 362.

[4] Charles Cornwallis, *An Account of the Baptism, Life, Death and Funeral of the most Incomparable Prince Frederick Henry, Prince of Wales* (London, 1751).

[5] Quoted in John Nichols, *The Progresses of King James The First* (London, 1828), 601.

[6] Quoted in Henry De Lafontaine, *The King's Musick* (London, 1909), 87.

[7] Andrew Parrott, 'Grett and Solompne Singing,' in *Early Music* 6, no. 2 (April 1, 1978): 184; Woodfill, *Musicians in English Society*, 149.

carryed home an organist and two men for playing on cornetts and sackbuts ... most exquisite in their severall faculties.[8]

The wind players for many of these services came from the fine civic wind bands, called waits. Civic pay records for performances by the waits in church are extant from Norwich (1638), Chester (1660s), and York (1602 and 1623), the last one reading, 'To the Waytes of York for playing in the Quire five services this year.'[9]

For the reader who may be surprised to find so many accounts of wind bands in the seventeenth-century church in England, let me point out that Parrott maintains that only one unquestionable reference can be found for this entire period which even mentions string instruments in the church.[10] Why, then, was there an almost exclusive preference for wind bands? One reason was the historic association of these instruments with the church, but a contemporary also offered the opinion that it was felt that wind instruments, and not strings, could play in tune!

> ... becaus *Entata* [stringed instruments] ar often out of tun; (Which soomtime happeneth in the mids of the Musik, when it is neither good to continue, nor to correct the fault) therefore, to avoid all offence (where the least shoolde not bee givn) in our Chyrch-solemnities onely the Winde-instruments (whose Notes ar constant) bee in use.[11]

The seventeenth century in England was a period of great religious upheaval and there were some opposed to any instrumental music in the church. The organ especially was held by many to be unsuitable, a view already long held by some. As early as the reign of Edward VI, the Lower House of Convocations listed organ playing among the '84 Faults and Abuses of Religion.'[12] During the reign of Elizabeth, a motion for the abolition of organ playing in churches failed by only a single vote.[13]

One of the objections to instrumental music in the church was that it obscured the words of the singers, the text being held more important than the music.

[8] William Dauney, *Ancient Scottish Melodies* (Edinburgh, 1838), 365.

[9] Bridge, 'Town Waits and their Tunes,' 71.

[10] Parrott, 'Grett and Solompne Singing,' 186.

[11] Charles Butler, *Principles of Musick* (1636), quoted in Parrott, ibid.

[12] Henry Davey, *History of English Music* (London: Curwen, 1921), 107.

[13] John Strype, *Annals of the Reformation* (London, 1709), 298–299.

… though it is not in Latin, yet by reason of the confusedness of voices of so many singers, with a multitude of melodious instruments … the greatest part of the service is no better understood, then if it weare in Hebrue or Irish.[14]

[14] John Cosin, 'The Correspondence of John Cosin, D.D.,' ed. George Ornsby, *Surtees Society* (London, 1869), LII, 166.

One preacher in Durham, in 1630, felt singing itself was inappropriate to the purpose of the service.

Our Durhamers have been so eager upon piping and singing, that instead of the Morning Prayer at 6. of the clock, which was wont to be read distinctly and plainly, for Schollers, and Artificers before they began their work, they brought in a solemne Service, with singing and Organs, Sackbuts and Cornets, little whereof could be understood of the people, neither would they suffer the Sacrament to be administered without a continuall noise of Musick, both instrumentall and vocal, to the great disturbance of these holy actions.[15]

[15] Peter Smart, *A Catalogue of Superstitious Innovations* (London, 1642), 9.

A large part of this concern was a puritanical desire to rid the service of everything extraneous to the simple presentation of the Anglican tenets. This same preacher, in a sermon in 1628, gave an example of this viewpoint.

This makes me call to remembrance, a strange speech little better than blasphemy, uttered lately by a young man, in the presence of his Lord, and many learned men: 'I had rather goe forty miles to a good service, then two miles to a Sermon.' And what meant he by a good service? his meaning was manifest; where goodly Babylonish robes were worn, imbroydered with images. Where he might heare a delicate noise of singers, with Shakebuts, and Cornets, and Organs, and if it were possible, all kinde of Musicke, used at the dedication of Nabuchodonosors golden Image … For if religion consist in Alter-ducking, Cope-wearing, Organ-playing, piping and singing … If I say religion consist in these and such like superstitious vanities, ceremoniall fooleries, apish toyes, and popish trinckets, we had never more Religion then now.[16]

[16] Peter Smart, *A Sermon Preached in the Cathedrall Church of Durham, July 7, 1628* (London, 1640), 22–24.

The following year, in a publication called, 'A Short Treatise of Altars, Altar-furniture, Altar-cringing and Musick of all the Quire, singing-men and Choristers,' Smart was even more vigorous in his views.

Why then are set before us so many objects of vanity, so many allurements of our outward senses, our eyes & eares, & consequently our minds from the meditation of Christs death & passion, and our sins which were the only cause of all our miseries & his lamentable suf-

> ferings. Can such paltry toyes bring to our memory Christ and his blood-shedding? Crosses, Crucifixes, Tapers, Candlesticks, gilded Angels, sumptous Organs, with Sackbuts & Cornets piping so loud at the Communion table, that they may be heard halfe a mile from the Church? No ... Such glorious spectacles, draw away from God the minds of them that pray, they further not, but hinder entire affections, and godly meditations.[17]

[17] Smart, *A Catalogue of Superstitious Innovations*, 19.

Those voices heard in favor of instrumental music in the church based their views, as such proponents always have, on the bible itself.

> Wherein doth our practice of singing and playing with instruments in his Majesty's chapel and our cathedral churches differ from the practice of David, the priests and Levites? Do we not make one sign in praising and thanking God with voices and instruments of all sorts?[18]

[18] Peacham, *The Compleat Gentleman*.

To some degree, the puritans had their say, for in ca. 1660 the organs were in fact suppressed and did not reappear generally until 1860! During this period the music in many smaller churches was provided by church bands, consisting of a half-dozen or so wind instruments, with an occasional cello.[19]

In the king's chapel, following the Restoration, cornetts found an even more important role for a time. Apparently the disruption of church boys' schools resulted in a shortage of boys to sing the upper parts, as mentioned by Matthew Locke in a treatise, 'The Present Practice of Music Vindicated,' in 1673.

[19] This fascinating story has been carefully chronicled by Kenneth H. MacDermott, in *The Old Church Gallery Minstrels* (London: SPCK, 1948) and in his manuscript correspondence, 'The Old Church Gallery Minstrels' (London, The British Museum [MS. Add. 47775]).

> For above a year after the opening of His Majesty's Chappell the orderers of the musick there were necessitated to supply the superior parts of their musick with cornets and men's feigned voices, there being not one lad for all that time capable of singing his part readily.

A similar reference was made by Hawkins:

> Upon the revival of the choral service, in the royal chapel especially, they were necessitated for want of treble voices, to make use of cornets, and on particular occasions sacbuts and other instruments.[20]

[20] Quoted in Lafontaine, *The King's Musick*, 482.

Charles II, who had lived part of his exile in Paris, introduced upon his restoration a group of strings into court life, modeled after Louis XIV's famous 'Twenty-four Violins.' This brings the first real tradition of using strings to accompany the English service, as can be accurately dated by the eyewitness, John Evelyn, in 1662.

> (One) of his Majesties Chaplains preachd: after which, instead of the antient grave and solemn wind musique accompanying the Organ was introduced a Consort of 24 Violins betweene every pause, after the French fantastical light way, better suited a Tavern or Play-house than a Church: This was the first time of change, & now we no more heard the Cornet, which gave life to the organ, that instrument quite left off in which the English were so skilfull.[21]

[21] *The Diary of John Evelyn*, 3:347–348, for December 21, 1662.

Another contemporary of the seventeenth century sheds some interesting light on the use of winds in the king's chapel after the restoration. First, on the introduction of the lower winds, heard at the festival of St. George at Windsor in 1661,

> the hymn was composed and set with verse and chorus by Capt. Cook—by whose direction some instrumental loud musick was at that time introduced, namely, two double sackbuts and two double courtalls—one sackbut and courtal before the four petty canons who began the hymn, and the other two immediately before the prebends of the College.[22]

[22] Elias Ashmole, quoted in Lafontaine, *The King's Musick*, 448.

The same observer, viewing the same service in 1674, gives an interesting comment on the placement of the winds in the choir.

> There were placed in the middle of the Choristers two Cornets & behind them a Sackbote, & last of all a Sackbut ... & Doctor Child the Organist alone in his Doctors habit.[23]

[23] Elias Ashmole, *The Autobiographical Notes of Elias Ashmole*, ed. Conrad Josten (Oxford, 1966), 4:1380.

Given the love of the English for ceremony, there were, in addition to the more regular usages of wind bands, occasional moments of the special splendor of trumpets and drums. The royal pay accounts for 1630 indicate seventeen trumpets performed during the Pentecost ceremony[24] and an eyewitness reports such instruments used in a Te Deum sung celebrating the Peace of Utrecht, in 1743.

[24] Lord Chamberlain Accounts, London (vols. 799, 459).

> As it was composed for a military triumph, the fourteen trumpets, two pair of common kettle drums, two pair of double drums from the Tower, and a pair of *double bass* drums, made expressly for this com-

memoration were introduced with great propriety. Indeed the last-mentioned drums, except in their destruction, had all the effect of the most powerful artillery.[25]

[25] William Thomas Parke, *Musical Memoirs* (New York: Da Capo Press, 1970), 38.

20 *Church Wind Bands in the German-Speaking Countries*

ONE OF THE MOST CHARACTERISTIC FEATURES of seventeenth-century German church music was the ever increasing participation by the local Stadtpfeifers, by whom is meant a wind band.[1] This was a very natural association for not only had civic wind players performed their watch duty for centuries in church towers,[2] but in turn performed spiritual music (Abblasen) from civic halls or clock towers. Therefore, when the town desired instrumental music in the church, it was the Stadtpfeifers who played their 'Instrumentalkonzert' during communion in the Protestant Church and for Offertory in the Catholic Church.[3]

But it was especially for the performance of so-called 'figural' music, the great multi-choral works for voices and instruments, that the wind players were needed,[4] perhaps for the purpose of helping the singers hold the pitch.[5] Indeed, they may have participated whenever such music was performed in some towns, for a document from Zwickau speaks of this practice, 'so oft man figurieret.'[6]

It is the use of wind instruments in this kind of music which is so extensively discussed by Praetorius[7] and Mattheson, the latter observing,

> There one uses works with three or four choirs, distributed in general as follows: In one choir very good trumpets and timpani are heard; one pair of timpani for six trumpets and two pair for twelve trumpets. In another choir are trombones, cornets and other wind instruments. In a third choir are singers, of an accompanied nature called *Capella* ... a fourth choir, yet again singers, is the main choir ... ; all will be conducted by the director.[8]

F. W. Marpurg wrote of similar multi-part wind band music, as part of a description of ideal church music he encounters in a dream during which he visits a foreign city.

> The same Ritornelle, and a brilliant unison composition, were given with much splendor by the trumpets, timpani, and horns. The (other) performing instruments were flutes, oboes, and bassoons. They had short Trios in several parts, which were played from the first choir and

[1] Arno Werner, in *Vier Jahrhunderte im Dienste der Kirchenmusik*, 220, says *only* winds, for the string instruments were usually played by burgers and students.

[2] Ehmann, *Tibilustrium*, 19, quotes a typical seventeenth-century application for a Stadtpfeifer position in which the applicant points to his service for a year in the tower of St. Stefan in Vienna.

> ... hab ich der Stadt Wien damals 1 Jahr auf S. Stephans Thurm für einen gesellen gedient.

[3] Arnold Schering, 'Einleitung,' *Denkmäler Deutscher Tonkunst* (Wiesbaden, 1958), xxix–xxx, ix.

[4] Braun, 'Entwurf für eine Typologie der "Hautboisten",' 55.

[5] Sittard, *Zur Geschichte der Musik ... am Württembergischen hofe* (Stuttgart, 1890), 1:302, quotes a contemporary document:

> ... und von den Instrumentisten zu merren (bessern) erhaltung des Toni, mit Zincken und Posannen ihr Assistenz darbei gelaistet werden.

[6] Quoted in Ehmann, *Tibilustrium*, 41.

[7] *Syntagma Musicum*, vol. 3, which I have quoted in the second volume of this series.

then from the second, always imitating intermittently through the tuttis. When an accompanied movement was repeated, it was not with the same instruments, but rather with the bassoon of one choir answering the oboes of the other and the oboes of one answering the bassoons of another. Only the flutes were now and then answering other flutes.[9]

Early during the seventeenth century, one finds the Stadtpfeifers playing, for the most part, on the principal Feast days of the church, for it was the use of these instruments which made these celebrations more 'festive.'[10] For such celebrations in Dresden in 1606, one finds the Stadtpfeifers playing crumhorns, recorders, flutes, dulcians, trumpets, and cornetts.[11] In Hamburg, a civic contract in 1613 calls for the civic wind players to 'ludt des nyen Contracts beide up dem Chore und Orgell uptowardende.'[12] The Jacobkirche in Hamburg employed 'Christianus dem Spelmann,' a player of discant and alto cornett in 1609 to play with the 'orgel und Chorales.'[13]

In the case of smaller towns, who might not be able to afford their own regular Stadtpfeifers, the civic wind bands of other towns were imported for these church festivities. Thus the Kantor in Waldheim brought in the Stadtpfeifers from Rochlitz in 1603 and the Kunstpfeifers from Liebenwerda helped out in Finsterwalde in 1612.[14]

---

[8] Quoted in Schering, 'Einleitung,' xx.

> Da macht man Stücke mit 3. à 4. Chören, und besetzet selbige gemeiniglich also: Auff einem Chor stehen v.g. Trompeter und Pauker, da imner zu 6 Trompeten ein Par, und zu 12 zwey Paar Pauken gehören. Auf dem and ern sind die Posaunen, Cincken und andere Blass-*Instrumenten*. Auff dem dritten ein Char Sänger mit zugehorigen *Accompagnement*, welches *Capella* heist: und auf dem Vierten abermahl ein Chor Sänger, welches das Haupt-Chor ist und aus *Concerti*sten bestehet; allda sind die vornehmsten *Symphoni*sten und wird die *Direction* geführet.

[9] *Kritische Briefe über die Tonkunst* (1760), 1:17 Brief.

> Die Ritornelle desselben, welche mit Trompeten und Pauken und mit Waldhörnern zu desto meherer Pracht ausgefüllet waren, waren kurz, und mit einem prächtigen Unisonostaze, welcher zum Zwischenspiel diente, untermischet. Die konzertierenden Instrumente waren Flöten, Hoboen und Fagotte. Sie hatten mehrerenteils kurze Trios, welche bald von dem ersten, bald von dem zweyten Chor vorgetragen, immer aber von dem anderen wieder nachgemacht und durch das Tutti unterbrochen wurden. Die Wiederholung eines konzertierenden Satzes geschah aber niemals mit eben denselben Instrumenten; sondern die Fagotte des eines Chores antworteten immer den Hoboen des anderen, und wiederum die Hoboen des einen den Fagotten des anderen Chores. Nur die Flöten wurden bisweilen wieder durch Floten beantwortet …

[10] Ehmann, *Tibilustrium*, 41.

[11] Grove 5:615.

[12] Liselotte Krüger, *Die Hamburgische Musikorganisation im XVII Jahrhundert* (Leipzig: Heitz, 1933), 57.

[13] Ibid., 58.

[14] Werner, *Kirchenmusik*, 219.

Already early in the century some churches began purchasing their own wind instruments for the Stadtpfeifers to use in the service. The church music director in Schweinfurt, in 1606, for example, acquired, 'two new cornetts, two trombones, two pair of crumhorns, two *Zezstück*, and two cornetts.'[15]

Beginning about 1620 one finds even stronger cooperation between the civic Stadtpfeifers and the church. One reads of four Stadtpfeifers engaged in the cathedral in Magdeburg in 1619 and a statement from the cathedral in Naumburg in 1626 mentions the service by the Stadtpfeifers, with their instruments, on fourteen Feast days.[16] Even in such small villages as Falkenhain, Mügeln, and Thalwitz one finds Stadtpfeifers playing for the same Feast days.[17]

For this period there are several extant Stadtpfeifer contracts which specifically mention the requirement of service in the church. One example from Rothenburg o.T. reads,

> The Stadtpfiefer should appear with their instruments as early as Vesper prayer time, on Sundays and Festival days, but also during the week as the Kantor requires, to help rehearse the music to be used the following Sunday.[18]

This practice of using the local civic wind band was so popular with the congregation that in those cases where the choir music director preferred the old 'a cappella' music he was sometimes replaced, as happened in Wittenberg in 1628.[19]

Another example of the purchase of instruments for church use can be seen in the Württemberg court chapel which maintained during this period (inventory of 1636) 'two Venetian cornetts, a quart-trombone, another trombone, and three cornetts.'[20]

When the Thirty Years War concluded with the Peace of 1648, one finds very strong cooperation throughout Germany between churches and the Stadtpfeifers.[21] Now even in the Reform Church winds appear in the service under pressure of public demand, although this service varied from town to town, especially in South German churches. There, for example, one finds Stadtpfeifers were 'obligat' in Friedberg, but completely missing in Alsfeld.[22]

[15] Ehmann, *Tibilustrium*, 42.

[16] Werner, *Kirchenmusik*, 219.

[17] Ibid.

[18] Quoted in Ehmann, *Tibilustrium*, 41.
> ... in den Sonn- und Feyertagen, so wol bey der Frue als Vesperpredigten in der Kirchen mit ihren Instrumenten erscheinen, zuvorderst aber alle wochen, auf das Cantoris erfordern, in der Singstund die Musicalische stuck so den folgenden Sonntag in der Kirchen gebraucht werden sollen, helfen probiren.

[19] Werner, *Kirchenmusik*, 219.

[20] Sittard, *Zur Geschichte der Musik ... am Württembergischen hofe*, 1:340.
> Zwei Venetianische Zincken
> Ein Quart Posaun umb 32
>   fl. erkaufft
> Ein andere Posaun
> Alle drey Zincken
>   ohne mundstück.

[21] Werner, *Kirchenmusik*, 219.

[22] Ibid.

To the North, one finds the Stadtpfeifers of Köln a. d. Spree in 1657 playing 'Psalmlieder' and other works in the cathedral in Berlin[23] and in Dresden a civic contract for 1675 requires the Stadtpfeifers to perform for a half-hour before the bells are rung on the three High Feast days, to perform the church music in the Sophienkirche and Frauenkirche whenever the superintendent was preaching, and to play once every six weeks in the church at Neustadt.[24] An interesting reference from Hamburg in 1650, describing a Service of Thanksgiving for the peace, gives the instrumentation of the civic wind band heard in the church as trombones, cornetts, and dulcians.[25]

As the Stadtpfeifers became more and more involved in church music during the seventeenth century, the church, in turn, became more and more involved in the affairs of the Stadtpfeifers. One can see in Zeitz that the consistory even had a voice in the audition process for new Stadtpfeifers.[26] The Church also was in a position to demand, in this same town, a puritanical 'keeping of the Sabboth,' preventing the Stadtpfeifers from weddings and outside playing opportunities on Sunday.[27]

From the last half of the seventeenth century one can find more churches purchasing their own instruments. The St. Wenzel Church in Naumburg in 1657 had no fewer than sixty instruments in its collection,[28] including a consort of eight crumhorns, trumpets, trombones, a consort of schreyerpfeife, and dulcians.[29] The court church records in Zeitz mention the possession of shawms in 1684–1689 and the new French oboe in 1691.[30]

It is only after 1700 that the strings begin to be more dominant in the German churches. One can see the arrival of these new instruments in an interesting inventory of the instruments owned by St. Thomas Church in Leipzig (which had purchased trumpets, trombones, and even timpani during the seventeenth century[31]) in the first years of the eighteenth century.

  1 large violin
  1 large spinet
  1 large Bombard and 4 smaller ones
  1 Quart-fagott
  6 trumpets and a small one in E♭
  3 old trombones (alto, tenor, and bass)
  2 'new' violins (purchased in 1701)[32]

[23] Curt Sachs, *Musik und Oper am Kurbrandenburgischen Hof* (Berlin: J. Bard, 1910), 73.

[24] Grove 5:615.

[25] Krüger, *Die Hamburgische Musikorganisation im XVII Jahrhundert*, 92.

  Dulcianene, Bassaunen und Zinken.

[26] Werner, *Städtische und fürstliche Musikpflege in Zeitz*, 40.

[27] Ibid., 43.

[28] Ibid., 220.

[29] Werner, 'Die alte Musikbibliothek und die Instrumentsammlung an St. Wenzel in Naumburg a. d. S.,' in *Archiv für Musikwissenschaft* 8 (1926): 390ff.

  Ein Stimmwerg Krumbhörner, alss 2 Bass, 2 Tenor, 2 Alt, 2 Discant ... Mundtstücke für Trompeten und Posaunen, für Krummhörner und Schreiarien, mit Rohren allerlei Instrumente.
  ……
  3 Discant-, 2 Alt- und 2 Tenor-Schreiarien ... Ersatzteile vom Dulcian ...

[30] Werner, *Städtische und fürstliche musikpflege in Weissenfels*, 95.

[31] Smithers, *The Music and History of the Baroque Trumpet*, 128.

[32] Schering, *Musikgeschichte Leipzigs*, 2:114.

It was still the civic musicians who, for the most part, performed on these instruments during their service in the church. There is one very interesting manuscript (ca. 1745) by Johann Schneider in which the horns and oboes during two movements put down their instruments and play violin![33]

During the Baroque the court wind bands also appeared in the church, sometimes in the town church, as in Köln where they helped out on a somewhat regular basis after 1723[34] and no doubt much more frequently in the private court chapels. As an example of the latter, one finds an ordinance by the Kapellmeister, Basilius Froberger, of the Württemberg court of Duke Johann Friedrich (1608–1628), issued on 1 September 1621, requiring the trombone and cornett players to appear without fail for the choir rehearsals during the week.[35]

The appearance of a court wind ensemble in church would have been especially characteristic of those towns dominated by an ecclesiastical court, where at least the aristocratic trumpets and timpani were a necessary status symbol of the church prince. A famous engraving of the interior of the Salzburg Cathedral in 1682 pictures three ensembles: trumpets and drums, trombones, and organ with strings[36] (see picture on following page). Marpurg describes such a ceremony in Salzburg, adding an interesting observation.

> The oboe and the transverse flute are heard rarely, but the waldhorn is never heard in the cathedral. All these gentlemen, therefore, join in playing the violins in the church.[37]

On those great occasions when civic, court, and church institutions all combined in celebration, no doubt one would hear all these various kinds of wind bands performing together. In such a case in Mainz in 1604, as part of a Te Deum sung celebrating a coronation, one heard alternating verses played by the civic wind band of cornett and trombones and the aristocratic trumpet and timpani ensemble.[38]

In those cases where the aristocratic trumpets could not yet read music, their participation in the church was restricted to the performance of memorized short intrada-like compositions. One might point to the fact that the *Psalm 136* of Schütz

33 Ibid., 100.

34 Braun, 'Entwurf für eine Typologie der "Hautboisten",' 56.

35 Sittard, *Zur Geschichte der Musik … am Württembergischen hofe*, 1:45.

> … wann Inn der Wochen mitt der gantzen Capell zuesammen gesungen, die Instrumentisten mit Ihren Pousaunen unnd Zinckhen, auch gewisslichen unnd ohne feehlen zugegen sehn, unnd Ihr stueckhen gepührlichen. vertretten.

36 Melchoir Kilsel, 'Festliche Musikaufführung im Salzburger Dom' (Salzburg, Museum Carolino Augusteum [Inv.Nr. 71/25]).

37 Quoted in Smithers, *The Music and History of the Baroque Trumpet*, 181.

38 Adam Gottron, *Mainzer Musikgeschichte*, 43.

212 Church Wind Bands

An engraving by Melchior Küsel, *Musical Festival in the Salzburg Cathedral*, 1682

contains a note at the end of the Bass part reading, 'Darauff wird stracks eine Intrada zum Final geblasen,' which is a cue for just such a performance.

Extant documents for the purchase of wind instruments by the monasteries and cloisters in the German-speaking countries indicate that some of them also used wind bands in their private celebrations. Gottron discusses several such purchases by such institutions in the Mainz area, including in one case the purchase of two cornetts and two bassoons in 1703.[39]

39 Ibid., 115.

One of the most extraordinary examples of such purchases is dated ca. 1720 from the Gottweig Abbey in Austria. Located some forty miles west of Vienna, this abbey had a musical tradition dating back to its foundation in 1094.[40] In their negotiations with the instrument maker Denner, three consorts of six instruments each were under consideration, one of oboes, one of flutes, and one of the new clarinets. They were given by Denner as follows:

40 Horace Fitzpatrick, 'Jacob Denner's Woodwinds for Gottweig Abbey,' *The Galpin Society Journal* 21 (March 1, 1968): 81ff.

1 Chor Hautbois mit 6 Stimmen alle von buxbaum
3 Primieur Hautbois à 5 fl.	15 fl
1 Taille	9 fl
2 Basson, à 22	44 fl

1 Chor Chalimou mit 6 Stimmen
3 Primieur Chalimou, à 3 fl	9 fl
1 Second Chalimou	7 fl
2 Basson, à 18	36 fl
Suma:	120 fl

1 Chor Flauden mit 6 Stimmen
3 Primieur Flauden, à ex 3 fl	9 fl
1 Second Flauden	6 fl
2 Basson, à 15 fl	30 fl
Zu diesen noch 1 Flaud d'Almanq	45 fl
Suma:	165 fl

It is interesting that the word 'Basson' seems to be used here as 'bass instrument.' In the oboe ensemble it probably was the instrument we call bassoon, as the oboe–taille–bassoon ensemble was a typical one for the seventeenth century, as the reader has seen. In the case of the clarinet and flute ensembles, the reference was probably to the bass of those families, which would also explain the variation in price given for the three sets of 'bassoons.' Fitzpatrick says the second reference is 'unequivocally a bass clarinet ... fifty years before the bass clarinet is thought to have been (first) invented' and observes further that the term 'Chalimou' appears for another three decades in Austrian church bands.[41]

Another Austrian monastery which enjoyed wind band music was the famous one at Melk. Here one notes the purchase in 1748 of two English horns and a bassoon; trumpets and timpani were used throughout the seventeenth century.[42]

Wind bands were used here on occasion for dinner music, as in 1743 when a report speaks of 'a very charming music with bassoon and horns which adds much decor to the total festivities.'[43] One extraordinary ceremony which seems to have been accompanied by the wind band was the ritual of 'Bleeding' (Phlebotomia), a health measure held twice a year and attended by the public! A monastery record for this event in September 1723 speaks of the wind band.[44]

> Only *eine kleine music* (the wind band[45]) [performed] by some three or at most four persons or instruments is allowed during the afternoons as well as evenings on the first and second days. The other musicians are not to appear either in the cloister or at the table. On the third day, however, *plenior Musica* may be permitted.

One may be certain that these wind players appeared in all ceremonial festivities as well. A case in point was the visit in 1743 of Maria Theresa, when one not only heard her personal trumpets and the local town wind band, but also the monastery trumpets and timpani and a wind band made up of students at the monastery all taking part in the welcoming festivities.[46]

The extant literature of the German Baroque Church for wind band is vast and diverse in forms. All of the large scale forms for voices and winds of sixteenth century Italy appeared in the following generations in Germany. The most direct representative was of course Schütz, who composed a number of such multi-choral works. But there are many other similar large scale works for voices and winds, mostly combinations of cornetts, trombones, and bassoons. These include compositions like Schütz's, based on the Psalms, by Ahle (d. 1673)

---

[41] Ibid.

[42] Robert Freeman, 'The Practice of Music at Melk Monastery in the Eighteenth Century' (Dissertation, University of California, Los Angeles, 1971), 103.

[43] Ibid., 207.

[44] Ibid., 151.

[45] This was another synonym sometimes used for a wind band, usually in the form of 'kleine Spiel,' with 'grosse Spiel' for larger 'orchestral' ensembles. (See Ehmann, *Tibilustrium*, 38) This usage seems consistent here for in another monastery document one finds '*Musica minor* with wind instruments only, performed by the four Thurner-musicians.' (Freeman, 'The Practice of Music at Melk Monastery in the Eighteenth Century,' 135)

[46] Freeman, 'The Practice of Music at Melk Monastery in the Eighteenth Century,' 206.

Schein (1625), and Werner (d. 1650); Masses by Ebner (1674), Stadlmayr (1631, 1642, 1643), Ulich (ca. 1690) and Vilhaver; the *Magnificat* by Ahle; Cantatas by Schwemmer (d. 1696) and Telemann; and additional large works by Altenburg, Buxtehude, Crüger, Forchheim, Frank, and Keiper. A collection, *Geistliche Harmonien* by Johann Horn (ca. 1630–1685), published in Dresden in 1681, carries an interesting note:

> If shawms are not available use flutes, and if there are no trumpets use cornetti, etc., letting the musical director make the most agreeable arrangements.

The smaller *concerti d chiesa*, including compositions for solo voices and smaller numbers of winds, were also carried on in the Italian tradition. The nine compositions for voices and winds among Schütz's *Symphoniae sacrae* (1629) are a perfect example, scored sometimes for consorts of trombones or bassoons and sometimes for heterogeneous collections of flutes, cornetti, trombone or bassoon. Similar works exist by Ahle (with Sinfonias for four bassoons!), Grandi, Hintze, Krieger, Christoph Peter, and Christian Sartorius.

A few church works include parts for horns, reflecting the approach of the *Harmoniemusik* tradition of the Classic period. These include works by Giovanni Hasse, Rahtgeber (1736), and Jungbauer. A wedding composition by Georg Riedel, composed in 1715, is scored for 2 'Cors de Chasse,' 2 oboes, trombone, and timpani.

There are also many examples of short wind band movements within larger church compositions. Buxtehude's *Ihr lieben Christen*, for example, contains a Sinfonia for three cornetts and three trombones. An Oratorio by Bollius contains sinfonias for flute consort and for two cornetts and bassoon.

Finally, one must mention the generation or so of German compositions which are, if not always in name, church canzonas for wind band after the Italian models.

21 Church Wind Bands in France

THE CONSERVATIVE CLERGY OF PARIS issued the *Ceremoniale parisiense* in 1662, a document based on the discussions of the Council of Trent, which warned against using any instrument but the organ in the church. This seems, indeed, to have retarded the introduction of string instruments in French church music, as one does not see violins introduced at Notre Dame in Paris until the end of the seventeenth century or in the case of Chartres and Nantes, the early years of the eighteenth century.[1]

Wind instruments, on the other hand, seem to have been continued to some degree, either as a necessity for choral support or for special ceremony. During the seventeenth century the clergy themselves in Nantes played the serpent, cornet, and crumhorns. The music master at the Chartres Cathedral, taught the dozen or so boys not only singing and composition, but also bassoon and serpent. In Paris one heard since 1651 a serpent accompanying the plainsong at Sainte-Chapelle.

The immediate court of Louis XIV probably placed themselves above the rulings of the clergy, as the use of instruments continued in all forms. Not only did the numerous Te Deums of a military or political nature demand trumpets and drums, but more aesthetic efforts also enjoyed wide experimentation with instruments. In the *Messe pour plusieurs instruments au lieu des orgues* by Marc-Antoine Charpentier, for example, one finds a 'Kyrie,' 'Domine Deus Agnus,' and 'Quoniam' for four-part woodwind ensembles and two other movements for two oboes and continuo. The 'Offerte' is for two ensembles, one of strings and the other a wind band (Choeur des instruments à vent).[2]

[1] Grove 14:194; 4:177; 13:21.

[2] H. Wiley Hitchcock, 'The Instrumental Music of Marc-Antoine Charpentier,' The Musical Quarterly 47, no. 1 (January 1, 1961): 58ff. The autograph is in Paris, Bibliothèque nationale (MS. Res. Vm 1.259/1, 67–78). This wind band is scored in four different clefs, including the so-called 'French Violin Clef,' as was the custom for French court wind band compositions.

22 Church Wind Bands in Italy

At the end of the sixteenth century, the use of wind bands in the church reached a tremendous artistic climax in the distinguished music composed for the musicians of St. Mark's Cathedral in Venice. This rich tonal splendor continues in the church ceremonies of the first several generations of the seventeenth century.

An eyewitness to some of these celebrations, Jean-Baptiste Duval, French ambassador to the Republic of Venice in 1607–1609, reported a procession on the eve of Ascension, 1608, with 'eight standards, six silver trumpets and oboes.'[1]

For the procession of Corpus Christi in 1608, he saw the fraternity of St. Theodore preceded by four trumpets dressed as Turks. The same procession the following year included 'six oboe players dressed in long robes with wide sleeves of dark blue or of rosy silk.' A water procession on Easter Sunday, 1608, featured the galley of the doge, pulled by smaller boats containing oboe bands.

Duval also reported the use of winds during the actual Mass, in one case 'different wind instruments were sounded, such as clarions, trumpets, oboes, and drums.'

Another visitor to Venice, the Englishman, Thomas Coryat, wrote of the music he heard inside St. Mark's at about the same time.

> At that time I heard much good Musicke in Saint Markes Church, but especially that of a treble violl which was so excellent, that I thinke no man could surpasse it. Also there were sagbuts and cornets as at St. Laurence feast which yielded passing good musicke.[2]

In a previous volume I have discussed the wind canzoni of Gabrieli and of the generations before his. This rich tradition continues for another generation or two in Italy during the seventeenth century. Original canzonas specified for winds were published by Riccio (1620), Picchi (1625), and Marini (1617 and 1626). In addition there are numerous extant prints which have no designated instrumentation, but were, in my opinion, almost certainly played by wind bands. Among these

[1] This and the following descriptions are quoted in Egon Kenton, *Life and Works of Giovanni Gabrieli* (American Institute of Musicology, 1967), 35ff.

[2] Ibid., 37.

are collections by Canale (1600), Mortaro (1600), Quagliati (1601), Bonelli (1602), Troilo (1606), Taeggio (1608), Rossi (1608), Bottaccio (1609), Bargnani (1611), Rovigo (1613), Bona (1614), Merula (1615), Lappi (1616), Picchi (1625), Marini (1629), and Frescobaldi (1628). In addition there are published collections of the music of several composers, the most interesting being that by Rauerij (Venice, 1608), which contains some Gabrieli works found nowhere else and the beautiful work for four bands by Massaino.[3] I beg the reader's patience in listing so many composers, but the purpose is to make an important and sometimes forgotten point: the well-known canzonas by Gabrieli are but the best known representatives of a vast repertoire of such works.

[3] This collection is available in a modern score from Leland Bartholomew, Music Department, Fort Hays State College, Fort Hays, Kansas.

In addition, the Italian church repertoire contains other instrumental forms, such as sonatas, intradas, and the *Symphonia* for two cornetts and trombone contained in the *Sacri armonici concentus* (1640) by Gregorius Urbanus. I suspect the cornett was frequently used during the first half of the seventeenth century in Italian churches as in the rest of Western Europe. One chaplain, Nicolo Rubini, was a famous cornettist, known as 'Il Cavaliere del Cornetto,' but his life was cut short by a murderer.[4]

[4] Grove 16:296–297.

There is also extant literature from the service of the seventeenth century for voices and winds. Examples include the collection of Masses (1634) by Chinelli for voices and trombones; the *Messe a cinque* by Polidori, for five-part chorus, cornetti, trombones, and organ; a *Pange lingua* by Bigaglia, for SATB chorus and three trombones; and eight *Cantate* for solo voice, oboe, and 'Flageoletto,' by Torri.

In the introduction to this volume I mentioned the *concerti da chiesa* by Franzoni. To this one might add the *Intonuit* (1614) by Usper for two voices and four trombones and the two collections of sonatas (1629 and 1644) for voices and winds by Castello, composed for St. Mark's. Other extant literature which may fall into this category include the *Concerti per sonare et cantare* (1607) by Radino, the *Seconda aggiunta alli concerti* (1607) by Lucino, and the *Il virtuoso ... can varati concerti Musicali* (1626) by Banchieri.

23 Church Wind Bands in the Spanish-Speaking Countries

IN THE CATHEDRAL IN GRANADA there were already in 1563 six wind players in regular daily service, playing on flutes, trumpets, trombones, and bassoons. During the seventeenth century cornetts, oboes, and horns were added to these instruments. After the basso continuo was introduced in the late sixteenth century, the bassoon became an indispensable part of its realization.[1]

In the royal chapel in Toledo, the pastoral chants were accompanied by four wind instruments, two oboes, a small 'bassoon-serpentine,' and bassoon.[2]

Among the extant Spanish literature for wind band and voices are three Masses by Francisco Soler (1625–1688).[3]

In nearby Portugal, during the seventeenth century wind bands of cornetts, sackbuts, and bassoons were the principal accompanying ensembles in the Badajoz Cathedral.[4]

This seventeenth-century preference for wind bands in Spanish cathedrals can be seen reflected in the export of this style to the New World. In Puebla, the second largest city in seventeenth-century Mexico, the cathedral used recorders, shawms, cornetts, sackbuts, and bassoons to double or even replace the voices; violins do not appear until the eighteenth century. Surviving documents indicate that one of the leading composers, Juan Gutiérrez de Padilla, maintained a shop in his home in which salaried workers produced 'ecclesiastical instruments,' bassoons, shawms, and recorders.[5]

Similarily, in Mexico City, a poem of 1691 by the celebrated Juana Ines de la Cruz, which was set to music by a leading composer, Antonio de Salazar (ca. 1650–1715), gives a typical ensemble as being 'clarino, trumpet, cornett, trombone, bassoon, and organ.'[6]

[1] Grove 7:627.

[2] Vander Straeten, *La Musique aux Pays-Bas*, 8:194–195.

[3] Copies in Spain, Barcelona, Biblioteca Central and Gerona, Archivo musical de la Catedral.

[4] Grove 4:817.

[5] Grove 15:441; 14:76.

[6] Grove 16:412.

Notes on the Instruments

Notes on the Instruments

AT THE BEGINNING OF THE SEVENTEENTH CENTURY one would have still found all the interesting and colorful woodwinds of the Renaissance, but by the end of the same century these same instruments have all disappeared and have been replaced by the modern woodwinds. Perhaps it was in part the increasing demands of the music itself, together with the competition of the range and flexibility of the new strings, which resulted in the most promising member of the Renaissance families (tenor flute, alto recorder, soprano shawm, and bass curtal) to be redesigned as the modern instruments. The less promising family members, together with whole families, such as the musically limited crumhorns, disappeared entirely.

Unfortunately, the details of the early prototypes and their makers were so poorly documented that we know little today of these historic transformations. The most distinguishing feature of the new instruments in general is that they were made in several detachable pieces and not from single pieces of wood as was the case with most of the earlier instruments.

The Oboe Family

At the beginning of this volume I have discussed the arrival of the new modern oboe and speculated on the possible influence of the musette on its internal construction.[1] Our knowledge of the seventeenth-century history of this instrument is complicated by the profusion of terms used by the early writers, including 'piffaro' (fife) and 'piva' (pipe) in Italy.[2] The earliest reference to the actual introduction of the oboe is found in a comment by James Talbot, writing ca. 1700.

> ... the present French Hautbois (is) not 40 years old & an improvement of the great French hautbois which is like our Weights.[3]

The lower oboes found in the Baroque, the taille, oboe da caccia and English horn, should perhaps be thought of as the same instrument in a musical sense: all were tenor oboes and

---

[1] I might also add that Jean Hotteterre, who was instrumental in the development of this new instrument, was foremost a maker of bagpipes.

[2] Don Smithers, *The Music and History of the Baroque Trumpet* (London: Dent, 1973), 239.

[3] Quoted in Josef Marx, 'The Tone of the Baroque Oboe,' *The Galpin Society Journal* 4 (June 1, 1951): 11. The reference to the English 'Weights' is no doubt the shawm used by the waits, sometimes referred to as 'Wait-pipe.'

probably all in F.[4] Our knowledge of the development of the modern tenor oboe, as well as the distinction between taille and English horn is made difficult by the fact that no first generation (1660–1695) instruments or verifiable pictures survive.[5] I might add, however, that Francois Lesure has discovered some very interesting drawings, by Jacques Cellier, of both the taille and haut contre examples of lower shawms, dating from ca. 1585.[6]

During the Classic period, one finds some *Harmoniemusik* for 2 oboes, 2 English horns, 2 horns, and 2 bassoons. This music should be thought of as the last generation of *Hautboisten* music in so far as texture is concerned, as though the sound of the wind band with the lower oboe was synonymous with the wind band itself. The new texture was the wind band without this tenor voice.

The Clarinet

One associates the arrival of the modern clarinet with the early years of the eighteenth century and already in 1732 Majer's *Museum Musicum* refers to a family of three members.[7] There are several Baroque manuscripts, notably the Trios by Graupner (1683–1760) for this combination.

The Flute

One new flute type appears during the Baroque, the 'Eunuch-flute.' This instrument had a tube open at one end, where it terminated in a bell, but closed at the other end by a piece of membrane stretched like the head of a drum and covered with a cap pierced with holes into which the player emitted his voice. According to Mersenne, music in four or five parts was performed on these instruments.[8]

---

[4] Reine Dahlqvist, 'Taille, Oboe da Caccia and Corno Inglese,' *The Galpin Society Journal* 26 (May 1, 1973): 68, writes,

> They were all the same instrument, but why it got several names is difficult to answer.

[5] According to Michael Finkelman, of Bala Cynwyn, Penna., who has made the first world organological study of the lower oboes in his catalog of instruments in European museums and private collections.

[6] These drawings are reproduced under 'Some Sixteenth-Century French Drawings,' *The Galpin Society Journal* 10 (May, 1957): 88ff.

[7] Quoted in Edgar Hunt, 'Some light on the Chalumeau,' *The Galpin Society Journal* 14 (March 1, 1961): 42.

> Man hat sonst *Discant, Alt-* oder *Quart-*Chalumeaux, wie auch *Tenor-* und *Bass-*Chalumeaux, theils mit dem Französischen/ theils mit Teutschem Ton/ und sind absonderlich *ratione* des schwehren Ansatzes/ sehr hart zu blasen/ die *Application* darauf *correspondiret* meistens mit denen Flöthen; Allein deren *Ambitus* erstrecket sich nicht viel über eine *Octav.* Wird derhalben vor unnöthig erachtet/ weitläufiger hievon zu melden/ zumalen/ wann eine Flöthen blasen kan/ wird man auch hier *praestanda praestiren Können.*

[8] Grove 6:292.

The Horn

At the beginning of this volume I have discussed the introduction of the horn as an indoor 'concert' instrument during the early years of the eighteenth century.

One can not date exactly when the period of experimentation with the earlier, smaller multi-coiled instrument finally produced the larger modern sized horn, but tapestries ca. 1665 at Fontainebleau clearly show such an instrument, as does a statue, ca.1670, at Schloss Moritzburg in Germany.[9] An advertisement in a London paper in 1682 seems to infer such an instrument was already known in England.[10]

Multi-part horn music in the hunt may have been common during the seventeenth century. A description from the early years of the reign of the Emperor Charles VI (1711–1740) reads,

> The Emperor and his family stood under the Imperial canopy and shot at the game driven toward it by the beaters. At the end of the hunt the Master and the assembled huntsmen came forward; the horns were sounded; and the Imperial party were presented with green twigs, which the Emperor and Empress pinned to their hats. Then they removed to the banquet (where they were serenaded with fanfares in as many as six parts).[11]

Similarly, an ensemble of no fewer than six horns on stage can be dated as early as an opera ca. 1708, the stage directions in the prologue reading,

> Six Macedonian Heroes, led on by six Hautboys … Six Persian Heros, which are led on by six Waldhorner.[12]

The Trumpet

In the treatises by Bendinelli, the last great Renaissance trumpeter, and Fantini, the first great Baroque trumpeter, one can see the beginning of the transition of this instrument to concert use in the modern sense.

There is a very interesting discussion of the seventeenth-century trumpet in Daniel Speer's *Instruction in the Musical Art* (1687), where he gives five indispensable qualities for good trumpet playing: healthy physical strength; strong, long continuing breath; a quickly moving tongue; a willing industry in

---

[9] Horace Fitzpatrick, *The Horn and Horn-Playing* (London: Oxford University Press, 1970), 4, 7.

[10] *The Loyal Protestant & True Domestick Intelligence*, Nr. 126, for March 7, 1681/2.

> William Bull, one of his Majestie's Trumpeters-in-Ordinary and Trumpet-maker, is removed from the Trumpet and Horn in Salisbury-Street near the Strand, to the Trumpet and Horn at the lower end of Hay-market near the Pall-mall-end; where any gentlemen may be furnished with Trumpets, French horns, Speaking Trumpets, and Flasks of all sort both Silver and Brass.

[11] Eduard Vehse, 'Geschichte des Oestreichischen Hofs und Adels,' in *Geschichte der Deutschen Hofe Seit der Reformation* (Hamburg, 1852), 2:246. See also, Ernst Paul, 'Musikalisches in der Jagd: die Jagd in der Musik,' in *Wild imd Weidwerk der Welt* (Vienna, 1955).

[12] Johann von Besser, *Schrifften in Gebundener und Ungebundener Rede* (Leipzig, 1720), quoted in Fitzpatrick, *The Horn and Horn-Playing*, 22.

constant practice, whereby the embouchure is conquered and preserved; and good, long trills, that are made with the chin, which must therefore be accustomed to trembling or shivering.[13] In addition, Speer gives an interesting discussion on the embouchure.

[13] This and the following quoted in Douglas Smith, 'A Short History of the Trumpet,' *The Instrumentalist* (January, 1972): 22–23.

> There are but few private persons who learn this instrument. Cause: it requires great bodily exertion, difficult for an incipient to perform. With a view to learn more easily how to blow the trumpet, he should at once accustom himself to apply the mouthpiece most accurately to the upper large or hanging lip, and not so as to touch the nose; for then the flesh of the large lip is apt to gather, and fill the cup of the mouthpiece, leaving no room for tonguing; yea, it even prevents the air from getting in; and though physical strength may not be lacking, it will gradually become exhausted, as the aperture for the breath is stopped up, and the breath cannot proceed. The correct embouchere, therefore, is the chief feature of trumpet blowing.
>
> ...
>
> Above all, an incipient shall accustom himself to draw in his cheeks, not blow them out, for this is not only unseemly, but hinders the breath from having it due outlet and causes a man pains at the temples, so that true teachers are accustomed to box the ears of their pupils to cure them of this bad habit.

As a final thought to the contemplation of Baroque wind band music, it is interesting to remember that the old ideas on the relationships of tonality and character were not quite forgotten. Charpentier, in his *Regles de composition* (ca. 1690) touches on these relationships.[14]

[14] Quoted in Smithers, *The Music and History of the Baroque Trumpet*, 237.

Why (use) different keys?

The principal reason is for the expression of the different passions for which the different feelings of the several keys are appropriate.

The key-feelings are (in part)

C major	Gay and warlike
D major	Joyous and very warlike
D minor	Grave and pious
E flat major	Cruel and harsh

Bibliography

Bibliography

Abbott, John S.C. *Italy, and the war for Italian independence.* New York, 1871.

Aber, Adolf. *Die Pflege der Musik unter den Wettinern und wettinischen Ernestinern, von den Anfängen bis zur Auflösung der Weimarer Hofkapelle, 1662.* Bückeburg: C.F.W. Siegal, 1921.

Adson, John. *Courtly Masquing Ayres: 1621.* London: London Pro Musica Edition, 1976.

Aerde, Raymond Joseph Justin Van. *Ménestrels communaux ... Malines, de 1312 à 1790.* Mechelen, 1911.

Altenburg, Detlef. *Untersuchungen zur geschichte der trompete im zeitalter der clarinblaskunst.* Regensburg: G. Bosse, 1973.

Altenburg, Johann. *Versuch einer Anleitung zur heroisch-musikalischen Trompeter- und Pauker-Kunst ...* Halle, 1795.

Arbeau, Thoinot. *Orchesography.* Translated by Mary Stewart Evans. New York: Kamin Dance Publishers, 1948.

Ashmole, Elias. *Elias Ashmole (1617-1692): his autobiographical and historical notes, his correspondence, and other contemporary sources relating to his life and work.* Edited by Conrad Hermann Josten. Oxford: Clarendon Press, 1966.

Ashton, John. *Social Life in the Reign of Queen Anne.* London: Chatto & Windus, 1911.

Ashton, Robert. *James I.* London: Hutchinson, 1969.

Bach, Johann, and E.H. Muller von Asow. *Briefe.* Regensburg: Bosse, 1950.

Baines, Anthony. *Woodwind Instruments and their History.* New York: Norton, 1962.

Barine, Arvède. *La Grand Mademoiselle.* New York, 1902.

Barnes, Clifford. "Instruments and Instrumental Music at the 'Theatres de la Foire'." *Recherches sur la Musique Francaise Classique* V (1965).

Barry, Gerat. *A Discourse of Military Discipline.* Brussels, 1634.

Beattie, John. *The English Court in the Reign of George I.* London: Cambridge University Press, 1967.

Beer, Johann. *Musicalische Discurse.* Nürnberg, 1719.

Benoit, Marcelle. *Musiques de Cour.* Paris: Picard, 1971.

———. *Versailles et les musiciens du roi.* Paris: Picard, 1971.

Bernhard, M.B. "Notice sur la confrérie des joueurs d'instruments d'Alsace." In *La Revue historique de la Noblesse.* Paris, 1844.

Binet, Etienne. *Essay des merveilles de nature, et des plus nobles artifices.* Rouen, 1626.

Birch, Thomas. *The Life of Henry Prince of Wales.* London, 1760.

Bottrigari, Ercole. *Il desiderio overo de' concerti di varii strumenti musicali,* 1594.

Boulenger, Jacques. *The Seventeenth Century.* New York: Putnam, 1920.

Boydell, Barra. *The Crumhorn and other Renaissance Windcap Instruments.* Buren: Knuf, 1982.

Braun, Werner. "Entwurf fur ein Typologie der 'Hautboisten'." In *Der Sozialstatus des Berufsmusikers vom 17. bis 19. Jahrhundert*. Kassel: Bärenreiter-Verlag, 1971.

Brenet, Michel. "French Military Music in the Reign of Louis XIV." Translated by Mariola Chardon. *The Musical Quarterly* 3, no. 3 (July 1, 1917): 340–357.

Bridge, Joseph C. "Town Waits and Their Tunes." *Proceedings of the Musical Association* 54 (1927–1928): 63.

Brixel, Eugen. *Das ist Österreichs Militärmusik: von der "Türkischen Musik" zu den Philharmonikern in Uniform*. Graz: Edition Kaleidoskop, 1982.

Brixel, Eugen, and Wolfgang Suppan. *Das Grosse Steirische Blasmusikbuch*. Wien: Molden, 1981.

Bryant, Arthur. *King Charles II*. London: Collins, 1955.

Bukofzer, Manfred. *Music in the Baroque Era: From Monteverdi to Bach*. New York: Norton, 1947.

Cambridge Modern History. New York, 1907.

Campian, Thomas. *The description of a Maske, presented before the kinges majestie at Whitehall* ... London, 1607.

Carpenter, Nan Cooke. *Music in the Medieval and Renaissance Universities*. Norman: University of Oklahoma Press, 1954.

Caus, Salomon De. *Institution harmonique*. Frankfurt, 1615.

Çelebi, Evliya. *Narrative of travels in Europe, Asia and Africa, in the Seventeenth Century*. Translated by Joseph von Hammer. London, 1834.

Cerone, Pietro. *El melopeo y maestro*. Naples, 1613.

Cleland, James. *The institution of a young noble man*. Oxford, 1607.

Clephan, R. Coltman. *The Tournament*. New York: Ungar, 1967.

Collinson, Francis M. *The Bagpipe: The History of a Musical Instrument*. London: Routledge & K. Paul, 1975.

Cornwallis, Charles. *An account of the baptism, life, death and funeral, of the most incomparable Prince Frederick Henry, Prince of Wales*. London, 1751.

Cosin, John. *The correspondence of John Cosin, D.D.* Edited by George Ornsby. London, 1869.

Crewdson, Henry Alastair Ferguson. *The Worshipful Company of Musicians*. London: Knight, 1971.

Croft-Murray, Edward. "The Wind-Band in England, 1540-1840." In *Music and Civilisation*. London: Trustees of the British Museum, 1980.

Dahlqvist, Reine. "Taille, Oboe da Caccia and Corno Inglese." *The Galpin Society Journal* 26 (May 1, 1973): 58–71.

Dart, Thurston. "The Repertory of the Royal Wind Music." *The Galpin Society Journal* 11 (1958): 70.

Dauney, William. *Ancient Scottish Melodies*. Edinburgh, 1838.

Davey, Henry. *History of English Music*. London: Curwen, 1921.

Degele, Ludwig. *Die Militärmusik, ihr Werden und Wesen, ihre kulturelle und nationale Bedeutung*. Wolfenbüttel: Verlag für musikalische Kultur und Wissenschaft, 1937.

Diderot, Denis. *Encyclopédie*. Neufchastel, 1765.

Digges, Thomas. *An Arithmetical Warlike Treatise*. London, 1590.

Dittersdorf, Karl von. *The Autobiography of Karl von Dittersdorf*. Translated by A. D. Coleride. London, 1896.

Donado, Giovanni Battista. *Della letteratura de' Turchi*. Venice, 1688.

Doras, Sabahattin. *Mehterhane: The Military Band of the Turkish Army*. Ankara: Türkiye Turing Ve Otomobil Kurumu, 1970.

Downs, Anneliese. "The Tower Music of a Seventeenth Century Stadtpfeifer: Johann Pezel's *Hora decima* and *Fünff-stimmigte blasende Music*." *Brass Quarterly* 7, no. i (1965): 4, 7.

Dugdale, Gilbert. *The time triumphant*. London, 1604.

Durant, Will, and Ariel Durant. *The Age of Voltaire*. New York: Simon and Schuster, 1965.

Ecorcheville, J. "Quelques Documents sur la Musique de la Grande Ecurie du Roi." *Sammelbände der Internationalen Musikgesellschaft* 3 (1903): 608–642.

Écorcheville, Jules. *Vingt suites d'orchestre*. Paris: Liepmannssohn, 1906.

Ede, Mary. *Arts and Society in England under William and Mary*. London: Stainer and Bell, 1979.

Ehmann, Wilhelm. *Tibilustrium*. Kassel: Bärenreiter-Verlag, 1950.

Elton, Richard. *The compleat body of the Art Military*. London, 1650.

Engel, Hans. *Musik und Gesellschaft: Bausteine zu einer Musiksoziologie*. Berlin-Halensee: Max Hesse, 1960.

Engelke, Bernhard. "Musik und musiker am Gottorfer Hofe". Universitatsbibliothek Kiel, n.d.

Etat de la France, 1702.

Evans, Willa. *Ben Jonson and Elizabethan Music*. New York: Da Capo Press, 1965.

Evelyn, John. *The Diary of John Evelyn*. Oxford: Clarendon Press, 1955.

Fabrum, Antonius. *Europäischer Staats- Cantzley*. Leipzig, 1700.

Farmer, Henry George. *Military Music*. London: William Reeves, 1912.

Farmer, Henry. *Handel's Kettledrums, and other papers on Military Music*. London: Hinrichsen, 1965.

———. *Memoirs of the Royal Artillery Band*. London: Boosey & Co., 1904.

Fitzpatrick, Horace. "Jacob Denner's Woodwinds for Göttweig Abbey." *The Galpin Society Journal* 21 (March 1, 1968): 81-87.

———. *The Horn and Horn-Playing*. London: Oxford University Press, 1970.

Fleming, Hans Friedrich von. *Der vollkommene Teutsche Soldat*. Leipzig, 1726.

Frederick II von Brandenburg. *Memoirs pour servir a l'histoire de Brandenbourg*, 1750.

Freeman, Robert. "The practice of music at Melk Monastery in the eighteenth century". Diss., University of California, 1976.

Furetière, Antoine. *Dictionaire universel*. The Hague, 1690.

Gerauth, W. *Musikgeschichte der Stadt Halle*. Halle, 1931.

Giegling, Franz. *Giuseppe Torelli*. Kassel: Bärenreiter, 1949.

Gottron, Adam. *Mainzer Musikgeschichte von 1500 bis 1800*. Mainz: Auslieferung durch die Stadtbibliothek, 1959.

Green, David. *Queen Anne*. London, 1970.

Grove, George. *The New Grove Dictionary of Music and Musicians*. Edited by Stanley Sadie. London: Macmillan, 1980.

Guignard, Claude. *L'ecole de Mars*. Paris, 1725.

Gülke, Peter. *Musik und Musiker in Rudolstadt*. Rudolstadt: Buchdruckerei F. Mitzlaff, 1963.

Halfpenny, Eric. "A Seventeenth-Century Oboe Consort." *The Galpin Society Journal* 10 (May 1, 1957): 60–62.

Hibbert, Christopher. *Charles I*. New York: Harper & Row, 1968.

Hind, Harold. *The British Wind Band*. Hinrichsen, 1952.

Hirsching, Friedrich. *Historisch-literarisches Handbuch berühmter und denkwürdiger Personen*. Leipzig, 1792.

Hitchcock, H. Wiley. "The Instrumental Music of Marc-Antoine Charpentier." *The Musical Quarterly* 47, no. 1 (January 1, 1961): 58–72.

Hunt, Edgar. "Some Light on the Chalumeau." *The Galpin Society Journal* 14 (March 1, 1961): 41–44.

Hutchings, Arthur. *The Baroque Concerto*. New York: Scribner, 1979.

Imbert, Gaetano. *La vita fiorentina nel '600*. Florence, 1906.

Isherwood, Robert. *Music in the Service of the King: France in the Seventeenth Century*. Ithaca, NY: Cornell University Press, 1973.

Jacquot, Jean, ed. *Les Fêtes de la Renaissance*. Paris: Centre National de la Recherche Scientifique, 1973.

Janssen, Johannes. *History of the German People*. New York: AMS Press, 1966.

Jones, Paul. *The Household of a Tudor Nobleman*. Urbana: University of Illinois, 1918.

Jonson, Ben. *The Works of Ben Jonson*. Edited by C.H. Herford and Percy Simpson. Oxford: Clarendon Press, 1925.

Kappey, Jacob Adam. *A Short History of Military Music*, 1894.

Kastner, Georges. *Manuel général de musique militaire à l'usage des armées françaises*. Paris, 1848.

Kellner, Altmann. *Musikgeschichte des Stiftes Kremsmünster*. Kassel Basel: Bärenreiter Verlag, 1956.

Kenton, Egon. *Life and Works of Giovanni Gabrieli*. American Institute of Musicology, 1967.

Kerber, G. "Musikalisches aus dem Nachlasse des Generals C.H. v. Czettritz." In *Monatshefte für Musikgeschichte*. Vol. 32, n.d.

Kinsky, Georg. "Doppelrohrblatt-Instrumente mit Windkapsel. Ein Beitrag zur Geschichte der Blasinstrumente im 16. u. 17. Jahrhundert." *Archiv für Musikwissenschaft* 7, no. 2 (June 1, 1925): 253–296.

Köchel, Ludwig. *Die Kaiserliche Hof-Musikkapelle in Wien von 1543–1867*. Hildesheim: G. Olms, 1976.

Krückeberg, Elisabeth. "Ein historisches Konzert zu Nurnberg im Jahre 1643." *Archiv für Musikwissenschaft* (1918 1919).

Krüger, Liselotte. *Die hamburgische musikorganisation im XVII. jahrhundert*. Leipzig: Heitz & Co., 1933.

De Lafontaine, Henry. *The King's Musick*. London, 1909.

Langwill, Lyndesay Graham. *Waits, wind band, horn*. London: Hinrichsen, 1952.

Leppert, Richard. "Musical Instruments and Performing Ensembles in Flemish Paintings of the Seventeenth Century". Indiana University, 1973.

Lobstein, Jean. *Beiträge zur Geschichte der Musik im Elsass und besonders in Strassburg: von der ältesten bis auf die neueste Zeit*. Strassburg, 1840.

MacDermott, Kenneth H. *The Old Church Gallery Minstrels*. London: SPCK, 1948.

Magalotti, Lorenzo. *Relazione d'Inghilterra*, 1668.

Mallet, Alain Manesson. *Les travaux de mars: ou, L'art de la guerre*. Paris: D. Thierry, 1691.

Markham, Francis. *Fiue decades of epistles of warre*. London, 1622.

Marolles, Michel. *Les mémoires de Michel de Marolles, abbé de Villeloin*. Paris, 1656.

Marpurg, Friedrich Wilhelm. *Kritische Briefe über die Tonkunst*, 1760.

Marsigli, Luigi-Ferdinando. *Il Sato Militare dell' Imperio Ottomano, Incremento e Decremento Del Medesimo Dell Signore Conte di Marsigli ...* Hague, 1732.

Marx, Josef. "The Tone of the Baroque Oboe: An Interpretation of the History of Double-Reed Instruments." *The Galpin Society Journal* 4 (June 1, 1951): 3-19.

Di Marzo, G. *Diari della città di Palermo*. Palermo, 1880.

Mattheson, Johann. *Das Neu-Eröffnete Orchestre*. Hamburg, 1713.

———. *Ehren-Pforte*. Hamburg, 1740.

McGrady, Richard. "The Court Trumpeters of Charles I and Charles II." *The Music Review* 35 (1974): 227.

Menestrier, Claude-François. *Des ballets anciens et modernes selon les règles du théâtre*. Paris, 1682.

———. *Des representations en musique anciennes et modernes*. Paris, 1681.

Menke, Werner. *History of the Trumpet of Bach and Händel*. London: W. Reeves, 1934.

Mersenne, Marin. *Harmonie universelle* [1635]. Translated by Roger Chapman. The Hague: M. Nijhoff, 1957.

Mishkin, Henry G. "The Italian Concerto before 1700." *Bulletin of the American Musicological Society*, no. 7 (October 1, 1943): 20–22.

Molmenti, Pompeo. *Venice*. London, 1908.

Morley-Pegge, Reginald. *The French Horn*. London: Ernest Benn, 1973.

Musikalische Nachrichten und Anmerkungen auf das Jahr 1770. Vol. 3. Leipzig, 1770.

Nagler, A.M. *Theatre Festivals of the Medici*. New Haven: Yale University Press, 1964.

Naylor, Edward W. *Shakespeare and music*. New York: Da Capo Press, 1965.

Nettl, Paul. "Equestrian Ballets of the Baroque Period." *The Musical Quarterly* 19, no. 1 (January 1933): 74–83.

Nichols, John. *The progresses and public processions of Queen Elizabeth. Among which are interspersed other solemnities, public expenditures, and remarkable events, during the reign of that illustrious princess*. Vol. 3. London, 1805.

———. *The Progresses of King James the First*. London, 1828.

Nickel, Ekkehart. *Der Holzblasinstrumentenbau in der Freien Reichsstadt Nürnberg*. Munich: Musikverlag Katzbichler, 1971.

Le Nouveau Mercure. Paris, January 1679.

Oepen, Heinz. *Beiträge zur Geschichte des Kölner Musiklebens, 1760–1840*. Köln: Arno Volk-Verlag, 1955.

Ogilby, John. *The relation of His Majestie's entertainment passing through the city of London, to his coronation*. London, 1661.

Panóff, Peter. *Militärmusik in Geschichte und Gegenwart*. Berlin: K. Siegismund, 1944.

Parke, William Thomas. *Musical Memoirs*. New York: Da Capo Press, 1970.

Parrott, Andrew. "Grett and Solompne Singing." *Early Music* 6, no. 2 (April 1, 1978): 182–187.

Pascha, Arif Mehmed. *Les anciens costumes de l'Empire Ottoman*. Paris: Imprimerie de A. Laîné et J. Havard, 1863.

Paul, Ernst. "Musikalisches in der Jagd: die Jagd in der Musik." In *Wild und Weidwerk der Welt*. Vienna, 1955.

Peacham, Henry. *The Compleat Gentleman*. London, 1622.

Pepys, Samuel. *The Diary of Samuel Pepys*. London, 1924.

Pillement, Georges. *Paris en fête*. Paris: B. Grasset, 1972.

Pougin, Arthur. *Dictionnaire historique et pittoresque du théâtre*. Paris, 1885.

Praetorius, Michael. *The Syntagma Musicum*. Translated by Hans Lampl. Vol. 3. University of Southern California, 1957.

Du Praissac, John. *The Art of Warre*. Cambridge, 1639.

Printz, Wolfgang Caspar. *Historische Beschreibung der edelen Sing- und Kling-Kunst*. Dresden, 1690.

———. *Musicus Vexatus*. Freyberg, 1690.

Prunières, Henry. *La musique de la chambre et de l'écurie sous le règne de François Ier*. Paris: F. Alcan, 1911.

Quincy, Charles Sevin de. *Histoire militaire du règne de Louis le Grand*. Paris, 1726.

Rasmussen, Mary. "Gottfried Reich …" *Brass Quarterly* 4, no. i (1960).

———. Historical Notes to *Sonata no. 25 from Hora Decima*. North Easton, MA, 1962.

Rausching, Hermann. *Geschichte der Musik und Musikpflege in Danzig*. Danzig: Kommissionsverlag der Danziger Verlags-Gesellschaft, 1931.

Reese, Gustave. *Music in the Renaissance*. New York: Norton, 1959.

Reschke, Johannes. *Studie zur Geschichte der brandenburgisch-preussischen Heeresmusik*. Berlin: VDI-Verl, 1936.

———. "Zur Geschichte der Deutschen Militarmusik des 17. und 18. Jarhunderts." *Deutsche Musik-Kultur* 2 (1937): 11.

Riedel, Herbert. *Musik und Musikerlebnis in der erzählenden deutschen Dichtung*. Bonn: H. Bouvier, 1959.

Rimbault, Edward F. *The Old Cheque-Book*. London, 1872.

Rousseau, Jean-Jacques. "Copiste." *Dictionnaire de Musique*. Paris, 1767.

Rouvel, Diether. "Zur Geschichte der Musik am Fürstlich Waldeckschen Hofe zu Arolsen." In *Kolner Beitrage zur Musikforschung*. Regensburg: G. Bosse, 1962.

La Ruelle. *Obsequies of Charles III*. Nancy, 1608.

Sachs, Curt. *Musik und Oper am Kurbrandenburgischen Hofe*. Berlin: J. Bard, 1910.

———. *The History of Musical Instruments*. New York: Norton, 1940.
Sainsbury, John. *A Dictionary of Musicians*. London, 1825.
Saint-Simon, Louis de Rouvroy. *Memoirs of Louis XIV and the Regency*. London: Dunne, 1901.
Sandford, Francis. *The history of the coronation of ... James II*. London, 1687.
Sandman, Susan. "Wind Band Music Under Louis XIV". Dissertation, Stanford, 1978.
Saredo, Luisa. "Il matrimonio di Vittorio Emanuele II su documenti inediti." In *Nuova Antologia*. Turin, 1885.
Saxe, Maurice comte de. *Les Reveries ou Memoires sur l'art de la guerre*. Hague, 1756.
Sbarra, Francesco. *La Germania Esultante, Festa a Cavallo*. Vienna, 1667.
Schein, Johann. *Venus Kräntzlein*. Wittemberg, 1609.
Schering, Arnold. "Die Leipziger Ratsmusik von 1650 bis 1775." *Archiv für Musikwissenschaft* (1921).
———. "Einleitung." *Denkmaler Deutscher Tonkunst* 29–30 (1958).
———. *Geschichte des Instrumentalkonzerts*. Leipzig, 1927.
———. *Musikgeschichte Leipzigs von 1650-1723*. Leipzig: Zentralantiquariat der Deutschen Demokratischen Republik, 1926.
Schmidt, Günther. *Die Musik am Hofe der Markgrafen von Brandenburg-Ansbach*. Kassel und Basel: Bärenreiter-Verlag, 1956.
Serauky, Walter. *Musikgeschichte der Stadt Halle*. Halle-Berlin: Buchhandlung des Waisenhauses, 1939.
Shakespeare, William. *Othello*, n.d.
Shedlock, J. "Coronation Music." *Proceedings of the Musical Association* 28 (1902): 141.
"Siege de Namur." *Mercure Galant*, May 1692.
Sievers, H. *Die Musik in Hannover*. Hannover: Sponholtz, 1969.
Sirman, Mitchel. "The wind sonatas in Daniel Speer's Musicalisch-türckischer Eulen-Spiegel of 1688". Diss., University of Wisconsin, 1972.
Sittard, Josef. *Zur Geschichte der Musik und des Theaters am Württembergischen Hofe*. Stuttgart, 1890.
Smart, Peter. *A Catalogue of Superstitious Innovations*. London, 1642.
———. *A Sermon Preached in the Cathedrall Church of Durham, Iuly, 7. 1628*. London, 1640.
Smith, Douglas. "A Short History of the Trumpet." *The Instrumentalist* (January 1972): 22–23.
Smithers, Don. *The Music and History of the Baroque Trumpet before 1721*. London: Dent, 1973.
Spreckelsen, Otto. *Die Stader Ratsmusikanten*. Stade: A. Pockwitz, 1924.
Springell, Francis. *Connoisseur & Diplomat*. London: Maggs Bros., 1963.
Stephen, Leslie. *Biographie National*. London, 1885.
Strunk, Oliver, ed. *Source Readings in Music History*. New York: Norton, 1950.
Strype, John. *Annals of the Reformation*. London, 1709.
Suppan, Wolfgang. *Lexikon des Blasmusikwesens*. Freiburg: Schulz, 1973.
Terry, Charles Sanford. *Bach: A Biography*. London: Oxford University Press, 1933.
Thouret, Georg. *Friedrich der Grosse als Musikfreund und Musiker*. Leipzig, 1898.

Thurston Dart. "Some Sixteenth-Century French Drawings." *The Galpin Society Journal* 10 (May 1, 1957): 88–89.

Titcomb, Caldwell. "Baroque Court and Military Trumpets and Kettledrums: Technique and Music." *The Galpin Society Journal* 9 (1956): 56.

Trichet, Pierre. *Traité des instruments de musique* [1640]. Bordeaux, n.d.

Turner, James. *Pallas armata*. London, 1683.

Valentin, Caroline. *Geschichte der Musik in Frankfurt a.M.* Frankfurt: Völcker, 1906.

Vander Straeten, Edmond. *La musique aux Pays-Bas avant le XIXe siècle*. Vol. 7. New York: Dover, 1969.

Vehse, Eduard. "Geschichte des östreichischen Hofs und Adels." In *Geschichte der Deutschen Hofe Seit der Reformation*. Hamburg, 1851.

Veit, Gottfried. *Die Blasmusik*. Innsbruck, 1972.

Vessella, Alessandro. *La banda*. Milano: Istituto editoriale nazionale, 1935.

Walpole, Horace. *A catalogue of the royal and noble authors of England*. London, 1758.

Walther, Johann. *Musikalisches Lexikon oder Musikalische Bibliothek*. Leipzig, 1732.

Ward, Ned. *The London Spy*. Edited by Arthur Hayward. New York: Doran, 1927.

Warwick, Alan Ross. *A Noise of Music*. London: Queen Anne Press, 1968.

Werner, Arno. "Die alte Musikbibliothek und die Instrumentsammlung an St. Wenzel in Naumburg a. d. S." *Archiv für Musikwissenschaft* 8 (1926).

———. *Städtische und fürstliche musikpflege in Weissenfels*. Leipzig: Breitkopf & Härtel, 1911.

———. *Städtische und fürstliche musikpflege in Zeitz bis zum Anfang des 19. Jahrhunderts*. Bückeburg & Leipzig: Siegel, 1922.

———. *Vier jahrhunderte im dienste der kirchenmusik*. Leipzig: Carl Merseburger, 1933.

Wienpahl, Robert. *Music at the Inns of Court during the reigns of Elizabeth, James, and Charles*. Ann Arbor: California State University, Northridge, 1979.

Winston, James. "Collections relating to Vauxhall Gardens". Oxford, n.d.

Woodfill, Walter L. *Musicians in English Society from Elizabeth to Charles I*. Princeton: Princeton University Press, 1953.

Wustmann, Gustav. *Quellen zur Geschichte Leipzigs*. Leipzig, 1889.

Zulauf, Ernst. *Beiträge zur Geschichte der Landgräflich-Hessischen Hofkapelle zu Cassel bis auf die Zeit Moritz des Gelehrten*. Cassel: Druck von L. Döll, 1902.

Index

Index

Index of Names

A

Adinari, Alessandro, poet, 65
Admirall of Castile 17th century Spanish noble, 75
Ahle, Johann, 1625–1673, German composer, 214ff
Aichinger, Grégor, 1565–1628, German composer, 60
Albergati, Pirro, 1663–1735, Italian composer, 14
Alberti, Domenico, 1710–1740, Italian singer, 14
Albinoni, Tomaso, 1671–1751, Italian composer for Hautboisten, 14
Albmeyer, Giorgio Cristoforo, German leader of Italian military band in 1722, 152
Aldobrandini, Giovanni, on Italian military trumpets in 1601, 151
Alessandro VIII, 1610–1691, Pope, trumpets in 1689, 73
Aleworth, John, civic musician hired by Rochester in 1640, 180
Alsloot, Dennis, van, 17th century Dutch painter, 153, 188
Altenburg, Ernst, 1688–1761, writer on trumpet performance practice in 1671, 68, 117ff, 215
Angermaier, Christoph, early 17th Century German furniture maker, 4
Anna d'Orléans, niece to Louis XIV, 71
Anne of Austria, 1601–1666, queen consort of Navarre, visits Paris in 1664, 46
Anne of Russia, 17th century, 110
Arbeau, Thoinot, 1519–1595, author of dance manual, 138
Archduke of Austria (1716), 123
Ariosto, Ludovico, 1474–1533, Italian poet, 46
Arundal, Earl of, 17th century English noble, 91
August der Starke, 1670–1733, King of Poland, has Turkish band in 1699, 124, 126
Augustus II of Poland, d. 1735, 110

B

Bach, J. S., 1685–1750, 13, 59, 66, 160, 162, 174
Banchieri, Adriano, 1568–1634, Italian composer, 220
Banister, John, 17th century English impresario, 179
Bargnani, Ottavio, 1570–1627, Italian composer, 220
Battalus, Prince (17th century), 124
Beauregard, François, French oboist in Berlin in 1681, 6
Beer, Johann, 1655–1700, Konzertmeister at Weissenfels, 60, 171
Beethoven, Ludwig van, 1770–1827, 103
Benda, Franz, 1709–1786, Czech composer, 131
Bendinelli, Cesare, famous Baroque trumpeter, 227

Biber, Heinrich, 1644–1704, Bohemian-Austrian composer, 169
Biedermann, Hans Christian, court trumpeter in Weimar (early 18th century), 162
Bigaglia, Diogenio, 17th century Italian composer, 220
Blanchet, Thomas, 17th century engraver, 38
Bollius, Daniel, 17th century German composer, 215
Bona, 17th century Italian composer, 220
Bonelli, Aurelio, 1569–1620, Italian composer, 220
Bottaccio, Paolo, 17th century Italian composer, 220
Bottrigari, Ercole, 1531–1620, Italian scholar, 13
Braithwaite, Richard, author of treatise on manners in 1621, 88
Brausi, Paolo, conductor of the Modena town band in 1608, 193
Bretagne, Duke of, last grandchild of Louis XIV, 43, 45
Briegel, Wolfgang, 1626–1712, German composer, 17
Burckart, Franz, 17th century composer of Hautboisten music, 19
Busino, Horatio, Venetian ambassador in London in 1618, 86ff
Buxtehude, Dieterich, 1639–1707, composer in Germany, 215ff

C

Campion, Thomas, 1567–1620, English masque composer in 1607, 85
Canale, 17th century Italian composer, 220
Castello, Dario, 1590–1658, Italian composer, 220
Cavalli, Francesco, 1602–1676, composer, 74
Çelebi (Efendi), Evilya, author on travels in 17th century Ottoman Empire, 107ff
Cellier, Jacques, artist drawings of the taille in 1660–1695, 226
Cerone, Domenico Pietro, 1566–1625 Italian composer, theorist, 4, 15
Cesti, Pietro, 1623–1669, Florentine composer, 62, 74
Chapman and Beaumont, Baroque playwrights with wind band, 184
Charles I, 1600–1649, King of England, 79, 90ff
Charles II of Spain, d. 1699, 151
Charles II, 1630–1685, King of England, 92ff, 148, 204
Charles III of Spain, 152
Charles III, 1543–1608, Duke of Lorraine, 27ff
Charles VI, Emperor, 1717–1740, 227

Charpentier, Marc-Antoine, 1643–1704, French composer, 217, 228
Chaumont, Lambert, 1630–1712, on his use of winds in church, 199
Chinelli, Giovani, 17th century Italian composer, 220
Christian IV, 1588–1648, King of Denmark, visits England in 1606, 79, 82
Christian of Weissenfels, Duke, 1712–1736, 60
Christianus dem Spelmann, cornettist in the Jacobkirche, Hamburg, 208
Cleland, James, author of treatise on manners in 1607, 89
Clemente IX, 1600–1669, Pope, trumpets in 1667, 72
Clemente X, 1590–1676, Pope, trumpets in 1670, 73
Clemente XI, 1649–1721, Pope, trumpets in 1700, 73
Cole, James, creator of a writing sampler illustrating a Wait band in 1742, 178
Corelli, Arcngelo, 1653–1713, Italian composer, 16, 19
Cornale, Lodouico, cornettist in Venice in 1608, 194
Coryat, Thomas, on church music in Venice in 1608, 219
Cosimo de Medici, 1519–1674, Duke of Florence, 74
Count de Monterey, 17th century Spanish noble, 75
Count Palatine of Germany, marriage in 1612, 69
Crüger, Johann, 1598–1662, German composer, 215
Cumberland, Earl of, 17th century English noble, 88

D

dall'Abaco, Felice, 1675–1742, Italian composer 14
Dalla Casa, Girolamo, d. 1601, conductor, Doge's band in Venice, 12
Daser, Ludwig, 16th century German composer, 60
Davenant, William, 1606–1668, English impresario, 179
Degensee, Jonas, father of a Stadtpfeifer applicant in 1607, 159
Denner, Jacob, 18th century German woodwind maker, 213
Descoteaux, flute player under Louis XIV, 39
Desjardins, Jean Baptiste, oboist of the *Les Grands Hautbois*, 34
Dietrichstein, Count as rider in a horse ballet in 1667, 62
Dittersdorf, Carl Ditters von, 1739–1799, at the court music for Maria Theresia, 63
Don Lord Duarte, 17th century Spanish noble, 75
Donizetti, Gaetano, 1797–1848, 103
Dryden, John, 1631–1700, English poet, 96
Duchatel, Frans, engraving of Dutch trumpets and timpani in 1660, 153
Duke of Brunswick, visits Venice water pageant in 1685, 73
Duke of Infantado of 17th century Spanish noble, 75
Duke of Württemberg (1603), 69
Duval, Jean-Baptiste, French Ambassador to Venice, 1607–1609, 219

E

Ebner, Wolfgang, 1612–1665, German composer, 215
Edward VI, 1537–1553, King of England, 202
Effendi, Achmet, ambassador to Berlin, 18th century, 110
Elizabeth I, 1533–1603, Queen of England, 90, 202
Elizabeth, daughter to King James I of England, 69
Elvigius, 17th century bassoonist in the Antwerp Cathedral, 199
Ereditario of Florence, marriage in 1661, 71
Eugene, Prince of Savoy, 1663–1736, 63
Evelyn, John, 1620–1706, English historian, 93ff, 182, 184ff [use of timpani on the River Thames], 192 [musicians on slave ship], 205

F

Fantini, Girolamo, 1600–1675, Italian author of trumpet treatise, 65, 71, 227
Fasch, Johann, 1688–1758, German composer, 17
Fattorini, Gabriele, fl. 1598–1609, Italian composer, 14
Ferdinand II, Emperor, 1578–1637, 66 [edict of 1623 regarding royal trumpets], 110
Ferdinand III, Emperor, 1608–1657, 61ff, 66 [edict of 1653 regarding royal trumpets]
Ferdinando II of Florence in 1661, 71
Ferrabosco II, Alfonso, 1575–1628, masque composer, 84, 94
Fick, 17th century composer of Hautboisten music, 19
Finger, Gottfried, 17th century German composer, 17
Fleming, Hans von, treatise on military music of 1726, 128ff
Foerster, 17th century German composer, 18
Forchheim, 17th century German composer, 215
Förster, Kaspar, 1616–1673, German composer, 18
Francisco de Sandoval y Rois, 17th century Spanish noble, 76
Franck, Melchior, 1579–1639, German composer, 215
François I, 1494–1547, King of France, 35
Franzoni, Amante, 1575–1630, Italian composer church music with winds, 14, 220
Frederick II ('the Great'), 1712–1786 of Prussia, 6, 126, 130
Freschi, Giovanni, 1640–1690, composer of the opera Berenice in 1680), 74
Frescobaldi, Girolamo, 1583–1643, Italian composer, 220
Friedrich Augustus II, 1696–1763, Elector of Saxony, 163
Friedrich Heinrich, Duke of Sachsen-Zeitz, b. 1668, (re his Hautboisten in 1698), 58
Friedrich I, 1688–1713, his military music, 125ff
Friedrich III, 1688–1713, of Berlin, 65
Friedrich Wilhelm I, 1713–1740, of Berlin, 8; 'the Soldier-King,' 60, 70, 122, 124; his military music, 110, 126ff
Friedrich Wilhelm, Elector, 1640–1688, 'the Great Elector,' 123ff

Froberger, Basilius, Kapellmeister at Württemberg in 1621, 211
Froidmont, Libert, d. 1653, Th.D at the University of Louvain, 199

G

Gabrieli, Giovanni, 1554–1612, Italian composer in Venice, 13, 14, 66, 219, 220
Galliard, Johann Ernst, 1687–1749, composer of a work for 24 bassoons, 179
Gallo (1762), German composer, 129
George I, 1714–1727, King of England, 99
Gillotot, François, 17th century, oboe student, 34
Goderick, Hans, church bassoonist in Alost, 1603–1605, 199
Gorner, Johann, 1702–1762, German composer, 160
Graf von Sparr (17th century), 124
Graf, Johann, 1669–1734, 'Hoboistenmeister' in Bamberg, 130
Grafe, Baroque German composer, 131
Grammont, French ambassador visiting Saxony in 1606, 61
Grandi, Alessandro, 1586–1630, Italian composer, 215
Graun, Carl, 1704–1759, of Hautboisten music, 19, 131, 169
Graupner, Christoph, 1683–1760, German composer, 17, 213
Gregori, Alberto, considered best trombonist in 17th century Italy, 193
Gregori, Giovanni, late Baroque Italian composer, 16
Guignard, Claude, 18th century French author of a military treatise, 141
Gussaghi (1608), Italian composer, 194
Gutiérrez de Padilla, Juan, 1590–1664, instrument maker in Mexico, 221

H

Hammerschmidt, Andreas, 1611–1675, German composer, 16
Handel, Georg, 1685–1759, German composer of music for Hautboisten, 8, 11, 18, 99ff. 106. 178
Harington, John Sir, 17th century English noble, 82
Hasse, Johann (Giovanni), 1699–1783, German composer, 18, 215
Hassler, Hans Leo, 1562–1612, 169
Haydn, Josef, 1732–1809, Austrian composer, 21
Heinrich, Baroque German composer, 131
Henry III, 1551–1589, King of France, 25, 35
Henry of England, Prince of Wales (1610), 82
Henry VIII, King of England, 90
Hentzschel, Caspar, on trumpet performance practice, 1620, 69

Hertel, Johann, 1727–1789, German composer, 18, 131
Hintze, Jacob, 1622–1661, German composer, 215
Horn, Johann, composer in Dresden in 1681, 215
Hotteterre, Jean, d. 1720, Paris instrument maker, 39
Howard, Lord, 17th century English noble, 88

I

Ines de la Cruz, Juana, 17th century Spainish poet, 221
Innocenzo X, 1574–1655, Pope, trumpets in 1644, 72
Innocenzo XI, 1611–1689, Pope, trumpets in 1676, 73
Innocenzo XII, 1615–1799, Pope, trumpets in 1689, 73
Isabella of Savoy, 193
Isabella, Archduchess visits Brussels in 1615, 187

J

James I, King of England from 1603–1625, 77ff, 181, 201
James II, 1633–1701, King of England, 96
Johann Friedrich, Duke at Württemberg, 1608–1628, 211
Johann Georg I of Saxony, Elector in 1606, 61
Johann von Sachsen-Halle, visits Leipzig in 1671, 69
Jonson, Ben, 1572–1637, masque composer, 78, 84ff
Jungbaer, 17th century German composer, 215

K

Kara Mustafa Pasha, 17th century attack on Vienna, 106
Karl VI, 1711–1740 of Austria, regarding the winds in his court, 63
Kastner, Georges, 1810–1867, French military historian, 134ff
Keiper, 17th century German composer, 215
Keiser, Reinhard, composer in Württemberg in 1720, 8
Keller, 17th century German composer, 17
Kellie, Edward, Master of the Chapel Royal in Scotland in 1632, 201
Kindermann, Johann, 1616–1655, German composer, 17, 169
Köchel, Ludwig, 1800–1877, botanist, amateur musicologist, 62
Krieger, Johann Philipp, 1649–1725, composer of mil. concert music, 129, 215
Krüger, 17th century German composer, 17
Kuhnau, Johann, 1660–1722, critical of Leipzig Stadtpfeifers, 162, 166, 170

L

La Barre, Michel de, flutist and government official in 1730, 38
Lamalle, Pierre (1672), composer, 199
Lang, Friderich, paid to restore Nürnberg crumhorns in 1620, 161
Lanier, Andrea, musician of Charles I, 90

Lanier, Nicholas, head of court music, Restoration England, 95
Lappi, Pietro of Brescia, Italian composer, 220
Leopold I, Emperor 1658–1705 and composer, 61ff, 152
Lionardo, Simone di, famous trumpeter in Florence, 17th century, 71
Locke, Matthew, 1621–1677, English composer, 94, 204
Lorraine, Duke of, as rider in a horse ballet in 1667, 62
Lottich, Jacob, poet in 1679 on Stadtpfeifer duties, 164
Louis de Rouvroy, Duke Saint-Simon, 1675–1755, diplomat, diarist, 27
Louis XIII, 1601–1643, King of France, 25ff, 90
Louis XIV, 1638–1715, the 'Sun God,' King of France, 5, 7, 10, 27ff, 35 [Les Grands Hautbois], 37 [Musettes et Hautbois du Poitou], 39 [Les Cromornes], 40 [Les Fifres et Tambours and Les Trompettes], 41 [Les Mousquetaires], 45, 75, 136ff, 217
Louis XV, 1710–1774, King of France, 47ff
Lubuissière, 17th century oboist and leader of Berlin court Hautboissten, 58
Lucino, 17th century Italian composer, 220
Luigi Ferdinando Marsigli, 17th century Italian military leader, 107
Lully, Jean Baptiste, 1632–1687, French composer, 46ff, 144

M

Magini, Francesso, Roman composer of a wind band work, 194
Mahmut II, Sultan, 103
Manesson-Mallet, Alain, 1630–1706, French treatise on the military, 140
Manfredini, Francesco, 1684–1762, Italian composer, 14
Maria Anna, daughter of Philip III of Spain, 61
Maria Theresia, Empress, 1717–1780, regarding her court winds in 1741, 63, 214
Marie Leszcynska of Poland, wife to Louis XV, 54
Marie-Thérèse, b. 1638, queen consort of France, 46
Marini, Biagio, 1594–1663, composer of incomplete wind band works, 194, 219ff
Markham, Gervase, 1568–1634, author of military treatise, 146ff
Marolles, Michel, de, 1600–1681, French writer, 192
Marpurg, Friedrich, 1718–1795, 207, 211
Marquis of Buckingham, early 17th century English noble, 87
Massaino, Tiburtio, 1550–1608, Italian composer, 220
Mattheson, Johann, 1681–1764, German writer on performance practice, 7, 59, 207
Maximilian I of Bavaria, 17th century, 4
Maximilian II, 1680–1726, [his military band], 125
Mersenne, Marin, 1588–1648, French encyclopedist, 6ff, 9, 37, 133ff, 226

Merula, Tarquinio, 1595–1655, Italian composer, 220
Mohammed II, 1451–1481, 106
Moliére (Jean-Baptiste Poquelin), 1622–1673, French playwright, 47
Möller, author of a military treatise in 1672, 73
Molter, Johann, 1696–1765, German composer, 13ff, 17ff,
Monteverdi, Claudio, 1567–1643, Italian composer, 74
Mortaro, Antionio, fl. 1587–1610, Italian composer, 220
Mozart, Wolfgang, 1756–1791, Austrian composer, 8, 103
Muffat, Georg, 1653–1704, German composer, 17, 19
Müller, Johann, German composer of music for Hautboisten in 1709), 9
Murat IV, Sultan, reign: 1623–1640, 108

O

Ogilby, John, observer of coronation of Charles II, 92

P

Paisible, James, late Baroque English composer, 98
Peacham, Henry, author of treatise on manners in 1622, 89
Pepusch, Gottfried, 1692–1736 German oboist & composer, 8, 58ff, 128
Pepusch, John Christophe, 58
Pepys Samuel, 1633–1703, England diarist, 95, 109, 183
Peri, 17th century Italian composer, 74
Peter the Great, 1682–1725, reorganizes Russian military music, 155
Peter, Christoph, 17th century composer, 215
Pezel, Johann, 1639–1694, German composer for civic music, 17, 165ff
Pfaffe, Carl, Stadtpfeifer applicant in 1745, 160
Pfeffel, Johann Andrea, engraving of military band in Vienna in 1712, 125
Philbert, flute player under Louis XIV, 39
Philidor, Jacques Danican, 17th century member of the Les Grands Hautbois, 36
Philip of Anjou, Baroque French noble, 151
Picchi, Giovanni, 1571–1643, Italian composer, 219ff
Polidori, Ortensio, 17th century Italian composer, 220
Potot, Pierre, French oboist in Berlin in 1681, 6
Praetorius, Michael, 1571–1621, Italian composer, conductor, 5, 13ff, 207
Preiner, Count as rider in a horse ballet in 1667, 62
Prowo, Pierre, 1708–1757, composer, 18
Purcell, Henry, 1659–1695, English composer, music for wind band, 98
Pureur, Chrétien, church trumpeter in Ieper in 1618, 200

Q

Quagliati, Paulo, 1555–1628, Italian composer, 220
Queen Anne, 1702–1727, of England, 99

R

Radino, Giovanni, d. 1607, Italian composer, 220
Rahtgeben, Jacob, 17th century German composer, 215
Rauverij (1608), Venice publisher, 220
Reiche, Gottfried, 1667–1734, German trumpeter, composer, 17, 163, 167ff, 171
Riccio, Giovanni, d. after 1621, Italian composer, 219ff
Riche, François le, French oboist in Dresden in 1699, 6
Richelieu, Cardinal, 1585–1642, statesman in France, 25
Riedel, Georg, a wedding composition with winds of 1715, 215
Roellig, 17th century composer of Hautboisten music, 19
Rolfe, Edward, English civic musician hired in Rochester in 1640, 180
Rossi, Luigi, 1597–1653, Italian composer, 220
Rousseau, Jean Jacques, 1712–1778, French philosopher, 36
Rovigo, 17th century Italian composer, 220
Rubini, Nicolo, famous Italian cornettist murdered in early 17th century, 220

S

Salazar, Antonio de, 1650–1715, composer of church music in Mexico, 221
Sallaert, Anthonis, painter of 1615 visit of Isabella to Brussels, 187
Sartorius, Christian, b. 1797, German composer, 215
Saxe, Maurice de, 1696–1750, French general, 111ff
Scarron, Paul, 1610–1660, French poet, 191
Schein, Johann, 1586–1630, German composer, 4, 161, 169, 215
Schmelzer, Heinrich, 1620–1680, Austrian composer for Leopold I, 62, 169
Schneider, Johann, German composer in 1745 of a church music, 211
Schubart, Christian F. Daniel, 1739–1791, German critic, 110
Schulz, 17th century composer, 17
Schumann, Christoph, 1726 Stadtpfeifer contract, 165
Schütz, Heinrich, 1585–1672, German composer, 16, 214ff
Schweickard von Kronberg, Johann, of Mainz in 1604, 57
Schwemmer, d. 1696, German composer, 215
Selijuk Sultan, 17th century, 106
Selim, Sultan, 1512–1520, 104
Selim III, 1789–1807, Sultan, 104
Servandoni, Chevalier, late Baroque English fireworks mechanic, 100
Shakespeare, 1564–1616, English playwright, 145
Smart, Peter, preacher in Durham in 1630, opposed to winds in church, 203
Smith, Mr., court trumpeter of Charles I, 91
Solar, Francisco, 1625–1688, Spanish composer, 221
Speer, Daniel, 1636–1707, German composer for civic music, 17, 168ff, 227ff

Sporck, Franz Anton, Count von, 1662–1738, (re the arrival of the horn indoors), 10
Stadlmayr, Johann, 1575–1648, German composer, 215
Stöckel, chief Stadtpfeifer in Altenburg (early 18th century), 162ff
Stölzel, Gottfried, 1690–1749, German composer, 17
Störl, Johann, Baroque German composer, 17, 131
Suleiman the Great, 1520–1566, 104

T

Taeggio, Francesco Rognoni, d. 1626, Italian composer, 220
Tagietti, Luigi, late Baroque Italian composer, 14
Talbot, James, 1700 reference to the new oboe, 225
Telemann, Georg, 1681–1767, German composer, 11, 19, 21, 123, 215
Theile, Johann, 1646–1742, instructor of Hautboisten bands, 125
Tollet, Thomas, late Baroque English composer, 98
Torelli, Giuseppe, 1655–1709, Italian composer, 13ff, 14
Torri, Pietro, 17th century Italian composer, 220
Trichet, Pierre, French 17th century treatise on the military, 144
Troilo, Antonio, Baroque Italian composer, 220
Trost, Johann, 17th century German composer for bassoon ensemble, 8
Turner, Sir James, comments on 17th century English military trumpet), 147ff

U

Urbano VIII, 1568–1644, Pope, trumpets in 1623, 72
Urbanus, Gregorius, composer of Italian church music with winds, 220
Usper (or Spongia), Francesco, 1561–1641, Italian composer, 220

V

Valdes (or Baldes), Francesco de, head of court minstrels, 17th century Spain, 75
Valentini, Giovanni, 1681–1753, Italian violinist, composer, 16
Van Ranst, Philippe, church bassoonist in the Netherlands, in 1619, 199
Venturini, Francesco, 1675–1745, Italian composer of Hautboisten music, 9, 19
Viadana, Lodovico, 1560–1627, Italian composer, 14
Vilhaver, 17th century Germany composer, 215
Vittorio Amadeo II, of Torino, 17th century son-in-law of Louis IV, 71, 151
Vivaldi, Antonio, 1678–1741, composer, Concerto grossi with winds in concertino, 16
Völckel, composer of 17th century hunting music, 61

W

Wagenseil, Georg, 1715–1777, Austrian composer, 20ff
Weigel, Christoph, engraving of Hautboisten band of Frederick William in 1720, 127
Werckmeister, Andreas, 1645–1706, composer, introduced Bach to equal tuning, 66
Wieland, 17th century composer of Hautboisten music, 19
William and Mary, 17th century England, 98
Witt, Friedrich, 1660–1717, German composer of Hautboisten music, 19

Z

Zedler, Johann Henrich, 1705–1751, German encyclopedist, 119

About the Author

Dr. David Whitwell is a graduate ('with distinction') of the University of Michigan and the Catholic University of America, Washington DC (PhD, Musicology, Distinguished Alumni Award, 2000) and has studied conducting with Eugene Ormandy and at the Akademie fur Musik, Vienna. Prior to coming to Northridge, Dr. Whitwell participated in concerts throughout the United States and Asia as Associate First Horn in the USAF Band and Orchestra in Washington DC, and in recitals throughout South America in cooperation with the United States State Department.

At the California State University, Northridge, which is in Los Angeles, Dr. Whitwell developed the CSUN Wind Ensemble into an ensemble of international reputation, with international tours to Europe in 1981 and 1989 and to Japan in 1984. The CSUN Wind Ensemble has made professional studio recordings for BBC (London), the Koln Westdeutscher Rundfunk (Germany), NOS National Radio (The Netherlands), Zurich Radio (Switzerland), the Television Broadcasting System (Japan) as well as for the United States State Department for broadcast on its 'Voice of America' program. The CSUN Wind Ensemble's recording with the Mirecourt Trio in 1982 was named the 'Record of the Year' by The Village Voice. Composers who have guest conducted Whitwell's ensembles include Aaron Copland, Ernest Krenek, Alan Hovhaness, Morton Gould, Karel Husa, Frank Erickson and Vaclav Nelhybel.

Dr. Whitwell has been a guest professor in 100 different universities and conservatories throughout the United States and in 23 foreign countries (most recently in China, in an elite school housed in the Forbidden City). Guest conducting experiences have included the Philadelphia Orchestra, Seattle Symphony Orchestra, the Czech Radio Orchestras of Brno and Bratislava, The National Youth Orchestra of Israel, as well as resident wind ensembles in Russia, Israel, Austria, Switzerland, Germany, England, Wales, The Netherlands, Portugal, Peru, Korea, Japan, Taiwan, Canada and the United States.

He is a past president of the College Band Directors National Association, a member of the Prasidium of the International Society for the Promotion of Band Music, and was a member of the founding board of directors of the World Association for Symphonic Bands and Ensembles (WASBE). In 1964 he was made an honorary life member of Kappa Kappa Psi, a national professional music fraternity. In September, 2001, he was a delegate to the UNESCO Conference on Global Music in Tokyo. He has been knighted by sovereign organizations in France, Portugal and Scotland and has been awarded the gold medal of Kerkrade, The Netherlands, and the silver medal of Wangen, Germany, the highest honor given wind conductors in the United States, the medal of the Academy of Wind and Percussion Arts (National Band Association) and the highest honor given wind conductors in Austria, the gold medal of the Austrian Band Association. He is a member of the Hall of Fame of the California Music Educators Association.

Dr. Whitwell's publications include more than 127 articles on wind literature including publications in Music and Letters (London), the London Musical Times, the Mozart-Jahrbuch (Salzburg), and 39 books, among which is his 13-volume *History and Literature of the Wind Band and Wind Ensemble* and an 8-volume series on *Aesthetics in Music*. In addition to numerous modern editions of early wind band music his original compositions include 5 symphonies.

David Whitwell was named as one of six men who have determined the course of American bands during the second half of the 20th century, in the definitive history, *The Twentieth Century American Wind Band* (Meredith Music).

A doctoral dissertation by German Gonzales (2007, Arizona State University) is dedicated to the life and conducting career of David Whitwell through the year 1977. David Whitwell is one of nine men described by Paula A. Crider in *The Conductor's Legacy* (Chicago: GIA, 2010) as 'the legendary conductors' of the 20th century.

'I can't imagine the 2nd half of the 20th century—without David Whitwell and what he has given to all of the rest of us.' Frederick Fennell (1993)

www.ingramcontent.com/pod-product-compliance
Lightning Source LLC
Chambersburg PA
CBHW082315230426
43667CB00034B/2769